A CHARTWELL-BRATT STU

COBOL for Mainframe and Micro

2nd Edition

Derek Watson

Department of Computing Science
University of Aberdeen

Chartwell-Bratt   Studentlitteratur

British Library Cataloguing in Publication Data
Watson, Derek
    COBOL for mainframe and micro - 2nd ed. - (A
    Chartwell-Bratt student text)
    1. Computer systems. Programming languages: COBOL
    language
    I. Title
    005.13' 3

ISBN 0-86238-211-4

© Derek Watson and Chartwell-Bratt Ltd, 1989

Chartwell-Bratt (Publishing and Training) Ltd
ISBN 0-86238-211-4

Printed in Sweden,
Studentlitteratur, Lund
ISBN 91-44-23512-7

Preface

This book is an introduction to programming in the COBOL language for students on information processing courses and on computing science courses which include a business computing section. It can also be used by someone who wishes to gain a knowledge of the language for their own interest. It assumes the student has a knowledge of computer terminology and also some knowledge of the basic concepts of programming. If the reader does not have this knowledge he or she is recommended to read a general introductory text to computing before starting on this book.

COBOL does not lend itself to the "Programming in Five Easy Lessons" type of treatment. Unlike many other programming languages where a runable program may require only a few lines of coding, the COBOL programmer has to acquire rather a lot of basic knowledge before he or she can write even the simplest program. This makes learning COBOL appear a formidable task, however, with a little patience and perseverance, simple programs can soon be written. This book proceeds to writing actual programs as soon as possible, just to encourage you and try to avoid the feeling of drowning in a flood of disjointed facts that many learners of COBOL experience.

The Second Edition has been extended to include COBOL 85 and the opportunity taken to amend some of the original text.

Acknowledgements

I greatfully acknowledge the support of Beryl, Ellen, Morag and Timon who had to put up with the birth pangs of this book. The text could never have been produced without the help of Denis Wilson whose knowledge of the text processing software was invaluable. I am also greatful to Chris Cotton who retrieved "lost" text files on a number of occasions and saved a considerable amount of time in the production of the second edition.

COBOL is an industry language and is not the property of any company or group of companies, or of any organization or group of organizations.

No warranty, expressed or implied, is made by any contributor or by the CODASYL Programming Language Committee as to the accuracy and functioning of the programming system and language. Moreover, no responsibility is assumed by any contributor, or by the committee, in connection therewith.

Derek Watson
December 1988

Contents

Contents

CHAPTER 1

COBOL and Programming

1.1 What is COBOL?

COBOL is the major computing language in use today. Over three quarters of the programs used in commerce and industry are written in this language. Anyone seeking to become a programmer in the area of information processing must be familiar with the language. Yet COBOL is subjected to a constant barrage of criticism, especially from academics, who are quick to point out its faults and disadvantages yet blind to COBOL's many advantages. Commercial computer users have been more satisfied, though changes are proposed from time to time and, less frequently, implemented. Commercial computer users continue to write their information processing systems in COBOL ignoring the frequent claims that better languages are available. The truth is that no one has yet produced a viable and generally acceptable improvement and it is likely to be some time before developments in fourth generation programming languages will produce one. Also, since COBOL has been in use for well over twenty years, user organisations have built up such an enormous financial investment in programs written in the language that the advantages of any future replacement will have to be great enough to persuade them to shoulder the very high cost of rewriting most of their existing software. In the meantime COBOL continues to be slowly revised to meet the changing needs of users and to satisfy the needs of most of them. An added boost has recently come from the development of COBOL compilers for microcomputers. As there are obviously going to be many more microcomputers installed than mainframes and minicomputers this will lead to a major expansion in the use of COBOL.

A major disadvantage of COBOL is that it is designed for batch processing. The standard specification of the language allows only the most primitive interactive programs. The great improvements in hardware of recent years have made interactive systems technically and economically feasible for all organisations and a great deal of systems and programming effort is now

1

involved in such systems. To overcome COBOL's shortcomings in this area software writers have either produced their own non-standard extensions for such things as screen handling on visual display units or written special software packages which are interfaced with standard COBOL programs. This book will deal with the screen handling facilities found in Micro Focus's series of COBOL compilers and IBM Personal Computer COBOL, both versions of the language specially written for microcomputers.

COBOL is a large language with a considerable number of commands, many of which, can be used in a variety of different ways. COBOL manuals are massive volumes stuffed with a mass of command statement formats and the rules for their use. We will do what in practice most programmers and programming departments do. We will use a subset of the language which provides enough facilities to cover normal programming requirements. Once you are familiar with this subset of COBOL, you should be able to understand the complexities of a COBOL manual. This involves omitting specialised or rarely used parts of the language, including the Report Writer which is sufficiently different from the rest of COBOL to be considered as virtually a separate programming utility. Some optional parts of those commands which are dealt with are also omitted for similar reasons.

1.2 History

COBOL is a problem oriented high level computer programming language designed specifically for commercial information processing. The word COBOL as an acronym for **CO**mmon **B**usiness **O**riented **L**anguage.

Every electronic computer has a basic machine code, which, by manipulating the electronic circuits within the machine carries out a series of operations. The means of allowing human beings to draw up the instructions for these operations is known as programming. In the 1950s, when the first commercial computers appeared on the market each manufacturer supplied his own means of programming - referred to as a language. Each of these languages, known as an Assembly Language, was unique to a particular make of computer. Not only were these languages highly complex and difficult to use but their uniqueness meant that programs written for one computer could not be transferred to another. Similarly, staff trained in programming one type of computer could not easily move (or be moved) to another.

These problems became particularly acute for the Government of the United States, by far the largest user of computers, so in April 1959 it summoned a meeting at the University of Pennsylvania Computing Centre of both governmental and private users and computer manufacturers to consider both the desirability and feasibility of establishing a common language for the programming of electronic computers for commercial applications. The meeting came to the conclusion that such a language was required and that it should be in English language form, making it easy to write and amend and also be self-documenting. It should also be independent of any one make of computer, making programs and programmers transferable from one installation to another. Unfortunately this compatibility has not been completely achieved.

The United States Department of Defence was given the job of specifying this language and in May 1959 called a meeting at the Pentagon in Washington which set up the COnference on DAta SYstems Languages (CODASYL). In April 1960 the first specification of the COBOL language was produced. This version was known as COBOL-60. Practical implementation showed that further modification and additions were required leading to the issue of a revised specification in the middle of 1961. COBOL was further revised in 1968 and again in 1974. By this time COBOL was now the responsibility of the American National Standards Institute and hence the latter is known as ANS COBOL 74. A further major revision was proposed for 1980, however, so much controversy was caused by the proposals for new facilities that the new standard did not come into effect until 1985 and is now called ANS COBOL 85. The COBOL 85 standard contains no radical changes to the previous one which is a disappointment to many who feel that COBOL is not responding to the dramatic developments that have been made in computing over the last twenty years. However, there has been a well organised campaign by a small number of users in the United States which has ensured that the original, much more radical proposals were watered down very considerably. COBOL 85, for the most part, lays down standard specifications for areas of the language which were not properly specified or were ambigous in previous standards. It also extends the capabilities of many existing statements and introduces a small number of new ones.

1.3 Program Design

When a programmer is given the job of writing a program to deal with a particular problem he or she faces two difficulties. One is to work out the logical solution of the problem, the other is the coding of that solution. These two separate operations are frequently confused by the inexperienced programmer. He or she is busy solving the logical problem and coding at the same time. Not surprisingly, this seldom achieves complete success. The program may eventually work but its messy and difficult to understand and change. The solution to the logical problem, or algorithm as it is called, is not correctly constructed and the coding is scrappy and inconsistant. It is essential to separate these two operations. This book is primarily concerned with the second operation, that of coding in COBOL, but we must first form some ideas as to what makes good program design and follow them throughout the programming examples in this book.

The medieval philosopher John of Occam is immortalised today by the saying "Entities should not be multiplied beyond necessity." Put in more modern English "Keep it simple!". This should be the motto of every programmer. Complexity for its own sake should always be avoided. Remember that your program is likely to be read by someone else, weeks, months, even years after the original program has been written. He or she has to understand the program fully so that amendments can be made easily, in the right place and with no adverse effect on the accuracy of the original program. This can only be done if the program is well written and easily understandable in the first place. In an ideal world every program should be documented giving a detailed commentary of every part of the program, explaining what is being done and why. However, program documentation is notoriously unreliable. Even if it was originally accurate, subsequent amendments and updates to the program are frequently poorly recorded or not recorded at all in the documentation. So it is all down to the understandability of the original program and the way it is designed. Remember that the maintenance programmer may be yourself so its in your own interest to design and write your program properly.

1.4 Top-down Design

An effective way of problem solving is using the top-down approach. This simply involves tackling a task by breaking it into a series of manageable chunks. We take the task as a whole and divide it up into several parts then look at each part in turn to see how it can be refined into lower levels. Each part is refined until a complete logical solution to the problem is reached. So we start from a general conception of the solution of the problem and work downwards progressively introducing more detail until we reach the bottom level which can be directly coded into a program. Although this is a commonsense approach, it is frequently ignored in the rush to write the program. However, the careful analysis and decomposition of a problem always pays off in the end with a well written, easily amended and easily understood program. The program can be written to reflect the top-down nature of the logic, as a series of modules invoked by a control module to which the logical path of the program always returns. Each module, except the control module, is called into use by a module immediately higher up the hierarchy and in almost all cases returns control back to the higher module.

Here is an example of a program to print an invoicing report.

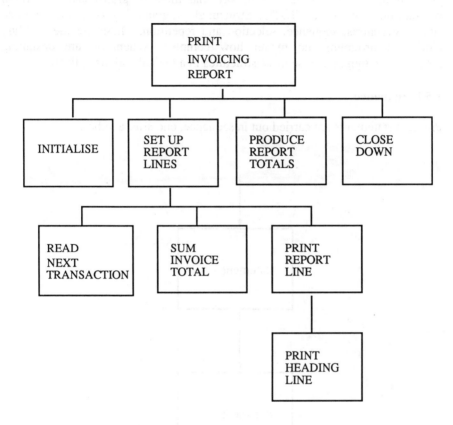

Fig. 1.1

1.5 Structured Programming

Structured programming allows the design of a program in a logical, systematic way which clearly shows the purpose of the program and thereby seeks to reduce the opportunities for errors and facilitate the future amendment of the program. Structured programming is often equated with GOTOless programming. This is not true. A disciplined use of GOTO is allowed. It is the wild, undisciplined use of this statement that has led to bad program design. But it is true to say that most programs can be written without the use of the GOTO. Structured programming is based on three simple structures, sequence, selection and repetition. These are the building blocks of programs, no matter how complex. When we are designing programs we must organise these structures in a logical and disciplined way

1.5.1 Sequence

Program statements are carried out in sequence, one after another.

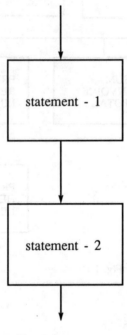

Fig. 1.2

1.5.2 Selection

A path is selected from two alternatives depending on whether a condition is true or false. Selection is represented as

6

IF condition THEN A ELSE B.

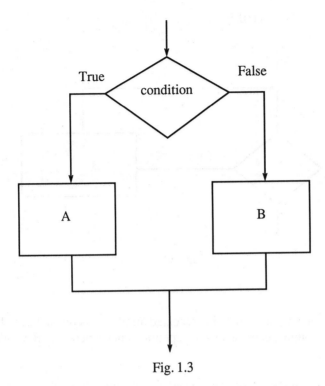

Fig. 1.3

If the condition is true, action A is carried out but if the condition is false, action B is carried out.

Taking the following as an example:

IF I have enough money THEN go by bus ELSE walk. If the condition is true i.e. I have enough money, the action following THEN is carried out but if the condition is false i.e. I do not have enough money", the ELSE action is carried out - I walk.

1.5.3 Repetition

This structure describes an operation which is carried out repeatedly while a certain condition remains true but ceases when the condition becomes false.

This is represented as

DO B WHILE A.

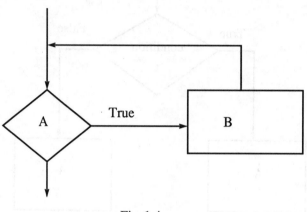

Fig. 1.4

In this case operation B will be repeated until A becomes false. If A was false at the commencement of the repetition then operation B would not be carried out at all.

These three structures are all that is needed to design a program. The skill of good programming is the ability to use these three simple structures to solve complex problems.

1.6 Pseudocode

Using the top-down approach we break the program into a series of units or modules. Each of these modules is designed in a structured way. The means of setting down on paper the logical steps differ. The traditional way is using flowcharts, but these have now gone out of favour. A better way is by using pseudocode. This is a description of the steps involved in the operation of the program using a simple subset of English. Here is an example of a program described in pseudocode which reads and prints all the records from a file.

```
MAIN
    Initialise
    While the input file is not at end of file
        Process-record
    Close-down
INITIALISE
    Open input file
    Open output file
    Set end-of-file marker to 0
    Read a record
    If end of file reached
        set end-of-file marker to 1
PROCESS-RECORD
    Set up the print line
    Write the print-line
    Read next record
    If end of file reached
        set end-of-file marker to 1
CLOSE-DOWN
    Set up end of processing message
    Write message
    Close files.
```

1.7 Design Methodologies

There are a number of design methodologies available either from text books or as commercial packages which allow the designing of programs in a formal way. The best known of these is probably JSP, Jackson Structured Programming, developed by Michael Jackson. JSP is a computer and programming language independent method of designing programs which uses a graphical method of setting down the relationship of the operations within a program and a special pseudocode called schematic logic to further describe these operations in detail. The designer uses these in a top down manner to design the algorithm of a program.

CHAPTER 2

Basic Elements of COBOL

2.1 Introduction

Although COBOL is designed to use English language statements, in practice, it uses only a very small subset of English and all statements are rigidly structured. This is because a COBOL program as written by a programmer has to be translated by another program called a compiler into a form which the central computing unit of the computer can operate upon. A simple, rigid structure makes this an easier task. The restrictions imposed by the hardware that was available at the time COBOL was designed is also obvious. The input medium was originally punched cards and the 80 column Hollerith punched card format has been imposed on the language. This also means that, up to the appearance of COBOL 85, all COBOL statements are written in capital letters. All COBOL 85 compilers and some recent COBOL 74 ones allow lower case letters to be used. The characters of each line of a COBOL program are distributed according to certain rules over 80 character positions and in some cases the position of a character in a particular column is very important. In order to facilitate the writing of COBOL programs a special coding sheet (Fig 2.2) is used to ensure that at least the format of each line is adhered to.

Before a start can be made to writing any programs the basic elements of the COBOL programming language have to be learned. Don't worry if you have difficulty understanding some of them. When you start writing programs their purpose should become clearer.

2.2 Statement Formats

In order to define the format of each COBOL statement a standard system of notation is used.

A certain number of words are known as **reserved words**. These have fixed meanings in the COBOL vocabulary. They are divided into two classes:

1   **keywords** which must be present and are indicated by being in capitals and underlined

    WRITE record–name–1

2   **optional words** which are present to keep the COBOL syntax close to natural English but can be omitted if the programmer wishes. In practice they usually are. These words are written in capitals and **not** underlined.

    PICTURE IS character–string.

Lower case words show where the programmer has to insert his or her own information. Where a choice has to be made the available choices are enclosed within braces (curly brackets).

$$\underline{\textbf{DISPLAY}} \quad \left\{ \begin{array}{l} \text{identifier–1} \\ \text{literal–1} \end{array} \right\}$$

Square brackets are used to enclose an optional item or clause and an elipsis . . . indicates the optional repetition of the immediately preceding information.

$$\underline{\textbf{ADD}} \quad \left\{ \begin{array}{l} \text{identifier–1} \\ \text{literal–1} \end{array} \right\} \left[\begin{array}{l} \text{identifier–2} \\ \text{literal–2} \end{array} \right] \cdots \underline{\textbf{TO}} \ \{ \ \text{identifier–m} \ [\ \underline{\textbf{ROUNDED}} \ ] \ \} \ \cdots$$

[ON **SIZE ERROR** imperative–statement–1]

[**NOT** ON **SIZE** ERROR imperative–statement–1]

[**END–ADD**]

The words ADD and TO are keywords and must be present. The programmer has to make a choice between using identifier-1 or literal-1. The presence of identifier-2 or literal-2 is optional depending on the context in which the statement is used. After identifier-2/literal-2 may follow, if required, identifier-3/literal-3, identifier-4/literal-4 etc. The ROUNDED keyword and the ON SIZE ERROR, NOT ON SIZE ERROR and END-ADD clauses are only present if they are needed within the context of the program.

Since this book covers two COBOL standards, COBOL 74 and COBOL 85, it is necessary to distinguish between functions which are available in COBOL 85 but not in COBOL 74. The method adopted in this book is to print all or part of a statement which is available in COBOL 74 and 85 in bold type-face and statements or parts of statements which are only available in COBOL 85 in normal type-face. So the ADD format shows that ADD . . .

11

TO and ON SIZE ERROR are available in both COBOL 74 and COBOL 85 but NOT ON SIZE ERROR and END-ADD are only available in COBOL 85.

2.3 Compilation

Electronic computers operate by means of groups of circuits each of which can be set to one of two different states. If we think of one of these states as representing 0 and the other representing 1, groups of these circuits are made to represent binary numbers. These binary numbers can themselves be grouped so as to represent data, not just numbers but alphabetic characters as well. So any information fed into a computer must be translated into binary numeric codes. The computer can interpret certain combinations of numbers as requiring it to carry out specific functions. The grouping together of these functions to process data is called programming. The basic numeric instructions are known as machine code. A free-standing set of instructions is called a program.

Early computers were programmed in machine code - a very difficult and time-consuming task. The advent of high-level programming languages, such as COBOL, removed most of the trouble by providing special translation programs called compilers. These compilers allowed programmers to write their programs in a form most convenient to themselves without having to know anything about the machine code requirements of the computer. The compiler does the translation - a process called compilation. The most convenient way to program a computer is to give instructions in English language statements and this is what COBOL does.

The set of statements written by a programmer is known as the source program. This is transferred to an input medium and submitted to the compiler which checks that the statements conform to the rules of the COBOL language and provides a list of any errors found. These are known as compilation errors and must be corrected before the program is submitted for compilation again. If the program is free from syntax errors, the compiler produces an object program which can be stored on any suitable storage device such as a magnetic disk or tape. The object program is the version of the user program which the computer itself can understand and is unintelligible to the programmer. When the program is to be run the object program must be loaded into the central processing unit of the computer and the appropriate starting instructions given.

2.4 Program Structure

A COBOL program is divided into four separate divisions each of which deals with a distinct function within the program. In order of appearance in a COBOL program the divisions are,

IDENTIFICATION DIVISION
ENVIRONMENT DIVISION
DATA DIVISION
PROCEDURE DIVISION

Not all these divisions need be present in a program, though in all but the most rudimentary programs they are. The ENVIRONMENT DIVISION, DATA DIVISION and PROCEDURE DIVISION can be subdivided into sections.

2.4.1 Identification Division

The IDENTIFICATION DIVISION contains descriptive information which identifies the source program, its author, the installation originating the program and the dates on which it was written and compiled.

2.4.2 Environment Division

The ENVIRONMENT DIVISION describes those parts of the program which are dependent upon the physical characteristics of the computer being used.

The CONFIGURATION SECTION describes the type of computer being used to compile and run the program.

The INPUT-OUTPUT SECTION deals with the definition of the input and output peripherals and the information needed to create the most efficient transmission and handling of data between the input/output media and the object program.

2.4.3 Data Division.

The DATA DIVISION contains descriptions of the format of files and data used in the program.

The FILE SECTION gives details of each of the files of data.

The WORKING-STORAGE SECTION describes the detailed formats of the data records as well as data which is used only within the program.

The LINKAGE SECTION describes data which is to be passed between programs without recording on magnetic media files.

2.4.4 Procedure Division.

The PROCEDURE DIVISION contains all the operations to be carried out during the data processing operation. These operations are written as statements making up sentences, paragraphs and sections.

2.5 Words, Identifiers and Literals

Since COBOL is designed to use English language it uses words, statements and sentences more or less in the same way as in general English usage but the grammatical rules are far stricter. Although bad grammar and spelling are acceptable in every-day usage as long as the meaning is clear this is not so in COBOL. The compiler applies the rules of grammar strictly and seldom makes any assumptions if rules are broken. So we will now take a look at how words are constructed and some special uses to which some of these words are put.

2.6 COBOL Character Set

When a COBOL program is written the programmer is allowed to use a group of characters known as the COBOL character set (Fig. 2.1). This is a subset of the full range of ASCII or EBCDIC characters which the computer can handle. This restricted character set applies only to the writing of the program statements. COBOL programs are able to process a much wider range of characters, e.g. lower case letters. In some versions all the characters in the computer's full character set may be output, including graphics characters but these must be treated as literals.

2.7 Word Formation

A word is composed of a combination of not more than 30 characters, chosen from the set characters consisting of the digits 0 through to 9 and the letters of the alphabet A through to Z. The hyphen - is also allowed but a word cannot begin or end with one, though more than one may be embedded within a word and they may be consecutive. For example COST-PRICE or LIST---PRICE. No special character such as * or $ can be used in a word. A word is ended by a space, period, right parenthesis, comma, semicolon or horizontal tab. If the terminator is not a space or tab then at least one space must follow the terminator. All words in COBOL are either reserved words which have pre-assigned meanings in COBOL or are programmer supplied names.

Character	Meaning
0 to 9	Digit
A to Z	Upper case letter
a to z	Lower case latter (COBOL 85 only)
	Space (blank)
+	Plus sign
-	Minus sign or hyphen
*	Asterisk
/	Stroke (vertigule, slash)
=	Equal sign
$	Dollar sign
,	Comma (decimal point - continental)
;	Semicolon
.	Period (decimal point)
"	Quotation mark
(	Left parenthesis
)	Right parenthesis
>	Greater than symbol
<	Less than symbol

Fig. 2.1

2.8 Identifiers

An identifier or data-name is a word assigned by the programmer to identify an item of data being used in the program. In other words each item of data or information that has to be processed must have a name applied to it and whenever that name is used the piece of data with that name is processed. An identifier always refers to a type of data, not to a particular value because the item referred to can assume a number of different values during the course of a program. An identifier must contain at least one alphabetic character. It is also adviseable to make identifiers as descriptive as possible as this makes the program easier to understand. Here are some examples of valid identifiers though the non-descriptive ones are not recommended for actual use.

Examples: D X475 NET EMPLOYEE-NAME
          PAYROLL-NUMBER LINE-OF-PRINT 123A456

Here are some examples of illegal identifiers and the reasons why they cannot be accepted.

Examples: DATE   reserved word
           ERROR!   ! is not in the COBOL character set
           COST PRICE   an embedded space
           FIELD-   ends with a hyphen

2.9 Literals

A literal is a value which is set up as a constant, that is, it does not change during the run of a program, unlike the value stored in an identifier which is expected to change. There are three different types of literal.

2.9.1 Numeric literal

This is a numeric value containing at least one and not more than eighteen digits. It may consist of characters 0 to 9, a plus or minus sign and a decimal point. It must, of course, contain only one sign character and one decimal point. The sign, if present, must appear as the leftmost character of the literal. If a numeric value is unsigned it is assumed to be positive. A decimal point may appear anywhere in the literal except as the rightmost character. In practice, it is not adviseable to have a leading decimal point. It is less likely to cause confusion if a leading zero is used followed by the decimal point. If a literal does not contain a decimal point it is considered to be a whole number.

Examples: 1506798 +12572.6 −256.75 0.16

2.9.2 Non-numeric literals

A non-numeric literal is a string of characters, usually alphabetic ones, contained within a pair of quotation marks. Any character which the implementation of COBOL supports can be used except the quotation mark itself. Any spaces enclosed within the quotation marks are included as part of the literal. A non-numeric literal must not exceed 120 characters in length and in practice it is advisable to keep such literals to an easily handled size.

Examples:　"EXAMINE CLOCK NUMBER"
　　　　　　"12345"
　　　　　　"page 144 missing"

2.9.3 Figurative constants

A figurative constant is a special form of literal. It represents a value to which a standard identifier has been assigned and as such falls into the category of reserved words. There are no quotation marks round a figurative constant. The two most widely used are SPACE and ZERO. In both cases the plural forms can be used - SPACES and ZEROS or ZEROES but there is no difference between the singular or plural forms in operation. The number of spaces or zeros actually represented in the program depends on the context. Other useful figurative constants are HIGH-VALUE and LOW-VALUE which produce the highest and lowest values respectively, which can be placed in a data field.

2.10 Punctuation

Since COBOL is designed to look like English language it uses punctuation in much the same way. But there is an additional use of punctuation in programming languages. This is to indicate to the compiler that certain actions have to be carried out. There are a number of rules to be obeyed.

A full stop, comma or semicolon used in the coding of a program must not be preceded by a space but must be followed by a space. Commas and semicolons may be used to separate a series of clauses or statements. They have no other effect and are not normally used by programmers. At least one space must appear between successive words or expressions. Two or more successive spaces are treated as a single space except when they appear in non-numeric literals. An arithmetic operator (+ - / * **) or an equal sign must be preceded and followed by a space. Be careful of this rule, especially if you have used the scientific languages such as Fortran, Pascal or BASIC where spaces are not necessary at this point. COBOL also allows the use of parenthesis - brackets - where the order of evaluation of an arithmetic expression or logical operation has to be specifically indicated. When they are used, a left parenthesis must not be followed by a space and a right parenthesis must not be immediately preceded by a space.

2.11 The COBOL Coding Sheet

The format of COBOL statements is not entirely free. Statements are designed to fit into an eighty column or character line. This is derived from the format of the Hollerith punched card which was the original medium for inputting programs. There are also additional restraints on where within the eighty character line certain types of data can be written. To simplify the coding process a special COBOL coding sheet should be used. It allows the programmer to see exactly where he or she is writing statements and reduces the problem which arises when using visual display units of not being sure what character position in a line the cursor is pointing to. Positions are referred to as columns in this book.

2.11.1 Columns 1 - 6 (Sequence number)

The sequence number identified the order in which the instructions are written. They must be numeric and in ascending sequence. Optionally they may be omitted altogether and in practice usually are. Systems software often demands that each instruction of a program is uniquely numbered for identification purposes, for example, a line editor requires to be given the number of the line of any statement that has to be amended. In this case the operating system or a system utility will automatically provide line numbers which double as sequence numbers. However, when this occurs, the programmer has to ensure that the number assigned is a six digit number. Any sequence error is indicated by the compiler but compilation continues.

2.11.2 Column 7 (continuation indicator)

A hyphen in this column indicates the continuation of a non-numeric literal from the previous line. The hyphen must be followed by a quotation mark before the remainder of the literal can be written. An asterisk (*) inserted in this column means that the following text is to be treated as a comment and not as a compilable statement. Other text in a COBOL program can be written over two or more lines without any continuation marker being required.

2.11.3 Columns 8-72 (Program text)

The source program statements are written in these columns. They are divided into two areas, area A starting at column 8 and area B starting at column 12. These areas are indicated by thick vertical lines on the coding sheet. Area A is reserved for division names, section names and paragraph names and some information about files and data. Area B contains the rest of the program text.

2.11.4 Columns 73 - 80 (Identification)

These columns may be used to identify either the program or groups of source lines. Any character in the COBOL character set may be used. Identification codes have no effect on compilation they provide only a visual check for the programmer. Normally these columns are left blank.

2.11.5 Character formation

There are a small number of characters in the COBOL character set which can give rise to ambiguity when they are written on a coding sheet. It is often difficult to distinguish between an O (the letter "oh") and 0 (zero). A common method used to differentiate between the two characters is to diagonally cross the zero e.g. $\emptyset$. Other confusing characters are I and 1 (one). So I must be written with a clear "top" and "bottom". The number 7 and character Z should have lines through the middle to distinguish them from a badly written 2, thus 7, Z. When a space has to be indicated either an up-turned triangle ∇ or a ∪ sign can be used. Even when you are writing unambiguous characters it pays to write clearly and carefully so that whoever is transcribing your program is less likely to make errors because of illegible coding.

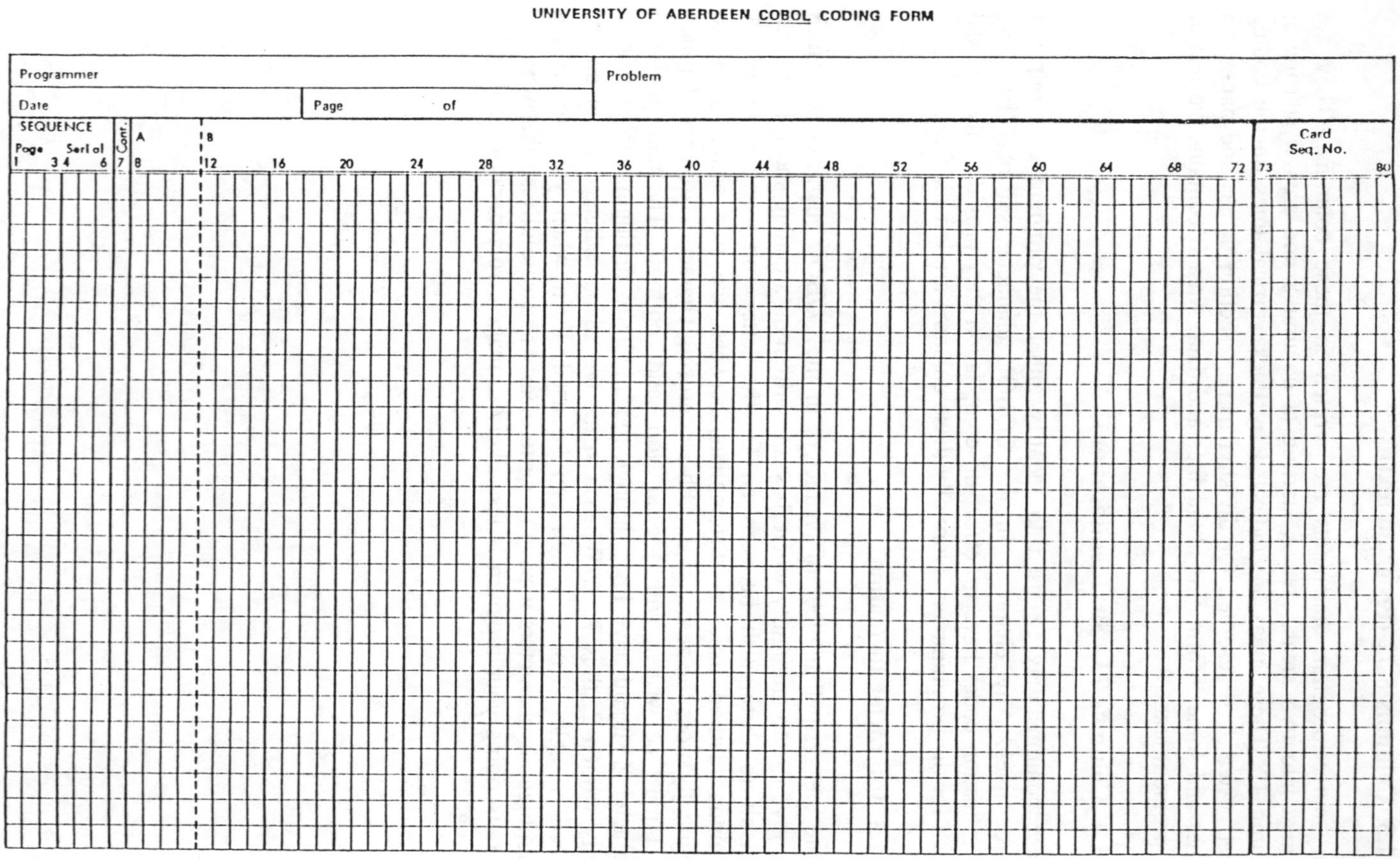
UNIVERSITY OF ABERDEEN COBOL CODING FORM
Programmer
Problem
Date
Page of
SEQUENCE
Page
Serial
1 3 4 6
Cont.
7
A
8
B
12 16 20 24 28 32 36 40 44 48 52 56 60 64 68 72
Card
Seq. No.
73 80

Fig. 2.2

CHAPTER 3

Starting Programming

3.1 Preparing a Program

There are two ways of entering a program into a computer. The first is by typing the program line by line into the computer via an on-line terminal, using a piece of software called an editor to receive and store the program on a magnetic disk. The compiler reads the source program from the disk and tries to compile it. If there are any errors in the program, a list of the errors is produced. Compilers detect two kinds of error, a fatal error and a non-fatal error. Fatal errors cause compilation to stop as a runnable object program cannot be produced. However, the compiler will continue if it finds non-fatal errors and produce a object program. A list of warning messages is produced telling the programmer what kind of errors the compiler detected. The resulting program will run but run-time errors may occur. It is always better to eliminate all non-fatal errors since this removes a potential cause of trouble when the program goes "live". Fig. 3.1 illustrates this process.

A microcomputer based system works in a similar way as an on-line terminal to a main-frame, though the program produced by the compiler may have to be run through a separate linking program before a runable object program is produced.

The second way of entering a program is by punching or encoding the source program using an off-line key-punching device which stores the program on a storage medium such as magnetic tape or disk. This must be read into the computer through a peripheral device which either feeds the program directly into the compiler or into a spooling program which creates a magnetic media file which is then read by the compiler.

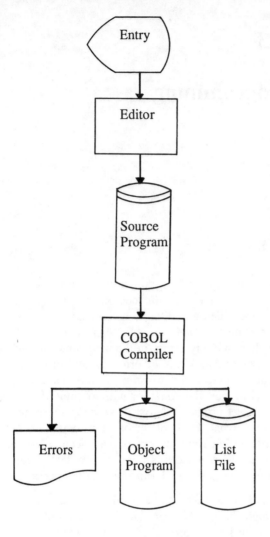

Fig. 3.1

3.2 A Simple Program

Let us start by looking at a very simple COBOL program (Fig. 3.2). This is just about the simplest usable program possible. The purpose of the program is to ask a user sitting at a terminal to type in his name and when this is done output a message. We will go through each of the lines in the program describing its function. The functions of all the statements will be described in much greater detail later, but for the present only information sufficient to explain this particular program will be given here. First, the program design expressed as pseudocode is as follows:

> MAIN
> output prompt message
> input name
> output reply message

Now for the program.

```
000100 IDENTIFICATION DIVISION.
000110 PROGRAM-ID. PROGRAM-1.
000120*
000130* THIS PROGRAM READS AN ITEM OF DATA AND DISPLAYS A MESSAGE.
000140*
000150 ENVIRONMENT DIVISION.
000160 CONFIGURATION SECTION.
000170 SOURCE-COMPUTER. IBM-PERSONAL-COMPUTER.
000180 OBJECT-COMPUTER. IBM-PERSONAL-COMPUTER.
000190 DATA DIVISION.
000200 WORKING-STORAGE SECTION.
000210 01    RECORD-1.
000220       03 FIELD-1           PICTURE X(6) VALUE "Hello ".
000230       03 NAME              PICTURE X(10).
000240       03 FIELD-2           PICTURE X(34)
000250                            VALUE " This is your first COBOL program".
000260 PROCEDURE DIVISION.
000270 MAIN.
000280       DISPLAY "Please type your name in."
000290       ACCEPT NAME
000300       DISPLAY RECORD-1
000310       STOP RUN.
```

Fig. 3.2

Each statement has a sequence number on the left side which identifies it uniquely. The original purpose was to sequence each punch card so that if a pack of cards was dropped then it could easily be put back into the correct sequence. Since punched cards are now a relic of the past, most compilers do not require sequence numbers. But on some computers the editing software uses the sequence number as a line number to identify the line being edited. The sequence number must always be six digits long or six spaces if no number is present. It is conventional to start the sequence at 000100 and increment by 10. This allows up to nine new statements to be inserted between two existing ones. If you wish to add more than nine then the program must be resequenced. Most computers which require sequence numbers have a program which will do this for you.

The program starts with the IDENTIFICATION DIVISION statement. This is followed by the PROGRAM-ID statement which is used to give the program a name with which to identify it. This program is called PROGRAM-1 but any non-reserved word would have done. If the name is longer than six characters only the first six are used. In this program, therefore, as far as the compiler is concerned, the program name is PROGRA. Statements 000120, 000130 and 000140 are comments. Commenting is achieved by putting an asterisk (*) in column 7 of a statement line. The remainder of the line is taken as a comment and has no effect on the compilation or running of the program. Line 000150 contains the ENVIRONMENT DIVISION heading statement and is followed on the next line by a section header, in this case the CONFIGURATION SECTION. This section specifies the type of computer being used to compile and run the program. The original idea of the designers of COBOL was to allow a program to be compiled on one type of computer - the source computer, and executed on a different one - the object computer. However, in practice, although some compilers may allow this, the majority assume that the source and the object computers are one and the same and for this reason some allow these statements to be omitted altogether. Whichever is the case, the compiler you use will accept only the computer names specified by the compiler author. In this program the computer being used is an IBM-PERSONAL-COMPUTER. Watch the hyphens, omitting them will cause a compilation error!

The DATA DIVISION starts at line 000190 with the division header statement. Though the DATA DIVISION can contain a number of sections only the WORKING-STORAGE SECTION is needed in this program. This section contains the description of a record. The record is used to contain the message which is printed when the program is executed. The record is given a name RECORD-1. The number 01 in columns 8 and 9 preceding the record name indicates that this is a record name statement. This number is called a level number. Level numbers are explained later, but for the present remember that any data name with 01 preceding it is a record and the entries on following lines with higher level numbers are part of this record. Notice that the record name and the record fields start in area B, at column 12. FIELD-1 has a PICTURE of X(6). This means that FIELD-1 is an identifier or name given to a piece of data which is six characters long and each character represented by X can be any numeric, alphabetic or punctuation character. This PICTURE clause is followed by an additional clause VALUE "Hello ", which puts the word "Hello " into FIELD-1. The next field of the record is NAME which occupies ten character positions. This time nothing is put in the field because there is no VALUE clause. After the name, we wish to print out the sentence, "This is your first COBOL program.". All the spaces are present in the literals so that when the contents of RECORD-1 are output the format of the sentence is correct.

The PROCEDURE DIVISION starts at line 000260. This consists of a single paragraph with the name of MAIN which contains a single sentence comprising four statements. Up to now the statements in PROGRAM-1 have been administrative in the sense that they are setting up the environment in which the program is to be run and describing the format of the data to be processed but not actually carrying out any processing. The PROCEDURE DIVISION statements carry out the processing operations on the data described in the DATA DIVISION. The DISPLAY statement causes the string of characters enclosed in quotation marks to be output on a terminal. When the programmer responds by typing a name followed by the RETURN or ENTER key, the ACCEPT statement stores the name in the area of RECORD-1 called NAME then executes the next DISPLAY statement which outputs the complete contents of RECORD-1 on the terminal. Notice that if the name typed in is less than the 10 character positions allocated to NAME then the unused character positions are filled with spaces. The STOP RUN statement ends processing. This program carries out the PROCEDURE DIVISION statements once, in the order in which they are written. There is no provision for repeating operations except by running the program again. Notice that the DISPLAY statement can be used in two different ways, the first version at 000280 outputs a literal - a string of characters bounded by quotation marks but the second version at line 000300 outputs the contents of a record. Many instructions in COBOL have several formats which increase the flexibility of the language but initially can be rather confusing. Pay attention to the positions of the full-stops. These are essential. Each COBOL sentence must be terminated by a full-stop as in English but a COBOL sentence may not always look like an English language sentence, especially in the IDENTIFICATION ENVIRONMENT AND DATA DIVISIONs.

3.3 Running a Program

Once a program has been compiled successfully, it can be run. The way in which this is done varies with different operating systems. In Fig 3.2 the message [C:\cobol] is a prompt from the PC-DOS operating system to indicate that it is waiting for instructions. The object program is run by typing in the name of the file containing the object program, cobp1. The program is then executed. Notice that, in common with most operating systems, PC-DOS uses the name of the file containing the object program not the name in the PROGRAM-ID paragraph of the program. These two names can be the same or completely different depending on the programmer.

In the printed output from PROGRAM-1, a gap appears between the end of the name "Derek" and the beginning of the sentence "This is your first COBOL program.". The reason for this is that "Derek" only fills five of the ten character positions set aside for NAME. The literal " This is your first COBOL program." has a space preceding "This" so that if a name happens to be ten characters long, there will be a space between it and the next sentence. If your name is longer than ten characters you will have to increase the size of NAME to hold it.

CHAPTER 4

Identification and Environment Divisions

4.1 Introduction

Let us now look in more detail at the IDENTIFICATION DIVISION and the ENVIRONMENT DIVISION. There is really very little to remember since most programs will contain almost identical IDENTIFICATION DIVISIONs and most of the ENVIRONMENT DIVISION will also be the same.

4.2 IDENTIFICATION DIVISION

The IDENTIFICATION DIVISION must be present in every ANS COBOL source program though most of the statements are optional. Also, since most of the statements in the division are for documentation purposes only, some compilers allow it to be omitted altogether.

4.2.1 Structure

The IDENTIFICATION DIVISION has the following general format:

    <u>IDENTIFICATION DIVISION</u>.

    [<u>PROGRAM–ID</u>. program–name.]

    [<u>AUTHOR</u>. author–name.]

    [<u>INSTALLATION</u>. [comment–entry] $\cdots$]

    [<u>DATE–WRITTEN</u>. [comment–entry] $\cdots$]

    [<u>DATE–COMPILED</u>. [comment–entry] $\cdots$]

    [<u>SECURITY</u>. [comment–entry] $\cdots$]

The program-name identifies the source program, object program and all listings produced during the compilation process. It may be any valid non-reserved COBOL word. If it is longer than six characters only the first six characters are used to identify the program. The first six characters must be letters or numbers.

A comment-entry is one or more sentences containing any combination of characters from the computer's character set. It may be extended over several lines if necessary. The comment-entry is for documentation purposes only and has no effect on the operation of the program. The purpose of each of the statements is self evident, except for SECURITY. The purpose of SECURITY entry is to provide a note of the level of security attached to the program by the user organisation. The statements present in the IDENTIFICATION DIVISION must be written in the specified order. The five comment-entry statements, AUTHOR, INSTALLATION, DATE-WRITTEN, DATE-COMPILED and SECURITY have been declared obsolete in COBOL 85. This means that they are supported by COBOL 85 but will be omitted from the next version of COBOL.

4.3 ENVIRONMENT DIVISION

The ENVIRONMENT DIVISION provides a standard method of describing the physical characteristics of the particular computer on which the program is to be compiled and run. It contains two sections, the CONFIGURATION SECTION and the INPUT-OUTPUT SECTION. The ENVIRONMENT DIVISION must be included in a program, but, like the IDENTIFICATION DIVISION, some compilers allow all or most of it to be omitted. The INPUT-OUTPUT SECTION is always optional.

4.3.1 Structure

The ENVIRONMENT DIVISION must follow the IDENTIFICATION DIVISION. In COBOL 74 it has the following general format:

> ENVIRONMENT DIVISION.
>
> CONFIGURATION SECTION.
>
> SOURCE–COMPUTER. source–computer–entry.
>
> OBJECT–COMPUTER. object–computer–entry.
>
> [SPECIAL–NAMES. special–names–entry.]
>
> [INPUT–OUTPUT SECTION.
>
> FILE–CONTROL. file–control–entry.]

In COBOL 85, the whole of the ENVIRONMENT DIVISION becomes optional and many of the statements within the division which are mandatory in COBOL 74 also become optional.

[ENVIRONMENT DIVISION.

[CONFIGURATION SECTION.

[SOURCE–COMPUTER. [source–computer–entry.]]

[OBJECT–COMPUTER. [object–computer–name.]]

[SPECIAL–NAMES. [special–names–entry.]]]

[INPUT–OUTPUT SECTION.

FILE–CONTROL. file–control–entry.]

4.3.2 CONFIGURATION SECTION

The CONFIGURATION SECTION documents the name of the computer used to compile and run the program and also allows the linking of specific hardware and operating system features to mnemonic names supplied by the programmer. The source-computer-entry and the object-computer-entry specify the name of the computers being used to compile the source program and run the object program. Each implementation of COBOL has specific names assigned for this purpose and these are to be found in the COBOL Reference Manual for the compiler you are using. Though, in theory, a program can be compiled on one computer with a certain range of facilities to be run on another with a different range of facilities, in most cases, the program will be run on the same or compatible computer as it was compiled.

Examples: SOURCE-COMPUTER. LEVEL-66-ASCII.
           OBJECT-COMPUTER. LEVEL-66-ASCII.

           SOURCE-COMPUTER. IBM-PERSONAL-COMPUTER.
           OBJECT-COMPUTER. IBM-PERSONAL-COMPUTER.

The SPECIAL-NAMES entry may contain a number of sentences depending on the implementation of COBOL being used. Commonly available ones are

[implementor–name IS mnemonic–name, · · ·]

[CURRENCY SIGN IS literal]

[DECIMAL–POINT IS COMMA] .]

The first option allows a system device or function to be linked to a mnemonic name made up by the programmer. This is often used in conjunction with ACCEPT and DISPLAY statements to specify where data is to be input from or output to.

Examples: SPECIAL-NAMES.
            PRINTER IS LST.
                . . .
                . . .
            PROCEDURE DIVISION.
                . . .
                . . .
            DISPLAY RECORD-1 UPON LST.

This will output data to a printer instead of the display screen as would normally happen with a DISPLAY statement.

The DECIMAL-POINT IS COMMA clause instructs the program to handle numeric data in the continental European format where the comma is used as a decimal point and the decimal point is used as a comma.

Examples: U.S./British   1,385.50
           European   1.385,50

COBOL always uses the U.S./British format unless this sentence is specified.

The CURRENCY SIGN IS option is used to specify the currency sign required if $ is unsuitable.

Example: CURRENCY SIGN IS "L".

Wherever a currency sign was required in the program we would use L. Special national currency signs such as the British pound sign are not usually available on computing hardware.

The INPUT-OUTPUT-SECTION will be dealt with in detail in chapter 7.

CHAPTER 5

Representing Data

5.1 DATA DIVISION

Before we proceed any further we must investigate the way COBOL handles the data being processed. COBOL basically processes records of data and the way in which COBOL looks at data is based on this concept. The designers of the language thought that this was the easiest way to describe the type of data used in commercial systems since it approximates fairly closely to the way data is stored in a business filing system.

The purpose of the DATA DIVISION is to describe the format of data and the context in which it is to be stored and handled. We saw from the simple program in chapter 3 that we must reserve areas of the computer's internal memory to store data. Any processing to be done on data by a program can only be done on data which has been stored in this way. In order to reference any item of data we must give it a name - an identifier in COBOL terminology - and describe in a special way how that data item is organised.

By placing the description of data to be processed in the DATA DIVISION and the statements that manipulate this data in the PROCEDURE DIVISION, COBOL allows the characteristics of any item of data to be changed without requiring any change to the PROCEDURE DIVISION statements, so long as the name that we have given to a data item has not been changed. For example, a data item with an identifier QUANTITY may be defined as being a four digit number allowing a maximum of 9,999 to be stored in it. At a later stage the field proves too small so it is increased to six digits in length, allowing a maximum of 999,999, but the name QUANTITY remains unchanged. All statements in the PROCEDURE DIVISION containing QUANTITY remain unaltered.

The DATA DIVISION commences with the words DATA DIVISION in area A of the coding sheet, followed by a full-stop. It contains a number of sections, two of which, the FILE SECTION and the WORKING-STORAGE

SECTION are the most commonly used.

5.2 Types of Data

There are two types of data. The first type is data held externally in files, which enters or leaves the internal memory of the computer according to program instructions. This type of data is held in the FILE SECTION of the program. The second type is data developed internally either as a result of actions carried out on external data or been generated in some way within the program. This type of data is placed in the WORKING-STORAGE SECTION. It can be held in records but records in the WORKING-STORAGE SECTION do not form part of any file. The data in the program in Fig. 3.2 is of this type.

5.2.1 Organisation of External Data

To facilitate the efficient and fast transfer of data into and out of the computer's central memory, data is organised into files which are in turn an organised collection of records. The relationship between records on a file can be that of common purpose, format or source.

There are two types of records, physical records and logical records. A physical record is a group of characters which is treated as a single unit when being transferred into, within and out of internal memory. A logical record is a collection of related data items. In a payroll system all the information which a company holds on an individual employee is an employee record. In a stock control system the details about a item of stock are grouped together to form an item record.

The distinction between physical and logical records is particularly important when dealing with files held on magnetic tape or magnetic disk. In this context the physical record is called a block. A block may contain one or many logical records but whenever data is transferred into internal memory from a magnetic disk unit the transfer is by block, even though only one logical record is required. The computer's operating system organises this action and ensures that the correct logical record is available to the program. Similarly, on output, several logical records may be grouped together to form a block (physical record) and only after a block is full does the physical transfer of data records to magnetic disk takes place. The area of the computer in which these blocks are either received or formed is called a buffer and the insertion or extraction of the individual logical records is known as packing and unpacking the buffer. When more than one record occurs in a block, the file is said to be blocked and the number of logical

32

records stored is the blocking factor.

The handling of the physical records is the responsibility of the operating software. Except when the programmer has to declare how many logical records form a physical record in the FILE SECTION, all other references to records in a COBOL program act upon logical records. Whenever a record is referred to in this book a logical record is meant. The physical record is referred to as a block.

5.3 Files and Records

A file is an organised collection of records. Each record contains one or more items of data. Consider the example of a company which maintains an inventory of all the products in its warehouse. Each product in stock has a record in a file which records all the information the company needs to know to carry out its business properly. Each record contains the following items of information:

> Product name
> Product description
> Unit of measure
> Unit price
> Unit cost
> Quantity on hand
> Quantity on order
> Estimated date of delivery.

5.4 Level Numbers

By grouping together all the individual records a file is formed. COBOL defines the relationship between the items of data in a record in a hierarchical manner. Each item is assigned a field in the record which is large enough to store the maximum value of the data item. A system of level numbers is used to indicate the relative positions of the data fields within the record. The record itself always has a level number of 01. Each of the fields within the record has a higher level number. The relationship between the fields is indicated by the level numbers. The level structure of the product record is as follows:

```
01  PRODUCT-RECORD.
    02 PRODUCT-NUMBER
    02 DESCRIPTION
    02 UNIT-PRICE
    02 COST-PRICE
    02 QUANTITY-ON-HAND
    02 QUANTITY-ON-ORDER
    02 DATE-OF-DELIVERY
```

The 01 level shows that the record is called PRODUCT-RECORD. This is a complete sentence and must be followed by a full-stop. The other entries are only partially complete and have no full-stop. The fields of the record are listed below the record name. Each has a level number of 02 which shows they are parts of the lower level number 01. Level numbers can be any value between 01 and 49. 01, as we have seen, has a special meaning but level numbers from 02 to 49 can be used for data groups and elements, so long as the correct hierarchy is preserved. Each of these fields is a data element, that is, a single undivided item of data. But any field of data may itself be divided into smaller units. An item which is subdivided in this way is called a data group. Each data group consists of a set of associated elements or of smaller data groups. The distinction between group and element is one of definition because most data elements could, if necessary, be further subdivided. Figure 5.1 shows a simple time-card for an employee.

Level 01	TIME CARD						
Level 02	NAME		EMPLOYEE	DATE			HOURS
Level 03	FORE	SURNAME	NUMBER	DAY	MONTH	YEAR	WORKED

Fig. 5.1

TIME CARD is a record. NAME is a data group consisting of two data elements, FORE and SURNAME. DATE is also a data group subdivided into the data elements DAY, MONTH and YEAR. EMPLOYEE NUMBER and HOURS WORKED are data elements since they are each single items with no subdivision. This record would have the following arrangement of levels in the DATA DIVISION.

```
01  TIME-CARD.
    02 NAME.
```

34

```
        03 FORE
        03 SURNAME
  02 EMPLOYEE-NUMBER
  02 DATE-1.
        03 DAY-1
        03 MONTH
        03 YEAR
  02 HOURS-WORKED
```

Those statements terminated by a full-stop are complete, those without require a PICTURE clause which will be dealt with later. By looking at this indented level arrangement we can see the relationship between the fields on record TIME-CARD. SURNAME is part of NAME immediately following FORE. HOURS-WORKED is the last field on the record and is a data element. The indenting is not required by the compiler and has no effect on the running of the program but it clearly shows the interrelationship between the fields of TIME-CARD. The identifiers DATE-1 and DAY-1 are used in the record description because DATE and DAY are reserved words, though MONTH and YEAR are not. This is something that the programmer has to be wary of when choosing identifiers. COBOL is not very consistent in this respect.

It is good programming practice to increment the level numbers in a record by more than one. This allows a higher level to be inserted into a record at a later date. In this book, the level numbers increase by two but it is also common practice to increase by a larger number, such as five.

5.4.1 Level 77 Items

COBOL allows single data items in the WORKING-STORAGE SECTION which are not part of a record or related to any other set of data, to be given a level number of 77.

Example: 77 INDEPENDENT

If level 77 descriptions are used in a program they must be written before any records are described. However, there is, in practice, no need to use 77 level items at all and you are not recommended to use them. An 01 level number can be used instead.

Example: 01 INDEPENDENT

You can also group independent items together into a record.

Example: 01 WORK-ITEMS.
                03 TEMP-1
                03 REPLY
                03 TEMP-TOTAL

5.5 PICTURE Clause (simple)

The PICTURE clause gives a general description of an elementary data item, showing the type of data to be stored and its size.

It has the format:

$$\left\{ \begin{array}{l} \underline{PICTURE} \\ \underline{PIC} \end{array} \right\} \text{ IS } \left\{ \begin{array}{l} \text{alpha--form} \\ \text{alphanumeric--form} \\ \text{numeric--form} \end{array} \right\}$$

5.5.1 Alpha-form

This option represents an alphabetic item. The type must be indicated by a string of characters A. An A indicates that the character position always contains any letter from A to Z or a space. No special characters are allowed, therefore, the name SMITH-JONES would be unacceptable because of the hyphen. When a number of characters have to be specified it is normal to place a repetition factor in brackets following the character type.

Example: NAME PICTURE A(10).
                instead of
                NAME PICTURE AAAAAAAAAA.

5.5.2 Alphanumeric-form

This option represents an alphanumeric item, that is, any character from the computer's character set, either numbers, letters or special characters. The type is indicated by one or more X characters. The size of the field is determined by the number of Xs in the PICTURE clause.

Example: ITEM-CODE   PICTURE X(5).
                LAST-NAME   PICTURE X(20).
                FLAG   PIC X.

36

5.5.3 Numeric-form

This option allows the description of a numeric item with or without a decimal point. Each numeric digit is represented by a 9. The position of a decimal point is indicated by the letter V. The computer does not actually store decimal points but has to be told where it is positioned in the string of numeric digits. This saves storage space in internal memory and on external files but it means that the programmer has to ensure that data being input and output is in the correct format. There is a facility to insert an actual decimal point when we have to print data but we will leave that till later. This implied decimal point, then, is represented by a V. Obviously there can only be one such character in a numeric PICTURE clause. If a number contains a + or - sign then its presence must be indicated by an S preceding the 9s. In certain types of numeric fields the sign character is compulsory but only required in others if the item contains a sign.

Example: TOTAL   PICTURE 999.
          AMOUNT   PICTURE IS S9(5).
          PRICE   PIC 99V99.
          COST   PIC 9(4)V99.

5.6 The Complete Record Description

We have now learned enough to complete the description of the time card in Fig. 5.1 and also the product record. PICTURE clauses can be added to each data element to complete the sentence. A data group never has a PICTURE clause.

```
01  TIME-CARD.
    02 NAME.
        03 FORE              PICTURE X(10).
        03 SURNAME           PICTURE X(20).
    02 EMPLOYEE-NUMBER       PICTURE 9(5).
    02 DATE-1.
        03 DAY-1             PICTURE 99.
        03 MONTH             PICTURE 99.
        03 YEAR              PICTURE 99.
    02 HOURS-WORKED          PICTURE 99V99.


01  PRODUCT-RECORD.
    03 PRODUCT-NUMBER        PIC 9(5).
```

03 DESCRIPTION	PIC X(20).
03 UNIT-PRICE	PIC 999V99.
03 COST-PRICE	PIC 999V99.
03 QUANTITY-ON-HAND	PIC S9(5).
03 QUANTITY-ON-ORDER	PIC 9(5).
03 DATE-OF-DELIVERY.	
05 DD	PIC 99.
05 MM	PIC 99.
05 YY	PIC 99.

5.7 FILLER Clause

There are many instances where a data item is present in a record description but the item is not subsequently referred to in a program. Rather than thinking up names for these items the identifier FILLER can be used any number of times. However, no operation can be carried out on any item with this name in the PROCEDURE DIVISION.

Example: 01 RECORD-1.

03 ITEM	PICTURE X(5).
03 FILLER	PICTURE X.
03 PRICE	PICTURE 99V99.
03 FILLER	PICTURE X(5).
03 AMOUNT	PICTURE 9(4).

As far as the program is concerned the items with identifier FILLER are blanks in the record. There may in fact be data present but this is not available for processing.

5.8 VALUE Clause

In the program in Fig. 3.2 the VALUE clause in the WORKING-STORAGE SECTION was used to set the contents of an identifier to a particular value so that when the identifier was displayed the pre-stored message was output. This clause is particularly useful for setting up page headings or messages and also for ensuring that identifiers are set to spaces or zeros prior to being used for processing. It is more efficient in storage space and execution time to set up such data in WORKING-STORAGE than to use PROCEDURE DIVISION statements. A VALUE clause can only be written for data items in the WORKING-STORAGE SECTION.

It has the format:

VALUE IS literal-1

```
Example:   01   HEADING-1.
                03 FILLER        PIC X(5)    VALUE SPACE.
                03 H-1-DD        PIC 99.
                03 FILLER        PIC X       VALUE "/".
                03 H-1-MM        PIC 99.
                03 FILLER        PIC X       VALUE "/".
                03 FILLER        PIC X(16)   VALUE SPACES.
                03 H-1-1         PIC X(22)   VALUE
                                             "MONTHLY SALES ANALYSIS".
                03 FILLER        PIC X(16)   VALUE SPACES.
                03 H-1-2         PIC X(5)    VALUE "PAGE ".
                03 PAGE-NUM      PIC 999     VALUE ZERO.
```

5.9 USAGE Clause

In a data description entry the USAGE clause is used to specify how an item is stored in the computer's internal memory.

It has the format:

```
                    ⎧ DISPLAY          ⎫
                    ⎪ COMPUTATIONAL    ⎪
        [USAGE IS]  ⎨ COMP             ⎬
                    ⎪ BINARY           ⎪
                    ⎩ PACKED-DECIMAL   ⎭
```

This is an optional clause. If it is omitted, as it usually is, the program automatically assumes that the item is DISPLAY. DISPLAY items are stored as a series of alphanumeric characters in a coding system determined by the manufacturer of the computer being used. This is normally ASCII or, if the computer is manufactured by IBM, EBCDIC. If arithmetic operations are carried out on a numeric data item held as DISPLAY, the data item has to be converted to binary before the calculation can take place. The result is converted back to DISPLAY. In most data processing applications this is not a problem. The time taken for the conversions is very small in comparison with the time taken for reading and writing records. However, if a lot of arithmetic operations are to be carried out, USAGE IS COMPUTATIONAL

(COBOL 74) or USAGE IS BINARY (COBOL 85) should be used. This causes data items to be stored in a binary format and no conversions are required when calculation is carried out. COMP is equivalent to COMPUTATIONAL. Manufacturers often offer a number of computational formats for various purposes, e.g. COMPUTATIONAL-3 which is a packed decimal format. COBOL 85 now has PACKED-DECIMAL which specified that numbers are stored in base 10, normally two numeric digits in a character position. COMPUTATIONAL can only be specified for a signed or unsigned numeric PICTURE. It may be specified at group or item level. But, if it is used at group level, all items in that group are also COMPUTATIONAL and you must take care that no clashes of data types takes place.

```
Example:01   BORROWER-RECORD.
             03 BORROWER-CODE    PIC X(5).
             03 LOAN-TYPE        PIC 9.
             03 LOAN-DETAILS     USAGE IS COMPUTATIONAL.
                05 LOAN-AMOUNT   PIC 9(5).
                05 LOAN-TERM     PIC 99.
                05 INTEREST-RATE PIC 99V99.
```

The first two data items, BORROWER-CODE and LOAN-TYPE, are USAGE IS DISPLAY by implication, i.e. if no USAGE is explicitly given then COBOL defaults to DISPLAY. Since the data group LOAN-DETAILS has USAGE IS COMPUTATIONAL, all items in the group are also COMPUTATIONAL. If an alphanumeric item had been present within the group, the compiler would have indicated an error.

CHAPTER 6

Procedure Division

6.1 Description

The PROCEDURE DIVISION is the division of a COBOL program which sets out the actual step-by-step instructions which tell the computer what processing is to take place. The PROCEDURE DIVISION can be composed of sections, paragraphs and sentences. Sections are often omitted and a program is divided into paragraphs and sentences only. A sentence is made up of one or more statements and we will start looking at the detailed structure of the PROCEDURE DIVISION by defining what is meant by a statement. Then we will build upwards, defining a sentence, a paragraph and a section. This division must begin with the words PROCEDURE DIVISION starting in column 8 of the coding sheet and followed by a full stop and a space.

6.2 Statements

A statement describes an operation which the computer is to perform such as carrying out an arithmetic calculation or sending data to a printer. A statement consists of a COBOL verb, or the word IF followed by any appropriate operands (i.e. identifiers, literals or file names) and any other COBOL names that are necessary, written according to the rules of COBOL. There are three types of statements, imperative, conditional and compiler-directing.

6.2.1 Imperative Statement

An imperative statement specifies an unconditional action to be taken by the program.

Example: WRITE OUTPUT-RECORD AFTER ADVANCING 2 LINES.

6.2.2 Conditional Statement

A conditional statement tests a specified condition to determine which path in a program is to be taken.

Example: IF QUANTITY IS EQUAL TO ZERO
         PERFORM NO-MORE-STOCK
    ELSE
         PERFORM STOCK-AVAILABLE.

6.2.3 Compiler-directing Statement

A compiler-directing statement instructs the compiler to carry out certain actions at compilation time. These statements are not compiled into the program and have no effect at run time.

Example: COPY "FILEX.DDS".

6.3 Sentences

A sentence is either a single statement or a series of statements ending in a full stop and a space. The separator between statements is one or more spaces. If there is more than one space, the compiler ignores the rest of the spaces. PROCEDURE DIVISION sentences must begin in area B of the COBOL coding sheet and they usually start at column 12.

6.4 Paragraphs

A paragraph contains one or more sentences. Each paragraph must begin with a paragraph name which is used for reference.

Example: PARAGRAPH-NAME-1.
        sentence-1.
        sentence-2.
    PARAGRAPH-NAME-2.
        sentence-3.
        sentence-4.

42

Paragraph names start in column 8 and terminate with a full-stop. Sentences may start on the same line as the paragraph name but you should not use this facility. A paragraph name should always stand out in the body of coding. A paragraph name follows the rules of word formation. It may contain any alphabetic character A through to Z, numbers and the hyphen. Numeric paragraph names are permitted but since the names should always be meaningful and should give some idea of the function of the paragraph, these types of names should be used with care. A paragraph name must be unique within a program.

6.5 Sections

A single paragraph or group of paragraphs can be assigned a section name for reference. The section name applies to all paragraphs following it until another section name is encountered or the end of the program is reached. The section name must begin at column 8 (area A) be followed by a space, the word SECTION and end with a full-stop. A section name must be followed by a paragraph name.

Example: READ-INPUT SECTION.
           READ-DATA.
                   sentence-1.
                   sentence-2.
                     . . .
           PROCESS-DATA.
                   sentence-n.
                   sentence-m.

CHAPTER 7

Sequential File Processing

7.1 Introduction

In Chapter 4 we saw how data is organised in records and how a record and its contents are described in a COBOL program. Now we must look at the way COBOL processes a file and find out what information must be provided. Examples are given of the use of each statement but since it is always easier to understand how COBOL works when you see the statements being used in the context of a program, we will use the simple report program PRINT-PRODUCTS (Figure 7.3) to illustrate sequential file processing. The program reads each record from a file called PRODUCT and prints selected data from the record in the form of a line of a report. The program is a simple one which takes no account of paging which will be covered in Chapter 14. The MOVE and PERFORM statements are new and will be dealt with in detail later. However, it is sufficient to know that MOVE copies the contents of one identifier to another and PERFORM causes a paragraph to be repeated until a certain condition arises and then the program proceeds to the statement following the PERFORM. The format of the report is drawn up on a format specification sheet which is used by the programmer as a blueprint for the record description in the program (Fig. 7.4).

7.2 Environment Division

The ENVIRONMENT DIVISION of the program contains an INPUT-OUTPUT SECTION which deals with the definition of the input/output devices and the information needed to create the most effective transfer of data between these devices and the program. The section has the following structure:

44

<u>INPUT–OUTPUT</u> <u>SECTION</u>.

<u>FILE–CONTROL</u>.

$$\underline{\text{SELECT}} \text{ file–name–1 } \underline{\text{ASSIGN}} \text{ TO } \left\{ \begin{array}{l} \text{device–name} \\ \text{literal–1} \end{array} \right\}$$

[[<u>ORGANIZATION</u> IS] <u>SEQUENTIAL</u>]

[<u>ACCESS</u> MODE IS <u>SEQUENTIAL</u>].

The headings INPUT-OUTPUT SECTION and FILE-CONTROL must start at area A of the coding sheet and the SELECT and its accompanying clauses start in area B. The INPUT-OUTPUT SECTION may be omitted altogether if no files are used by the program as happens in the program in Fig. 3.2. A SELECT sentence must be given for each file used in the program. The file-name must be unique within each program and must have a File Description (FD) entry in the DATA DIVISION. Conversely, each file named in an FD entry must be named in a SELECT statement.

Examples: SELECT PRODUCT-FILE ASSIGN TO DISK.
SELECT REPORT-FILE ASSIGN TO PRINTER.
SELECT CUSTOMER-FILE ASSIGN TO "CUSTOMER".

If the ORGANIZATION IS SEQUENTIAL and ACCESS MODE IS statements are omitted then the program assumes that it is dealing with sequentially organised files which are to be accessed sequentially. In COBOL 85 the ORGANIZATION IS clause is optional. Notice that ORGANIZATION is spelt with a Z not an S. The device-names are decided by the authors of the compiler and vary from computer to computer. The SELECT . . . ASSIGN sentence links the file handling software of the computer's operating system to the program. This is the part of a COBOL program where the greatest differences occur between the various COBOL compilers. You must read the appropriate entries in the COBOL Reference Manual for the particular computer you are using. In the example, the device names DISK and PRINTER have a particular meaning to some compilers but others might require device names such as SYSIN and SYSOUT. COBOL 85 allows a literal to used in place of a device name. Depending on the implementation, this could be the name of a file stored on the magnetic media.

7.3 File Descriptions

The File Description entry in the DATA DIVISION sets out the physical characteristics of a file. It starts with the letters FD in columns 8 and 9 and the remainder of the description follows in or after column 12. The whole description is terminated by a full-stop. No full-stop may appear after any but the last clause of the FD entry. There are a number of different clauses which can appear in an FD entry but only two are necessary at the present time.

FD file–name

$$\left[\text{LABEL} \begin{Bmatrix} \underline{\text{RECORD}} \text{ IS} \\ \underline{\text{RECORDS}} \text{ ARE} \end{Bmatrix} \begin{Bmatrix} \underline{\text{STANDARD}} \\ \underline{\text{OMITTED}} \end{Bmatrix} \right]$$

$$\left[\underline{\text{VALUE}} \ \underline{\text{OF}} \ \underline{\text{FILE–ID}} \text{ IS } \begin{Bmatrix} \text{identifier–}1 \\ \text{literal–}1 \end{Bmatrix} \right]$$

The file-name refers to the file in the SELECT clause which is being described. The LABEL RECORD IS STANDARD is required by some compilers when the file is held on magnetic disk or tape. All files in auxiliary storage have header and trailer labels at the beginning and end of the file.

Header label	record 1	record 2	record 3	Trailer label

Fig. 7.1

Special processing takes place on these labels either to make sure that the correct file is made available to the program or that writing to the file has been completed successfully. When this clause is used the VALUE OF FILE-ID clause is normally present. This clause tells the operating system the actual name recorded on the header label. If the file is to be read, the operating system searches for a file with the correct name. If the file in question is to be created by a program, the operating system writes the header label with the given file-name. Some COBOL 74 compilers do not require this statement as the device-name in the SELECT clause is sufficient to identify the peripheral used. COBOL 85 treats it and the LABEL RECORD IS statement as obsolete statements which must be allowed in a program but will be deleted from the language at the next revision. Files referenced in the

program are linked to the operating system by way of the device name in the
ASSIGN clause. COBOL 85 allows a literal to be used in place of a device
name. This allows the name of the external file to be specified at that point
making the VALUE of FILE-ID clause redundant. Some COBOL 74
implementations also work this way. If the file described is for a slow
peripheral, such as a printer, then LABEL RECORD IS OMITTED is used,
because there are no header labels on these types of files and therefore the
VALUE OF FILE-ID clause must not be present. All this sounds
complicated but we will use a section of coding from the program in Fig. 7.3
as an example.

```
000160 INPUT-OUTPUT SECTION.
000170 FILE-CONTROL.
000180     SELECT PRODUCT-FILE ASSIGN TO DISK.
000190     SELECT REPORT-FILE ASSIGN TO PRINTER.
000200 DATA DIVISION.
000210 FILE SECTION.
000220 FD  PRODUCT-FILE
000230     LABEL RECORDS STANDARD
00024      VALUE OF FILE-ID "PRODUCT".
000250 01  INPUT-RECORD              PIC X(51).
000260 FD  REPORT-FILE
000270     LABEL RECORDS OMITTED.
000280 01  REPORT-LINE               PIC X(80).
```

The first FD at line 000220 describes a file called PRODUCT-FILE which
contains a set of records which are to be read, one by one, into the program.
The file-name is the one in the first SELECT clause. The file has been
assigned to DISK, so the operating system will look for the file on a
magnetic disk. LABEL RECORDS STANDARD tells the operating system
that it can process the file labels normally and the VALUE OF FILE-ID
"PRODUCT" gives the name on the header label of the file. Notice that the
program knows the file as PRODUCT-FILE but the operating system knows
the same file as PRODUCT. This allows the programmer to write a program
with file-names that suit his program without knowing about the actual name
of the file. If a file with a different name but the same record format as
PRODUCT is to be processed then only the VALUE OF FILE-ID
"PRODUCT" has to be changed. Elsewhere in the program the file is called
PRODUCT-FILE and this does not have to be changed. It is possible to read
in a file-name at program run time if the identifier is used in the VALUE OF
FILE-ID clause instead of the literal. The second FD describes a REPORT-
FILE which is a file of data to be sent to a printer. A printed document, even
though it may contain only one character, is a file in the COBOL meaning of

the word. A line of print is a record and one or more lines make up a file. The items printed in the line form the data fields. Since this is a print file then LABEL RECORD IS OMITTED and there is no VALUE OF FILE-ID clause.

A file may contain records in a number of different formats. The record description(s) follow immediately after the end of the FD sentence. Where there are more than one record description these form templates that specify different layouts for the same area of internal memory. In the programming example PRINT-PRODUCTS two ways of describing records in a file are used. In PRODUCT-FILE the records are all of the same format which is described in PRODUCT-RECORD. The full description of PRODUCT-RECORD is given in the FILE SECTION. But in REPORT-FILE there are three different formats of records. Each of the two lines of headings have to be described as separate records. They are called FIRST-HEADING-LINE and SECOND-HEADING-LINE. The record containing the data extracted from PRODUCT-FILE is set up as REPORT-RECORD. These three records are described in the WORKING-STORAGE SECTION and the record in the FILE SECTION is described as a record with a single field of 80 characters. In this example the length of the line of print is set at 80 characters. Another popular size is 132 characters. The idea behind this arrangement is that when a record is to be printed, the data is placed into the fields in the records in the WORKING-STORAGE SECTION then the whole record is moved from the WORKING-STORAGE SECTION into the record description in the FILE SECTION and printed from there.

This may seem a complicated system but there are a number of advantages. One reason which is important in the present example is that VALUE clauses are not allowed in the FILE SECTION. Therefore, setting up page headings as we have done in FIRST-HEADING-LINE and SECOND-HEADING-LINE is not possible in the FILE SECTION. So when print files are described which invariably have headings to be set up, the most efficient way of dealing with this is to set up the headings and the print line details in WORKING-STORAGE SECTION and then move the records as required into the FILE SECTION. Another reason is to deal effectively with the way that COBOL behaves when the end of an input file is encountered which presents problems if the record being processed is described in the FILE SECTION. This will be dealt with in greater detail later. Henceforth we will follow the rule that the FILE SECTION is for files and the WORKING-STORAGE SECTION is for records. In future examples records read into a program will also be passed into the WORKING-STORAGE SECTION and accessed from there by the program.

Fig. 7.2 illustrates this process.

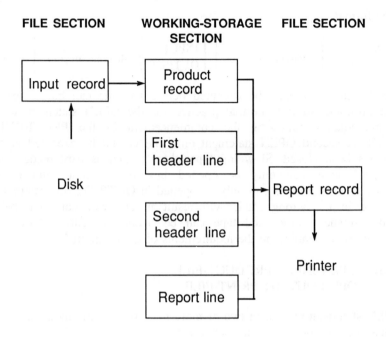

Fig. 7.2

7.4 Opening and Closing Files

Before a file can be used either for reading or writing it has to be opened. This means that the operating system checks to make sure that the device specified in the SELECT statement is operating and available to the program. When processing has stopped all the files opened in the program must be closed before the program terminates.

7.4.1 OPEN Statement

The OPEN statement makes a file available for processing.

It has the format:

$$\underline{\text{OPEN}} \left\{ \begin{array}{l} \textbf{INPUT} \\ \textbf{OUTPUT} \end{array} \right\} \text{ filename--1} \cdots \left[\left\{ \begin{array}{l} \textbf{INPUT} \\ \textbf{OUTPUT} \end{array} \right\} \text{ filename--m} \cdots \right] \cdots$$

The OPEN statement must be executed before any file can be referenced within a program, so it is normal practice for the OPEN statement to be placed immediately following the commencement of the PROCEDURE DIVISION. A second OPEN statement on a file cannot be executed unless that file has been closed. Slow input peripherals such as card readers and paper tape readers can only be opened in INPUT mode, and output peripherals such as printers can only be opened in OUTPUT. Any attempt to open a file in the wrong mode will result in an error condition being signalled. Magnetic disks and tape can be opened in either INPUT or OUTPUT mode depending on the requirements of the program.

Examples: OPEN INPUT PRODUCT-FILE.
OPEN OUTPUT PRINT-FILE.

The OPEN statement may open two or more files in the same mode and both modes may be present in the same statement.

Examples: OPEN INPUT BF-MASTER-FILE AMENDMENT-FILE.
OUTPUT CF-MASTER-FILE.

The OPEN statement does not make an input record available for processing, only a READ statement can do that, but on a sequential file the OPEN statement always ensures that the first record on the file is ready to be read. In the example program PRINT-PRODUCTS (Fig. 7.3) the input PRODUCT-FILE and the output REPORT-FILE are opened in the first sentence of the PROCEDURE DIVISION.

7.4.2 CLOSE Statement

When the processing of a file is complete the file must be closed. This releases the file from the control of the program and frees it for use by other programs.

It has the format:

<u>CLOSE</u>   filename--1 [filename--2] $\cdots$

The CLOSE statement can only be executed for a file which has been previously opened.

Examples: CLOSE PARTS-FILE.
CLOSE PRODUCT-FILE REPORT-FILE.

7.5 Input/Output Statements

The Input/Output statements are used to transfer records into and out of a program.

7.5.1 READ Statement

The READ statement makes the next logical record available from an input file.

It has the format:

READ   file–name–1 **RECORD** [**INTO** identifier]

[**AT END** imperative–statement–1]

[**NOT** AT **END** imperative–statement–2]

[**END–READ**]

The file-name-1 must be defined by a File Description (FD) entry in the DATA DIVISION and the record read from the file is placed in the record area described in the FD entry. The record remains there until the next READ or the end of file condition is reached.

Example: READ PRODUCT-FILE RECORD
AT END MOVE 1 TO END-OF-FILE-MARKER.

In program PRINT-PRODUCTS the READ statements at 000850 and 01050 cause the next available record on the input file PRODUCT-FILE to be read and placed in PRODUCT-RECORD where it can be processed by the other PROCEDURE DIVISION statements. When the INTO identifier option is used the record is read into the FD record area then copied into the identifier which should be the name of a record in the WORKING-STORAGE SECTION. So the record read from the input file now exists in two separate record descriptions in the DATA DIVISION. If, on the execution of a READ statement, the end of a file is detected, the imperative statements in the AT END clause are carried out. Files have different terminators. Magnetic media files have end-of-file labels placed at the end of the file by the

51

operating software. Other types of input will have a terminator suitable for the operating system in use. After the AT END action has been taken no input record is available in the FD record area. However, if the READ . . . INTO option is used then the last record read before the end-of-file label was encountered will still be available in the WORKING-STORAGE record area. This is one important reason why it is strongly recommended that this option be used every time. Any attempt to read a record from a file after the AT END action has been taken for that file will result in a run-time error.

Example: READ MASTER-FILE INTO INPUT-1
          AT END
          MOVE RECORD-COUNT TO PRINT-RECORD-COUNT
          MOVE END-MESSAGE TO PRINT-MESSAGE
          GO TO END-OF-PARAGRAPH.

If the AT END path is taken, all the statements following up to the next full-stop are included as part of the AT END operation. The program then executes the following sentence. If the end of the file is not encountered the program proceeds to the next sentence, ignoring any statements within the scope of the AT END statement. This is one of the places in COBOL where you have to be careful where you place the full-stop. If it is not placed in the right position after the AT END the program will not operate as you expect. COBOL 85 has the NOT AT END clause in addition. The NOT AT END clause specifies any action that has to be taken when the AT END condition has not occurred. It allows the programmer to carry out operations out only when the AT END condition has not arisen.

Example: READ PRODUCT-FILE RECORD INTO PRODUCT-REC
          AT END MOVE "Y" TO END-OF-FILE
          NOT AT END PERFORM PROCESS-RECORD.

END-READ is a scope terminator. The purpose of scope terminators will be explained later.

7.5.2 WRITE Statement

The WRITE statement sends a record to an output file either on magnetic tape or disk, punched card, paper tape or printer.

It has the format:

WRITE record–name–1 [<u>FROM</u> identifier–1]

$$
\left[\ \left\{ \begin{array}{l} \textbf{\underline{BEFORE}} \\ \textbf{\underline{AFTER}} \end{array} \right\} \textbf{ADVANCING} \left\{ \begin{array}{l} \left\{ \begin{array}{l} \textbf{identifier–2} \\ \textbf{integer–1} \end{array} \right\} \left[\begin{array}{l} \textbf{LINE} \\ \textbf{LINES} \end{array} \right] \\ \left\{ \begin{array}{l} \textbf{mnemonic–name–1} \\ \textbf{\underline{PAGE}} \end{array} \right\} \end{array} \right\}\ \right]
$$

[<u>END–WRITE</u>]

When a record is being written to magnetic media, card or paper tape only the record-name, and the FROM option if required, is specified. The BEFORE/AFTER ADVANCING clause is only used when the record is to be printed and controls the line feed mechanism of the printer.

Example: WRITE REPORT-1.

An OPEN statement on a file must have been executed before the first WRITE statement to that file. The record referred to in record-name-1 is no longer available for processing after a WRITE statement has been executed on that file. When the FROM identifier-1 option is used, identifier-1 should be the name of a record in the WORKING-STORAGE SECTION. Data is copied from identifier-1 to record-name-1 then written to the appropriate output device. After the execution of the WRITE statement, though the data in record-name is no longer available, the data in identifier-1 still remains.

Example: WRITE OUTPUT-RECORD FROM PAY-SLIP.

The BEFORE/AFTER ADVANCING option is used to enable the programmer either to move the paper on the printer a number of lines or to perform a recognition throw to a specified line, before or after a line is printed. If this option is used for a given file every WRITE statement for that file must contain this option. Identifier-2 must be numeric.

Examples: WRITE TOTAL-LINE AFTER ADVANCING 2 LINES.
            WRITE SECOND-HALF BEFORE 1.

Remember! You always READ a file but WRITE a record.

The program PRINT-PRODUCTS prints two lines of heading and a line of data extracted from each record read from the input file. The first heading line is contained in the record in WORKING-STORAGE SECTION called FIRST-HEADING-LINE. The statement

WRITE REPORT-LINE FROM FIRST-HEADING-LINE AFTER PAGE

causes the contents of FIRST-HEADING-LINE to be copied into REPORT-LINE and passed from there to a printer. AFTER PAGE causes the printer to throw the paper to the top of a page before it prints the contents of REPORT-LINE.

WRITE REPORT-LINE FROM SECOND-HEADING-LINE AFTER ADVANCING 1 LINE.

causes the contents of SECOND-HEADING-LINE to be copied to REPORT-LINE and printed after the printer has thrown one line. The other print statement

WRITE REPORT-LINE FROM REPORT-RECORD AFTER ADVANCING 2 LINES.

causes the contents of REPORT-RECORD which have been set up by the preceding MOVE statements to be copied to REPORT-LINE and printed after the printer has moved on two lines. This means that there will be one blank line between each line of print.

7.6 Input and Output Data

Input and output data is treated as alphanumeric data by a COBOL program. When data is read into a record area either in the FD or WORKING-STORAGE SECTION no checking takes place to see if the format of the data in the record corresponds to the PICTURE clauses declared in the program. So, it is quite possible to read a product description into a quantity field. This error would not be detected until the program attempted to do some arithmetic operation with the quantity field. Since the computer does not check the data, the program must. It is essential to check that all the data is valid before any processing takes place. The first example program PROGRAM-1 did not check the data being input. It is assumed to be correct. This is not acceptable for general use but we will wait until validation is dealt with in Chapter 11 before including it in our programs. Programs which read data from master files on magnetic media, such as PRODUCT, can assume with safety that the data has already been checked before the master file records were created.

7.7 Program PRINT-PRODUCTS

The program design is expressed in the following pseudocode.

START-UP
    open files
    set end-of-file marker to 0
    write headings
    read a record
    if end of file reached
        set end-of-file marker to 1
PROCESS-RECORDS
    while the input file is not at end of file
        set up report line
        write out report line
        read next record
        if end of file reached
            set end-of-file marker to 1
CLOSE-DOWN
    set up end message
    write end message
    close files.

The records stored on the file PRODUCT are as follows:

```
80036HEATHER BELL WHISKY HALF BTL  00549004670070000000000000003261
80037HEATHER BELL WHISKY BTL       00739006110035000500026078500932
80120GLEN CALLETER WHISKY HALF BTL 00459003990000000035020078500252
80122GLEN CALLETER WHISKY BTL      00683005800012500000000000000121
80131DUNVEGAN WHISKY BTL           00925008050005000020240785006100
80163SKEAN DHU WHISKY BTL          00895007990012300000000000000679
81032LOUIS XIV BRANDY BTL          00873007920009800000000000001395
81047CHAMBORD BRANDY HALF BTL      00628005370005200100010088500685
```

The program prints a report (Fig. 7.5) in the format set out on the format layout sheet given in Fig. 7.4. Layout sheets of this type are used to set down the design of a report. They are used by a programmer as the blueprint for coding that report. Each line of the layout represents one line of the report and each square represents one character on a line. Headings and fixed messages are written as and where they are to appear on the printout. The position of variable data is indicated by an X or a 9 in each character position to be occupied by a data item. Each alphabetic or alphanumeric character is indicated by an X. Each numeric character is indicated by a 9. Using the data from the file PRODUCT and writing the program to conform to the requirements of the layout in Fig. 7.4, we will get the following output, starting at the top of a page.

The listing of the program is as follows:

```
000100 IDENTIFICATION DIVISION.
000110 PROGRAM-ID. PRINT-PRODUCTS.
000120 ENVIRONMENT DIVISION.
000130 CONFIGURATION SECTION.
000140 SOURCE-COMPUTER. ABC-1.
000150 OBJECT-COMPUTER. ABC-1.
000160 INPUT-OUTPUT SECTION.
000170 FILE-CONTROL.
000180      SELECT PRODUCT-FILE ASSIGN TO DISK.
000200      SELECT REPORT-FILE ASSIGN TO PRINTER.
000220 DATA DIVISION.
000230 FILE SECTION.
000240 FD   PRODUCT-FILE
000250      LABEL RECORDS STANDARD
000260      VALUE OF FILE-ID "PRODUCT".
000270 01   INPUT-RECORD                      PIC X(67).
000280 FD   REPORT-FILE
000290      LABEL RECORDS OMITTED.
000300 01   REPORT-RECORD                     PIC X(80).
000310 WORKING-STORAGE SECTION.
000320 01   PRODUCT-RECORD.
000330      03 PRODUCT-NUMBER                 PIC 9(5).
000340      03 DESCRIPTION                    PIC X(30).
000350      03 UNIT-PRICE                     PIC 999V99.
000360      03 COST-PRICE                     PIC 999V99.
000370      03 QUANTITY-ON-HAND               PIC 9(5).
000380      03 QUANTITY-ON-ORDER              PIC 9(5).
000390      03 DATE-OF-DELIVERY.
000400         05 DD                          PIC 99.
000410         05 MM                          PIC 99.
000420         05 YY                          PIC 99.
000425      03 QUANTITY-SOLD                  PIC 9(5).
000430 01   REPORT-LINE.
000440      03 FILLER                         PIC X(3) VALUE SPACES.
000450      03 RL-PRODUCT-NUMBER              PIC 9(5).
000460      03 FILLER                         PIC X(4) VALUE SPACES.
000470      03 RL-DESCRIPTION                 PIC X(30).
000480      03 FILLER                         PIC X(5) VALUE SPACES.
000490      03 RL-QUANTITY-ON-HAND            PIC 9(5).
000500      03 FILLER                         PIC X(5) VALUE SPACES.
000510      03 RL-QUANTITY-ON-ORDER           PIC 9(5).
000520      03 FILLER                         PIC X(4) VALUE SPACES.
000530      03 RL-DD                          PIC 99.
000540      03 FILLER                         PIC X  VALUE "/".
000550      03 RL-MM                          PIC 99.
000560      03 FILLER                         PIC X  VALUE "/".
000570      03 RL-YY                          PIC 99.
000580 01   FIRST-HEADING-LINE.
```

```
000590        03 FILLER                       PIC X(3) VALUE SPACES.
000600        03 FILLER                       PIC X(7) VALUE "PRODUCT".
000610        03 FILLER                       PIC X(11) VALUE SPACES.
000620        03 FILLER                       PIC X(11) VALUE "DESCRIPTION".
000630        03 FILLER                       PIC X(14) VALUE SPACES.
000640        03 FILLER                       PIC X(29) VALUE "QUANTITY   QUAN
000650-                                        "TITY  ESTIMATED".
000660 01  SECOND-HEADING-LINE.
000670        03 FILLER                       PIC X(3) VALUE SPACES.
000680        03 FILLER                       PIC X(6) VALUE "NUMBER".
000690        03 FILLER                       PIC X(37) VALUE SPACES.
000700        03 FILLER                       PIC X(18
000710        03 FILLER                       PIC X(9) VALUE "D-O-D".
000720 01  SUMMARY-RECORD.
000730        03 FILLER                       PIC X(34) VALUE SPACES.
000740        03 SUMMARY-MESSAGE              PIC X(13).
000750 01  END-OF-FILE-MARKER                 PIC 9.
000760 PROCEDURE DIVISION.
000770 START-UP.
000780        OPEN INPUT PRODUCT-FILE
000790             OUTPUT REPORT-FILE.
000800        MOVE ZERO TO END-OF-FILE-MARKER.
000810        WRITE REPORT-RECORD FROM FIRST-HEADING-LINE
000820             AFTER ADVANCING PAGE.
000830        WRITE REPORT-RECORD FROM SECOND-HEADING-LINE
000840             AFTER ADVANCING 1 LINE.
000850        READ PRODUCT-FILE RECORD INTO PRODUCT-RECORD
000860             AT END MOVE 1 TO END-OF-FILE-MARKER.
000870 PROCESS-RECORDS.
000880        PERFORM PRINT-AND-READ UNTIL END-OF-FILE-MARKER = 1.
000890 CLOSE-DOWN.
000900        MOVE "End of Report" TO SUMMARY-MESSAGE.
000910        WRITE REPORT-RECORD FROM SUMMARY-RECORD
000911             AFTER ADVANCING 2 LINES.
000920        CLOSE PRODUCT-FILE REPORT-FILE.
000940        STOP RUN.
000950 PRINT-AND-READ.
000960        MOVE PRODUCT-NUMBER TO RL-PRODUCT-NUMBER
000970        MOVE DESCRIPTION TO RL-DESCRIPTION
000980        MOVE QUANTITY-ON-HAND TO RL-QUANTITY-ON-HAND
000990        MOVE QUANTITY-ON-ORDER TO RL-QUANTITY-ON-ORDER
001000        MOVE DD TO RL-DD
001010        MOVE MM TO RL-MM
001020        MOVE YY TO RL-YY.
001030        WRITE REPORT-RECORD FROM REPORT-LINE
001040             AFTER ADVANCING 2 LINES.
001050        READ PRODUCT-FILE RECORD INTO PRODUCT-RECORD
001060             AT END MOVE 1 TO END-OF-FILE-MARKER.
```

Fig. 7.3

UNIVERSITY OF ABERDEEN

PRODUCT NUMBER	DESCRIPTION	QUANTITY ON HAND	QUANTITY ON ORDER	ESTIMATED D-I-A
99999	XXXXX...XXXX	99999	99999	99/99/99
99999	XXXXX...XXXX	99999	99999	99/99/99

Fig. 7.4

58

PRODUCT NUMBER	DESCRIPTION	QUANTITY ON HAND	QUANTITY ON ORDER	ESTIMATED D-O-D
80036	HEATHER BELL WHISKY HALF BTL	00700	00000	00/00/00
80037	HEATHER BELL WHISKY BTL	00350	00500	26/07/85
80120	GLEN CALLETER WHISKY HALF BTL	00000	00350	20/07/85
80122	GLEN CALLETER WHISKY BTL	00125	00000	00/00/00
80131	DUNVEGAN WHISKY BTL	00050	00020	24/07/85
80163	SKEAN DHU WHISKY BTL	00123	00000	00/00/00
81032	LOUIS XIV BRANDY BTL	00098	00000	00/00/00
81047	CHAMBORD BRANDY HALF BTL	00052	00100	01/08/85

End of Report

Fig. 7.5

CHAPTER 8

Moving And Repeating

8.1 Moving Data

A considerable part of programming is taken up with the moving data from
one storage location in main memory to another. This is done to transfer data
from one record to another or to preserve data which would otherwise be lost
or overwritten. The format of data can deliberately be changed just by
moving an item of data defined as having one type of PICTURE clause to an
identifier which has a different PICTURE.

8.1.1 MOVE Statement

The MOVE statement transfers a data item from one data area in a program
to one or more other data areas.

It has the format:

$$\underline{\text{MOVE}} \left\{ \begin{array}{l} \text{identifier--1} \\ \text{literal--1} \end{array} \right\} \underline{\text{TO}} \ \{ \ \text{identifier-2} \ \} \ \cdots$$

The data value in identifier-1 or the literal is transferred to identifier-2 then,
provided the option is used, to any other identifier in the list. The contents of
identifier-1 remain unchanged by the execution of the statement and the
original contents of identifier-2 etc. are lost. So MOVE essentially copies
data.

Examples: MOVE INPUT-1 TO OUTPUT-1

60

	INPUT-1	OUTPUT-1
Before	25	38
After	25	25

MOVE 1 TO LINE-COUNT PAGE-COUNT

	LINE-COUNT	PAGE-COUNT
Before	54	23
After	01	01

MOVE "WEEKLY TOTALS" TO PRINT-AREA-1

	PRINT-AREA-1
Before	DAILY TOTALS
After	WEEKLY TOTALS

There are a number of restrictions which apply to this statement. The most important are detailed below.

8.1.2 Alphanumeric to Alphanumeric

When a smaller data area is moved to a larger one the receiving area is filled up from left to right and any positions left over are filled with spaces. This is useful as it means you do not have to set an alphanumeric data area to spaces before moving variable length character strings into it.

Examples: MOVE CODE-1 TO AREA-1

CODE-1				AREA-1					
A	B	2	8	A	B	2	8		

If the receiving one is less than the sending one then the additional characters are lost.

Example: MOVE CODE-1 TO SUM

CODE-1				SUM		
A	B	2	8	A	B	2

8.1.3 Numeric to Numeric

Numeric items are aligned at the decimal point. Leading unused character positions are set to zero. Additional characters are truncated.

Example: MOVE PRICE TO TOTAL-1 TOTAL-2

PRICE					TOTAL-1						TOTAL-2			
3	5	0	2	5	0	0	0	3	5	0	2	5	0	2	5

The ^ sign indicates the position of the decimal point. Whole numbers (integers) are treated as if a decimal point followed the right-most (units) number.

8.2 MOVEs in PRINT-PRODUCTS

The program PRINT-PRODUCTS (Fig. 7.3) contains a number of MOVE statements. The first one is

MOVE ZERO TO END-OF-FILE-MARKER.

This has the effect of placing zero in the identifier END-OF-FILE-MARKER. END-OF-FILE-MARKER is used by the program to indicate when all the records have been read from PRODUCT-FILE. It is initially set to zero to indicate that there are records to be processed but when the end-of-file label is detected, END-OF-FILE-MARKER is set to 1 by the MOVE statement in the AT END clause of the two READ statements. The sentence

MOVE "End of Report" TO SUMMARY-MESSAGE.

moves a literal "End of Report" to SUMMARY-MESSAGE. This is a different way of setting up a description or heading. The other method is to use VALUE clauses as in FIRST-HEADING-LINE and SECOND-HEADING-LINE.

Each file has its own record area which is used for passing records into and out of the program. The statement

READ PRODUCT-FILE RECORD INTO PRODUCT-RECORD
    AT END MOVE 1 TO END-OF-FILE-MARKER.

causes a record to be read and its contents stored in PRODUCT-RECORD. In order to set up the detail lines of the report, items of data are moved from the fields in the input area PRODUCT-RECORD to the fields set aside to receive them in the output record area REPORT-RECORD.

62

```
MOVE PRODUCT-NUMBER TO RL-PRODUCT-NUMBER
MOVE DESCRIPTION TO RL-DESCRIPTION
MOVE QUANTITY-ON-HAND TO RL-QUANTITY-ON-HAND
MOVE QUANTITY-ON-ORDER TO RL-QUANTITY-ON-ORDER
MOVE DD TO RL-DD
MOVE MM TO RL-MM
MOVE YY TO RL-YY.
```

Remember that a MOVE statement copies data from one place to another. The data in the source variable remains intact and can be used again. Once this transfer is completed the record can then be printed.

8.3 Repeating Statements

Normally each statement in a COBOL program is executed once, then the program passes to the following statement. However, in most programs we want to repeat at least some of the sequences of statements. In the program PRINT-PRODUCTS we are processing all the records on the PRODUCT-FILE, therefore, we want the paragraph PRINT-AND-READ to be executed once for each record on the file. In other words, PRINT-AND-READ has to be repeated a number of times equal to the number of records on the file. The signal to stop reading records is given when the AT END clause is executed. The sentence

PERFORM PRINT-AND-READ UNTIL END-OF-FILE-MARKER = 1.

causes the paragraph PRINT-AND-READ to be repeated until END-OF-FILE-MARKER is set to 1. Originally END-OF-FILE-MARKER was set to zero by the statement

MOVE ZERO TO END-OF-FILE-MARKER.

END-OF-FILE-MARKER is set to 1 by the AT END clause of a READ statement. So PRINT-AND-READ will be PERFORMed, i.e. repeated, until the end-of-file condition is detected and END-OF-FILE-MARKER is set to 1.

The UNTIL condition is tested before PRINT-AND-READ is performed. If PRODUCT-FILE had contained no data records at all, just a header label and a trailer label then the end-of-file condition would have been detected by the READ statement immediately before the PERFORM statement and PRINT-AND-READ would not have been performed at all. The program would pass on to the next executable statement following the PERFORM statement. Within PRINT-AND-READ the next record is read at the end of the paragraph so that when the PERFORM ... UNTIL statement is executed again the program knows whether there are more data records to be processed or not.

This arrangement is known as "read ahead" and is very important when you are constructing a repetition of statements to process records on a sequential file. Careful thought must be given on what to do when a file ends. It is also essential to cope with the rather uncommon condition of a file with no data records on it, only the header and trailer labels. Careless programming can lead to a program trying to process a trailer label or whatever data is left in the input record area. This will certainly produce nonsensical output and probably cause the program to fail. So learn the good programming habit of reading the first record on the file immediately after the opening of the file and each subsequent record immediately after the previous one has been processed. The logical format of a read and process loop is

    read a record
    while the input file is not at end-of-file
        process record
        read next record

8.4 PERFORM Statement

We have seen how the PERFORM statement in PRINT-PRODUCTS is used to allow a sequence of PROCEDURE DIVISION statements to be repeated. However, PERFORM is a very powerful statement with a number of optional facilities. COBOL 85 introduces a major enhancement to PERFORM which further complicates matters. We will start by dealing with the syntax of the most commonly used versions which operate in both COBOL 74 and COBOL 85.

Format 1:

$$\underline{\text{PERFORM}} \quad \text{procedure–name–1} \quad \left[\left\{ \begin{array}{l} \underline{\text{THROUGH}} \\ \underline{\text{THRU}} \end{array} \right\} \text{procedure–name–2} \right]$$

The PERFORM statement transfers control from one part of a program to another, executes one or more sentences within a specified procedure then returns control to the sentence in the program immediately following the PERFORM. Control is passed to procedure-name-1 which is executed statement by statement until the end of the procedure is reached. A procedure-name can be a paragraph name, as in PRINT-PRODUCTS, or a section name. In the latter case all the paragraphs within the section are performed. If the THRU/THROUGH option is used, all the procedure-names between procedure-name-1 and procedure-name-2 are performed.

64

Example: PERFORM CALCULATE-1.
           PERFORM CALCULATE-1 THRU CALCULATE-3.

        CALCULATE-1.
           statement-1
           statement-2
           . . .
           statement-n.
        CALCULATE-2.
           statement-1
           statement-2
           . . .
           statement-n.
        CALCULATE-3.
           statement-1
           statement-2
           . . .
           statement-n.
        CALCULATE-4.

The first PERFORM statement executes paragraph CALCULATE-1. The program knows that it is at the end of a paragraph when it reaches another paragraph name, in this case CALCULATE-2. The second PERFORM statement performs all the paragraphs CALCULATE-1, CALCULATE-2, CALCULATE-3 and stops performing when the paragraph name CALCULATE-4 is reached. It is, however, recommended to avoid the use of THROUGH/THRU whenever possible. If a series of paragraphs have to be performed, set them up as a SECTION and PERFORM the section name.

8.4.1 UNTIL Option

Format 2:

$$\underline{\text{PERFORM}} \quad \text{procedure–name–1} \quad \left[\left\{ \begin{array}{l} \underline{\text{THROUGH}} \\ \underline{\text{THRU}} \end{array} \right\} \text{procedure–name–2} \right]$$

$$\underline{\text{UNTIL}} \text{ condition–1}$$

The PERFORM statement is executed and the condition following UNTIL is examined. If it is found to be true the program passes on to the statement immediately following. If the condition is false the range of the PERFORM is executed and the condition re-examined.

65

Examples: PERFORM READ-RECORD UNTIL RECORD-COUNT = 100.

When this statement is executed, the program looks at RECORD-COUNT to see if it equals 100. If not, the procedure READ-RECORD is performed then READ-COUNT is examined again. If it is still not equal to 100 READ-RECORD is performed again and so on until RECORD-COUNT contains 100 then the program moves on to the following statement. If READ-COUNT had contained 100 when the PERFORM was first executed, the program would have immediately passed on to the next statement without performing READ-RECORD. Care must be taken to ensure that READ-COUNT does sooner or later reach 100 or the program will keep performing READ-RECORD indefinitely.

Format 2 (COBOL 85)

$$\underline{\text{PERFORM}} \quad \text{procedure-name-1} \quad \left[\left\{ \begin{array}{c} \underline{\text{THROUGH}} \\ \underline{\text{THRU}} \end{array} \right\} \text{procedure-name-2} \right]$$

$$\left[\text{WITH } \underline{\text{TEST}} \left\{ \begin{array}{c} \underline{\text{BEFORE}} \\ \underline{\text{AFTER}} \end{array} \right\} \right] \underline{\text{UNTIL}} \text{ condition-1}$$

COBOL 85 allows the programmer to specify whether the test for the terminating condition is done BEFORE or AFTER each execution of the specified procedure. COBOL 74 has no WITH TEST clause. Its test is implicitly BEFORE. PERFORM WITH TEST BEFORE is a "do while" construct. This means that the procedure is performed as long as a condition is true. When it becomes false, the procedure is not performed. PERFORM WITH TEST AFTER is a "do until" construct. The condition is tested after the procedure has been performed, so there is always one pass through the procedure. A "do while" construct can have zero passes through the procedure. If the WITH TEST clause is omitted the program defaults to WITH TEST BEFORE to preserve compatibility with COBOL 74.

8.4.2 TIMES Option

Format 3:

$$\underline{\text{PERFORM}} \quad \text{procedure-name-1} \quad \left[\left\{ \begin{array}{c} \underline{\text{THROUGH}} \\ \underline{\text{THRU}} \end{array} \right\} \text{procedure-name-2} \right]$$

$$\left\{ \begin{array}{c} \text{identifier-1} \\ \text{integer-1} \end{array} \right\} \underline{\text{TIMES}}$$

The PERFORM statement is executed the number of times specified by integer or the contents of identifier. Integer or the contents of identifier must be positive. Identifier must be described as a number without a decimal point in the DATA DIVISION. If the value of integer or identifier is zero or negative control passes immediately to the next statement following the PERFORM. Take care not to alter the contents of identifier-1 within the performed procedure.

Examples: PERFORM DATA-CHECK THROUGH DATA-CORRECT
                    COUNT-1 TIMES.
            PERFORM READ-RECORD 100 TIMES.

8.5 PERFORM In COBOL 85

The COBOL 74 version of PERFORM is what is called an "out-of-line" PERFORM. That means the statements to be repeated must be written as a separate procedure elsewhere in the program and the PERFORM statement transfers control out of line to the procedure then return back to the original line of control. COBOL 85 includes an "in-line" PERFORM when the programmer need not create a separate procedure but may include the statements to be performed within the PERFORM statement itself. All the PERFORM formats have an "in-line" option.

Format 1:

PERFORM [imperative–statement–1 END–PERFORM]

Format 2:

PERFORM $\left\{ \begin{array}{l} \text{identifier–1} \\ \text{integer–1} \end{array} \right\}$ TIMES [imperative–statement–1 END–PERFORM]

Format 3:

PERFORM $\left[\text{WITH TEST} \left\{ \begin{array}{l} \underline{\text{BEFORE}} \\ \underline{\text{AFTER}} \end{array} \right\} \right]$ UNTIL condition–1

[imperative–statement–1 END–PERFORM]

To illustrate the use of the "in-line" PERFORM we will rewrite part of program PRINT-PRODUCTS (Fig. 7.3). Instead of writing

PERFORM PRINT-AND-READ UNTIL END-OF-FILE-MARKER = 1.

we can write

PERFORM UNTIL END-OF-FILE-MARKER = 1
    MOVE PRODUCT-NUMBER TO RL-PRODUCT-NUMBER

```
            MOVE DESCRIPTION TO RL-DESCRIPTION
            MOVE QUANTITY-ON-HAND TO RL-QUANTITY-ON-HAND
            MOVE QUANTITY-ON-ORDER TO RL-QUANTITY-ON-ORDER
            MOVE DD TO RL-DD
            MOVE MM TO RL-MM
            MOVE YY TO RL-YY
            WRITE REPORT-RECORD FROM REPORT-LINE
                AFTER ADVANCING 2 LINES
            READ PRODUCT-FILE RECORD INTO PRODUCT-RECORD
                AT END MOVE 1 TO END-OF-FILE-MARKER
    END-PERFORM.
```

The statements which are part of procedure PRINT-AND-READ are now
incorporated within the PERFORM statement. The "in-line" PERFORM
performs all statements whether they are terminated by a full-stop or not, up
to the scope terminator END-PERFORM.

8.5.1 In-line or Out-of-line?

Whether a programmer uses the "in-line" or "out-of-line" PERFORM depends
on personal preference, but, in general, the "in-line" is useful when a small
number of statements have to be repeated and "out-of-line" when more
substantial amounts of coding are involved. Also, the "out-of-line" method of
performing procedures makes the overall logical structure of the program
clearer. However, against this, can be weighed the nuisance of hunting
through a long program listing trying to find a procedure.

8.5.2 Scope Terminators

Scope terminators are introduced in COBOL 85 for the first time in COBOL
although they have been a feature of other programming languages for some
time. At the simplest level, scope terminators are substitutes for full-stops and
are primarily used in situations where an actual full-stop cannot be used. This
happens most commonly in decision statements (see Chapter 10), but we have
already encountered the scope terminators END-READ and END-WRITE
when discussing READ and WRITE statements. Their format is always the
same, the word END followed by a statement verb joined by a hyphen. The
scope terminator END-PERFORM is used to delimit the scope of any
imperative statements within "in-line" PERFORM. Since imperative
statements within the scope of an "in-line" PERFORM can be complete
sentences with full-stops this character obviously cannot be used to delimit
the scope of PERFORM, hence the need for END-PERFORM. The
importance of scope terminators to other statements will be discussed when
the need arises.

CHAPTER 9

Processing Numeric Data

9.1 Arithmetic Statements

Arithmetic statements allow a program to carry out the basic arithmetic operations on numeric data items and send the results of calculations to different places. COBOL is not designed as a number crunching language though it can deal with fairly complicated mathematical procedures if required. All arithmetic statements must be written in area B of the coding sheet.

9.2 ADD Statement

The ADD statement adds two or more numeric data items and stores the result. There are two formats in both COBOL 74 and COBOL 85 but there are differences between the two versions of the language.

Format 1 (COBOL 74 and 85):

$$\underline{\text{ADD}} \quad \begin{Bmatrix} \text{identifier–1} \\ \text{literal–1} \end{Bmatrix} \quad \begin{bmatrix} \text{identifier–2} \\ \text{literal–2} \end{bmatrix} \quad \dots \quad \underline{\text{TO}} \quad \text{identifier–m}$$

The values of all the identifiers (including identifier-m) and the literals are added together. The resulting answer is placed in identifier-m. The contents of the fields preceding the TO remain unchanged.

Examples: ADD OVER-TIME TO WEEKLY-HOURS
            ADD 1 TO PAGE-NUMBER.

Format 2 (COBOL 74):

$$\text{ADD} \quad \begin{Bmatrix} \text{identifier-1} \\ \text{literal-1} \end{Bmatrix} \quad \begin{bmatrix} \text{identifier-2} \\ \text{literal-2} \end{bmatrix} \quad \dots \quad \underline{\text{GIVING}} \quad \text{identifier-m}$$

At least two identifiers and/or numeric literals must follow the word ADD and the initial value of the identifier-m is excluded from the addition.

Examples: ADD ON-HAND ON-ORDER GIVING TOTAL-STOCK
            ADD 328 625 UNIT-VALUE GIVING RESULT

In COBOL 74 the word TO does not appear in format 2. Compilers will flag an error if it is included. However COBOL 85 has a different format which includes TO.

Format 2: (COBOL 85)

$$\text{ADD} \quad \begin{Bmatrix} \text{identifier-1} \\ \text{literal-2} \end{Bmatrix} \dots \quad \underline{\text{TO}} \quad \begin{Bmatrix} \text{identifier-2} \\ \text{literal-2} \end{Bmatrix} \quad \underline{\text{GIVING}} \quad \text{identifier-3} \; [\; \text{ROUNDED} \;]$$

Example: ADD ON-HAND TO ON-ORDER GIVING TOTAL-STOCK.

9.3 SUBTRACT Statement

The SUBTRACT statement subtracts one value or the sum of several values, from another value. There are two formats.

Format 1:

$$\underline{\text{SUBTRACT}} \quad \begin{Bmatrix} \text{identifier-1} \\ \text{literal-1} \end{Bmatrix} \quad \begin{bmatrix} \text{identifier-2} \\ \text{literal-2} \end{bmatrix} \quad \dots \quad \underline{\text{FROM}} \quad \text{identifier-m}$$

In its simplest form literal-1 or the contents of identifier-1 are subtracted from identifier-m and the result of the operation is placed in identifier-m.

Examples: SUBTRACT A FROM B

70

	A	B
Before	5	8
After	5	3

SUBTRACT 10 FROM C

	C
Before	28
After	18

In its more complicated form, the SUBTRACT statement operands preceding the FROM are added before being subtracted from identifier-m. The result is placed in the identifier following the FROM.

Example: SUBTRACT A B FROM C

	A	B	C
Before	5	8	28
After	5	8	15

Format 2:

$$\textbf{SUBTRACT} \left\{ \begin{array}{l} \text{identifier--1} \\ \text{literal--1} \end{array} \right\} \left[\begin{array}{l} \text{identifier--2} \\ \text{literal--2} \end{array} \right] \cdots \textbf{FROM} \left\{ \begin{array}{l} \text{identifier--m} \\ \text{literal--m} \end{array} \right\}$$

$$\textbf{GIVING} \ \ \text{identifier--n}$$

The result of the subtraction using the GIVING option is placed in identifier-n. In this case the contents of identifier-m remain intact. The FROM operand may be a numeric literal in this case.

Examples: SUBTRACT A FROM B GIVING C

	A	B	C
Before	5	8	28
After	5	8	3

SUBTRACT A B FROM C GIVING D

	A	B	C	D
Before	5	8	28	1
After	5	8	28	15

SUBTRACT A B FROM 100 GIVING D

	A	B		D
Before	5	8		1
After	5	8		87

SUBTRACT A B FROM 100 GIVING D E

	A	B		D	E
Before	5	8		1	1
After	5	8		87	87

9.4 MULTIPLY Statement

The MULTIPLY statement multiplies two numeric data items. It has two formats.

Format 1:

$$\underline{\text{MULTIPLY}} \left\{ \begin{array}{l} \text{identifier--1} \\ \text{literal--1} \end{array} \right\} \ \underline{\text{BY}} \ \text{identifier--2}$$

This version of the statement multiplies identifier-1 by identifier-2 and places the result in identifier-2.

Example: MULTIPLY A BY B

	A	B
Before	5	8
After	5	40

Format 2:

$$\underline{\text{MULTIPLY}} \left\{ \begin{array}{l} \text{identifier--1} \\ \text{literal--1} \end{array} \right\} \ \underline{\text{BY}} \ \left\{ \begin{array}{l} \text{identifier--2} \\ \text{literal--2} \end{array} \right\} \ \underline{\text{GIVING}} \ \text{identifier--3}$$

72

This version of the statement multiplies identifier-1 by identifier-2 and places the result in identifier-3. If the second operand is a numeric literal the GIVING option must be used.

Examples: MULTIPLY A BY B GIVING C

	A	B	C
Before	5	8	3
After	5	8	40

MULTIPLY A BY 100 GIVING B

	A	B
Before	5	8
After	5	500

Care must be taken to ensure that the results field is large enough to receive the whole answer. A simple rule is that the number of digits in the product of two numbers never exceeds the sum of the number of digits in the original numbers.

9.5 DIVIDE Statement

The DIVIDE statement divides one numeric data item by another. It has three formats.

Format 1:

$$\textbf{DIVIDE} \quad \begin{Bmatrix} \text{identifier--1} \\ \text{literal--1} \end{Bmatrix} \quad \underline{\textbf{BY}} \quad \text{identifier--2}$$

[**REMAINDER** identifier–3]

The first item is divided by the second and the result placed in the second. Note that the second item must be an identifier. To use a literal would be illogical as there would be nowhere to store the result of the division. If the remainder is required then the REMAINDER option must be used. This places the remainder in identifier-3.

Examples: DIVIDE A BY B

73

	A	B
Before	8	4
After	8	2

DIVIDE 24 BY A

	A
Before	8
After	3

Format 2:

$$\text{\underline{DIVIDE}} \left\{ \begin{array}{l} \text{identifier--1} \\ \text{literal--1} \end{array} \right\} \text{\underline{BY}} \left\{ \begin{array}{l} \text{identifier--2} \\ \text{literal--2} \end{array} \right\} \text{\underline{GIVING}} \quad \text{identifier--3}$$

[**REMAINDER** identifier--4]

The GIVING option causes the result of the division to be placed in identifier-3. This format of DIVIDE must be used if the divisor is a literal. Also care must be taken in all division statements to ensure that the divisor is never zero, because this, at best, will give unpredictable results or, more likely, cause the program to fail with a run-time error.

Example: DIVIDE A BY B GIVING C

	A	B	C
Before	8	4	10
After	8	4	2

There is another version of the DIVIDE statement which follows a different general format. This was the original COBOL divide and its rather awkward construction was designed so that the result would always be placed in the last identifier as with other arithmetic statements. The DIVIDE . . . BY version overwrites the divisor rather than the dividend which is rather illogical, so the artificial DIVIDE . . . INTO version was used. Programmers disliked the original version and user pressure forced the inclusion of the version of DIVIDE which corresponds to normal day-to-day usage of the operator.

Format 3:

$$\text{\underline{DIVIDE}} \begin{Bmatrix} \text{identifier--1} \\ \text{literal--1} \end{Bmatrix} \text{\underline{INTO}} \begin{Bmatrix} \text{identifier--2} \\ \text{literal--2} \end{Bmatrix}$$

$$\text{\underline{GIVING}} \quad \text{identifier--3}$$

$$[\text{\underline{REMAINDER}} \quad \text{identifier--4}]$$

Examples: DIVIDE A INTO B

	A	B
Before	4	8
After	4	2

DIVIDE A INTO B GIVING C

	A	B	C
Before	4	8	10
After	4	8	2

DIVIDE A INTO B GIVING C REMAINDER D

	A	B	C	D
After	4	9	10	0
Before	4	9	2	1

The REMAINDER option is not available in some compilers.

9.6 More Complicated Calculation

Most business applications of computers involve relatively small amounts of simple calculation. Nevertheless, some jobs do require complex arithmetical operations and in these cases the use of ADD, SUBTRACT, MULTIPLY and DIVIDE statements can lead to very cumbersome programs. The COMPUTE statement offers a much more compact way of specifying arithmetic operations. Indeed, programmers are sometimes recommended to use COMPUTE for all arithmetic operations, especially by those brought up on languages such as Fortran.

9.7 COMPUTE Statement

The COMPUTE statement assigns to a data item the value of a numeric data item, literal or the result of an arithmetic expression.

It has the format:

$$\underline{\text{COMPUTE}} \ \text{identifier--1} \ = \ \begin{Bmatrix} \textbf{identifier--2} \\ \textbf{numeric--literal} \\ \textbf{arithmetic--expression} \end{Bmatrix}$$

When identifier-2 or numeric-literal are used, the COMPUTE statement amounts to nothing more than a MOVE. The normal use of COMPUTE is with an arithmetic expression, i.e. a combination of identifiers, arithmetic operators, numeric-literals and parentheses.

The five arithmetic operators are the symbols:

+	addition
-	subtraction
*	multiplication
/	division
**	exponentiation

An operator must always be preceded and followed by a space.

Examples: A^2 A ** 2

$$\left[\frac{X+Y}{Z}\right] \quad (X + Y) / Z$$

If no spaces surround the operator they would be interpreted as part of an identifier and in most cases rejected during compilation. If you are used to languages such as Basic or Fortran which do not require a space here, be careful.

9.8 Precedence

The order of operation of the operators in an expression is assumed to be:

unary plus or minus

76

unary plus or minus
exponentiation
multiplication and division
addition and subtraction.

The plus and minus signs are the only unary operators. The unary operator is an operator with only one operand. Its purpose is to set that operand either positive or negative e.g. - A. The unary plus or minus sign must be the first character of the arithmetic expression or must be preceded by a left parenthesis.

Example: - A + B / C +D ** E * F - G
           is evaluated as
           (- A) + (B / C) + ((D ** E) * F) - G

When the order of a sequence of consecutive operations is on the same level the order of operations is assumed to be from left to right.

Example: A / B * C
           is evaluated as
           (A / B) * C

This assumed precedence can be overridden by the use of parenthesis (brackets).

Examples: A / (B * C)

           2(a+b)   2 * (A + B)
           Note that implied multiplication is not allowed.

           $\dfrac{A+B}{C+D}$ (A + B) / (C + D)

           $U^{(n-1)}$ U ** (N − 1)

           $\dfrac{a}{bc}$ A / (B * C)

           $\dfrac{ABX}{A^2 + X^2}$ A * B * X / (A ** 2 + X ** 2)

Exponentiation is only allowed for positive, integers. Two operators cannot

9.9 Arithmetic Expressions

An arithmetic expression must begin with either a unary operator, a left parenthesis, an identifier or a literal. It must end with a right parenthesis, an identifier or a literal. The meaning of the = sign in the COMPUTE statement is "make equal to".

Examples: COMPUTE A = B + C
             COMPUTE OVERTIME-PAY = (HOURS-WORKED - 40) *
                 RATE * 1.5
             COMPUTE QUARTER-AVERAGE = (JAN + FEB + MAR) / 3

The last statement may also be written

ADD JAN FEB MAR GIVING MONTHS
DIVIDE MONTHS BY 3 GIVING QUARTER-AVERAGE.

9.10 Program PRINT-DAY

The program PRINT-DAY (Fig. 9.1) illustrates the use of COMPUTE to process a more complicated algorithm than is usual in commercial data processing. The algorithm works out the day of any date from 1752. The result of the evaluation of the date entered is placed in WEEKDAY, 0 for Saturday, 1 for Sunday through to 6 for Friday. This number is converted by the series of IF statements to a day name. We have not yet dealt with these statements but there meaning is obvious. The day and month are each entered as two digits. The year is entered in full i.e. 1985. The algorithm works for any date from September 1752 when there was a change from the Julian to the Gregorian calendar in Britain. Notice that the data is not validated on entry, so it is possible to enter a nonsensical date such as 30 February 1985. To guard against this problem each value should be tested for reasonableness when it is entered. In fact it is essential that any program accepting raw data from a keyboard or other input device checks that the data is correct before any processing takes place on that data. But we will leave validation until later.

```
000100 IDENTIFICATION DIVISION.
000110 PROGRAM-ID. PRINT-DAY.
000120*
000130* This program works out the day of the week for a date
000140* It copes with all dates. See Practical Computing
000150* March 1985 Page 8 and December 1982.
000160*
000170 ENVIRONMENT DIVISION.
```

```
000140* It copes with all dates. See Practical Computing
000150* March 1985 Page 8 and December 1982.
000160*
000170 ENVIRONMENT DIVISION.
000180 CONFIGURATION SECTION.
000190 SOURCE-COMPUTER. ABC-1.
000200 OBJECT-COMPUTER. ABC-1.
000210 DATA DIVISION.
000220 WORKING-STORAGE SECTION.
000230 01    DATE-1.
000240      03 D                    PIC 99.
000250      03 M                    PIC 99.
000260      03 Y                    PIC 9(4).
000270 01    WORK-ITEMS.
000280      03 J                    PIC 9(5).
00290       03 K                    PIC 9(5).
000300      03 R                    PIC 9(5).
000310      03 W                    PIC 9(5).
000320      03 WEEKDAY              PIC 99.
000330*
000340 PROCEDURE DIVISION.
000350 MAIN.
000360      DISPLAY "Day".
000370      ACCEPT D
000380      PERFORM FIND-DAY UNTIL D IS EQUAL TO ZERO.
000390      STOP RUN.
000400 FIND-DAY.
000410      DISPLAY "Month".
000420      ACCEPT M
000430      DISPLAY"Year".
000440      ACCEPT Y.
000450      IF M IS LESS THAN 3
000460          ADD 12 TO M
000470          SUBTRACT 1 FROM Y.
000480      COMPUTE  J = D + 13 * (M + 1) / 5
000490      COMPUTE  K = 5 * Y / 4 - Y / 100 + Y / 400
000500      ADD J K GIVING W.
000510      DIVIDE W BY 7 GIVING R REMAINDER WEEKDAY.
000520      DISPLAY "This date falls on a ".
000530      IF WEEKDAY IS EQUAL TO 0
000540          DISPLAY "Saturday"
000550      ELSE
000560          IF WEEKDAY IS EQUAL TO 1
000570              DISPLAY "Sunday"
000580          ELSE
000590              IF WEEKDAY IS EQUAL TO 2
000600                  DISPLAY "Monday"
000610              ELSE
000620                  IF WEEKDAY IS EQUAL TO 3
000630                      DISPLAY "Tuesday"
```

```
000680                    IF WEEKDAY IS EQUAL TO 5
000690                        DISPLAY "Thursday"
000700                    ELSE
000710                        DISPLAY "Friday".
000720        DISPLAY "Day".
000730        ACCEPT D
```

Fig. 9.1

9.11 Size Errors

When arithmetic statements are being executed care must be taken to ensure
that the PICTURE into which the answer is placed is suitable. The alignment
of the decimal point must correspond to that of the fields being calculated.
Also the result field must be of sufficient length to accommodate the answer.
If the number of places calculated for the result, after decimal point
alignment, is greater than the number of places in the data item which is to
receive the result, the extra numbers are simply dropped off. This is known as
truncation.

Example: result   784.369
           result   item PICTURE   99V99
           result   item value   84.36

9.11.1 ROUNDED option

If there is any doubt about the size of a result of a calculation and truncation
following the decimal point is likely to lead to an unacceptable error, the
ROUNDED option should be used after the arithmetic statement. This
simply involves writing the word ROUNDED after the data name of the
result.

Example: MULTIPLY QUANTITY BY PRICE GIVING TOTAL ROUNDED.

This will ensure that the value in TOTAL, should it exceed the PICTURE
size of TOTAL, will be rounded up if the extra digit is greater than or equal
to 5 and down if it is less than 5.

Calculated results	PICTURE	Value after rounding	Value after truncating
-12.36	S99V9	-12.4	-12.3
-6.42	S9V9	-6.4	-6.4
65.6	99V	66	65
8.432	9V9	8.4	8.4
.0055	V999	.006	.005

Fig. 9.2

The ROUNDED option can, of course, be used deliberately to round numbers in calculating percentages or values to the nearest pound etc. ROUNDED can be used with all arithmetic statements, but remember, only the identifier which receives the result of the operation can be followed by ROUNDED. You should also be very careful when you use ROUNDED because repeated rounding during a series of arithmetic operations can give rise to an unacceptably large rounding error.

9.11.2 ON SIZE ERROR Option

If there are too many numbers to the left of the decimal point, the leading numbers are truncated after alignment on the decimal point. This creates a size error. We can avoid this problem by adding an ON SIZE ERROR clause to the arithmetic statement.

It has the format:

[ON SIZE ERROR imperative–statement]

If the ON SIZE ERROR option has been specified and a size error condition arises, the contents of the receiving field are not altered and the imperative statement following ON SIZE ERROR is executed. If the ON SIZE ERROR option has not been specified and a size error condition arises, no assumption can be made about the result. The program will continue uninterrupted.

Example: MULTIPLY WEEKS-PAY BY 52 GIVING YEARS-PAY ROUNDED
                  SIZE ERROR PERFORM OVERFLOW-ERROR.

It is worth noting that the use of ON SIZE ERROR changes an arithmetic statement from an imperative statement to a conditional statement.

81

9.12 NOT ON SIZE ERROR Option

In COBOL 74 the program proceeds to the next sentence if an ON SIZE ERROR clause is present but no size error is detected. COBOL 85 provides an additional clause which allows the programmer to specify special action to be taken if no size error has been detected.

It has the format:

[NOT ON SIZE ERROR imperative–statement]

Example: MULTIPLY WEEKS-PAY BY 52 GIVING YEAR-PAY ROUNDED
                    ON SIZE ERROR PERFORM OVERFLOW-ERROR
                    NOT ON SIZE ERROR PERFORM FIND-TAX.
          ADD SUB-TOTAL TO GRAND-TOTAL
                    ON SIZE ERROR PERFORM TOTAL-OVERFLOW
                    NOT ON SIZE ERROR PERFORM PRINT-TOTAL.

9.13 Scope Terminators

In COBOL 85 each arithmetic statement has a scope terminator. This is useful when both an ON SIZE ERROR and a NOT ON SIZE ERROR are used. Take the following example:

    ADD SUB-TOTAL TO GRAND-TOTAL
        ON SIZE ERROR
            ADD FIELD-1 TO FIELD-2
            MOVE ERROR-MESSAGE TO PRINT-LINE
        NOT ON SIZE ERROR
            PERFORM SUM-ROUTINE.
    END-ADD.

This is perfectly clear. There are two ADD statements, one nested within the other. The inner one is activated only if the ON SIZE ERROR path of the outer ADD is taken. But another programmer later amends the program and removes MOVE ERROR-MESSAGE TO PRINT-LINE giving

    ADD SUB-TOTAL TO GRAND-TOTAL
        ON SIZE ERROR
            ADD FIELD-1 TO FIELD-2
        NOT ON SIZE ERROR
            PERFORM SUM-ROUTINE.
    END-ADD.

Now the NOT ON SIZE ERROR becomes part of the inner ADD statement. This drastically changes the logic of the code. The solution is to use a scope terminator.

```
ADD SUB-TOTAL TO GRAND-TOTAL
    ON SIZE ERROR
        ADD FIELD-1 TO FIELD-2
        END-ADD
    NOT ON SIZE ERROR
        PERFORM SUM-ROUTINE.
END-ADD.
```

The END-ADD after the inner ADD statement ends the scope of that statement and leaves the NOT ON SIZE ERROR attached to the outer ADD, as was originally intended.

CHAPTER 10

Making Decisions

10.1 Program Flow

The execution of statements within a program is sequential, in other words, when one statement is completed the computer passes on to the next one in the program and so on until all the statements are executed. There are situations, however, when we have to select one out of two or more courses of action. The selection of each of the alternatives available depends on the conditions in operation when the program is executed. The program must contain sets of instructions for each of the different situations that can arise. This requires the use of a conditional statement. A conditional statement is a means of altering the flow of a program according to conditions prevailing at the time of execution of that statement. It forms one of the most important abilities of the computer, that of making decisions. These are, of course, second-hand decisions since they have already been made by the programmer.

In COBOL the IF statement is used to carry out selection and transfer control from one part of the PROCEDURE DIVISION to another. This statement has two basic formats allowing the option of carrying out one-way, two-way and multiway selection.

10.2 One-way Selection

The IF statement evaluates a condition and causes alternate actions to be carried out depending on whether the condition is true or false.

It has the format:

$$\text{IF condition--1} \begin{Bmatrix} \text{statement--1} \\ \underline{\text{NEXT}}\ \underline{\text{SENTENCE}} \end{Bmatrix}$$

If the value of the condition is TRUE the statement immediately following the condition is executed.

Example: IF PRODUCT-CODE IS EQUAL TO "AB21"
                    PERFORM PROCESS-AB21.

If the value of the condition is FALSE the program skips to the first statement of the next sentence without carrying out any action. In the example, the program would not PERFORM PROCESS-AB21 if PRODUCT-CODE was not equal to AB21. It is very important to ensure that the full stop indicating the end of the condition statement is in the correct place.

In the previous example only a single statement is executed if the condition is TRUE. But it is possible to execute many such statements as long as they form a single sentence.

Example: IF PRODUCT-CODE IS EQUAL TO "AB21"
                    MOVE 1 TO PAGE-NUMBER
                    MOVE HEADING-1 TO PR-HEADING
                    PERFORM GET-DATE
                    PERFORM WRITE-HEADER
                    PERFORM PROCESS-AB21.

When the condition is TRUE in this example all the statements up to the end of the sentence are executed. Then the program passes to the next sentence. If the condition is FALSE then the five statements up to the end of the sentence are skipped and the program passes to the next sentence.

10.3 Two-way Selection

In a one-way selection the statement or statements following the condition are either executed or not depending on the condition being TRUE or FALSE. In a two-way selection one statement or set of statements is executed if the condition is TRUE and a different set of statements is executed if the condition is FALSE. This form of the IF statement has the format:

$$\underline{IF}\ \ condition\text{--}1\ \left\{ \begin{array}{l} statement\text{--}1 \\ \underline{NEXT\ SENTENCE} \end{array} \right\}$$

$$\underline{ELSE}\ \left\{ \begin{array}{l} statement\text{--}2 \\ \underline{NEXT\ SENTENCE} \end{array} \right\}$$

When the ELSE option is used the statements following are executed when the condition is FALSE.

Example: IF PRODUCT-CODE IS EQUAL TO "AB21"
                    PERFORM PROCESS-AB21
               ELSE
                    PERFORM PROCESS-OTHERS.

The effect of this example is to test the contents of PRODUCT-CODE. If it is equal to AB21 (i.e. the condition is TRUE) the procedure PROCESS-AB21 is performed. If the content of PRODUCT-CODE is not equal to AB21 (i.e. the condition is FALSE) then the procedure PROCESS-OTHERS is performed. Whether the condition is TRUE or FALSE the program flow passes on to the next sentence after executing the appropriate statement.

10.4 Test Conditions

A test condition is an expression which may be true or false, depending on the circumstances existing when the expression is evaluated. There are four types of test conditions; the relation test, sign test, class test and condition-name test.

10.4.1 Relation Test

A relation test involves the comparison of two operands, either of which may be a data-name, literal or an arithmetic expression.

It has the format:

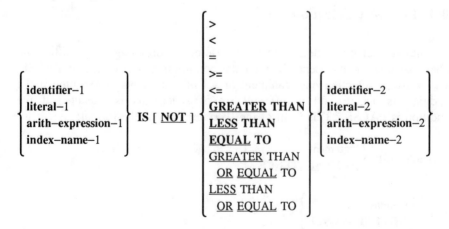

The comparison of two literals is not permitted. A figurative constant may be used in place of either literal in the relation test. GREATER THAN OR EQUAL TO and LESS THAN OR EQUAL TO are additions found in COBOL 85 but not in COBOL 74.

Symbols may be used in place of words and may be preceded by NOT, if required.

Examples: IF AGE IS LESS THAN 18
                    ADD 1 TO MINOR-COUNT.
               IF AGE < 18
                    ADD 1 TO MINOR-COUNT.
               IF QUANTITY > ZERO
                    ADD QUANTITY TO TOTAL.
               IF HOURS-40 IS GREATER THAN ZERO
                    ADD OVERTIME TO WAGES.
               IF AGE NOT < 18
                    ADD 1 TO MAJOR-COUNT
               ELSE
                    ADD 1 TO MINOR-COUNT.

10.4.2 Comparison of Numeric Items

When a comparison of numeric items takes place the lengths of the fields are ignored. The items are compared algebraically, after they have been aligned on their decimal points. Therefore, 35, 0035 and 35.00 are considered identical.

10.4.3 Comparison of Non-numeric Items

For non-numeric items a comparison results in the determination that one of the items is less than, equal to or greater than the other with respect to the binary collating sequence of the computer being used. If the two non-numeric items are the same length their characters in corresponding positions are compared from left to right until either a pair of unequal characters or the end of the items is encountered. The item containing the higher binary value is the greater. For example BROWN comes before SMITH because B has a lower binary value then S.

If the items are of different lengths, the shorter is considered the smaller except where the additional length of the longer is filled with spaces.

Examples: WILLIAMS comes before WILLIAMSON
               WILLIAMS is equal to WILLIAMS∇∇

When non-numeric items are of different lengths the shorter is padded out with spaces so that comparison takes place internally between two items of equal length. When mixed alphabetic and numeric (alphanumeric) items are being compared, care must be taken in considering the relative positions in the collating sequence of letters and numbers. The collating sequence of different computers may vary depending on whether ASCII or EBCDIC is used for individual characters.

10.4.4 Class Condition Test

The class test permits the testing of the contents of a data field to see if its contents are numeric or alphabetic.

It has the format

$$\text{IF identifier--1 IS [\underline{NOT}]} \left\{ \begin{array}{l} \textbf{NUMERIC} \\ \textbf{ALPHABETIC} \\ \text{ALPHABETIC--LOWER} \\ \text{ALPHABETIC--UPPER} \end{array} \right\}$$

The identifier is NUMERIC if it contains only the digits 0 to 9, with or without an operational sign (+ or -). To be termed ALPHABETIC in COBOL 74 the identifier must contain only the upper case letters A to Z or space. COBOL 85 changes the meaning of ALPHABETIC to cover both upper and lower case letters of the alphabet. Two extra classes, ALPHABETIC-LOWER and ALPHABETIC-UPPER are added. An identifier is ALPHABETIC-LOWER if it contains lower case a to z or space. An identifier is ALPHABETIC-UPPER if it contains upper case A to Z or space. Only a data item with a 9 picture can be tested for NUMERIC or NOT NUMERIC. The fact that an item has a numeric picture clause does not guarantee that its contents are numbers. So it is quite possible to accidently place alphabetic characters in a numeric field and only find the error when the program tries to carry out an arithmetic operation on the data. It is therefore, not only sensible but essential to check that a field which should contain numeric data does indeed do so.

Alphabetic and alphanumeric fields can be tested for ALPHABETIC or NOT ALPHABETIC. But ALPHABETIC is not the same as NOT NUMERIC. NOT NUMERIC means that the field contains any non-numeric character from the computer character set. So special characters such as * / , are NOT NUMERIC and NOT ALPHABETIC. The data item tested must be an elementary one.

Examples: IF UNIT-PRICE IS NUMERIC

MOVE 0 TO ERROR-SWITCH
ELSE
    PERFORM PRINT-ERROR-MESSAGE.
IF DESCRIPTION IS NOT ALPHABETIC
    PERFORM DESCRIPTION-ERROR.

10.4.5 Sign Test

The sign test determines whether the value of a numeric item is negative, zero or positive.

It has the format

$$\underline{IF} \; \left\{ \begin{array}{l} \text{identifier} - 1 \\ \text{arithmetic-expression} - 1 \end{array} \right\} \; [\; \underline{NOT} \;] \; \left\{ \begin{array}{l} \underline{POSITIVE} \\ \underline{NEGATIVE} \\ \underline{ZERO} \end{array} \right\}$$

Needless to say, only a signed numeric data item can be tested for NEGATIVE.

Examples: IF FIELD-1 IS POSITIVE
                DIVIDE FIELD-1 INTO AMOUNT GIVING ANSWER.
            IF UNIT-PRICE IS NOT ZERO
                MULTIPLY QUANTITY BY UNIT-PRICE GIVING COST.
            IF STOCK-QUANTITY IS NEGATIVE
                PERFORM ORDER-MORE.

10.5 Multiway Selection

Two-way selection allowed us to select from two alternatives. But we may wish to select from more than two. This is where we use multiway selection. The general logic of the IF statement is

            IF condition-1
                statements-1
            ELSE
                statements-2.

Statements-1 and statements-2 may themselves be IF statements.

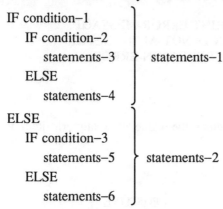

```
IF condition-1
    IF condition-2
        statements-3            statements-1
    ELSE
        statements-4
ELSE
    IF condition-3
        statements-5            statements-2
    ELSE
        statements-6
```

The order of execution of these statements is as follows. If condition-1 is TRUE then IF condition-2 is executed. If this is also TRUE then statements-3 are executed and the program proceeds to the next sentence. If condition-2 is FALSE then statements-4 is executed and the program proceeds to the next sentence. However, if condition-1 is FALSE then the ELSE part containing the expanded sentences-2 is executed. Condition-3 is tested and if it is TRUE then statements-5 is carried out and the program proceeds to the next sentence. If condition-3 is FALSE then statements-6 is executed and the program proceeds to the next sentence. Note that a full-stop always comes at the end of the complete IF statement.

In the previous arrangement, statements-1 and statements-2 each contain IF ... ELSE statements and there is no reason why statements-3, statements-4, statements-5 and statements-6 could not too. But a word of caution before we get too carried away. Nesting IF statements must be carried out with great care. It is absolutely essential that a program is written in such a way that its logic is easy to follow so that the program can be checked for correctness and any future alteration can be carried out easily. Therefore, multi-level nesting is not recommended.

Example: IF ERROR-CODE IS EQUAL TO "NO"
                MOVE ZERO TO QUANTITY-SHIPPED TOTAL-SHIPPED
                IF RECORD-CODE = "I"
                    PERFORM NEW-PRODUCT-SCREEN
                    PERFORM INPUT-INVOICE
                        UNTIL ANSWER IS EQUAL TO "NO"
                ELSE
                    PERFORM NEW-CREDIT-SCREEN
                    PERFORM INPUT-CREDIT
                        UNTIL ANSWER IS EQUAL TO "NO"

```
ELSE
     IF ERROR-CODE IS EQUAL TO "YES"
        PERFORM ERROR-ROUTINE
     ELSE
        DISPLAY "Unknown error code found " ERROR-CODE.
```

If ERROR-CODE is equal to "NO", zeros are moved to QUANTITY-SHIPPED and TOTAL-SHIPPED then RECORD-CODE is tested to see if it is equal to "I". If this condition is TRUE NEW-PRODUCT-SCREEN is performed and INPUT-INVOICE is performed until ANSWER is set to "NO". If RECORD-CODE is not equal to "I" then NEW-CREDIT-SCREEN is performed and INPUT-CREDIT is performed until ANSWER is set to "NO". If ERROR-CODE is not equal to "NO" the program skips to the ELSE part where ERROR-CODE is tested to see if it is equal to "YES". If this condition is TRUE then ERROR-ROUTINE is performed. If the condition is FALSE the error message is displayed.

10.6 NEXT SENTENCE

In the format of the IF statement the reserved words NEXT SENTENCE appear. As the phrase suggests, these words cause the program to skip to the next sentence following the IF sentence. This facility is seldom used, since, in a one-way selection, if a condition is FALSE the program automatically skips to the next sentence. However, in two-way or multiway selection we may wish to come out of an IF statement prematurely. Suppose, in the previous example, that PERFORM NEW-PRODUCT-SCREEN is executed but in the course of execution an error condition is found. This causes ERROR-INDICATOR to be set to 1. In this case we do not want to PERFORM INPUT-INVOICE UNTIL ANSWER IS EQUAL TO "NO" but to go to the next sentence. This piece of coding can be altered to

```
IF RECORD-CODE IS EQUAL TO "I"
   PERFORM NEW-PRODUCT-SCREEN
   IF ERROR-SWITCH IS EQUAL TO 1
      NEXT SENTENCE
   ELSE
      PERFORM INPUT-INVOICE
         UNTIL ANSWER IS EQUAL TO "NO".
```

10.7 Compound Conditions

It is often convenient to combine two or more tests into one conditional statement. For this purpose we use the logical operators AND, OR and NOT. Two or more simple conditions combined by AND, OR or both constitute a compound condition. AND means both conditions have to be satisfied. OR means either or both conditions have to be satisfied. Thus A OR B is TRUE when A is TRUE or B is TRUE or both A and B are TRUE.

Examples: IF QUANTITY > 9999 OR PRICE < ZERO
            DISPLAY "CARD IN ERROR" CARD-REC.
            IF A-CODE IS LESS THAN 20 AND B-CODE = C
            OR B-CODE = D
            PERFORM PROCESS-1
            ELSE
            PERFORM PROCESS-3.

You must take care to ensure that the order of evaluation of a compound condition statement is what you are expecting. When a condition contains both AND and OR, AND takes precedence over OR when the statement is executed.

Example: IF A > B OR A = C AND D = ZERO
           is evaluated as if it were
           IF (A > B) OR ((A = C) AND (D = ZERO))

Parentheses may be used to specify the order in which conditions are evaluated and overrule the natural precedence.

Example: IF (A > B OR A = C) AND D = ZERO
           is evaluated as
           ((A > B) OR (A = C)) AND (D = ZERO).

10.8 Condition Name Entry

COBOL has the very useful facility of giving a name to a condition and using this name rather than the complete condition in IF statements. A condition-name is assigned to an elementary data item by adding a special 88 level number entry to its description in the DATA DIVISION.

It has the format:

$$88 \text{ condition–name} \left\{ \begin{array}{l} \textbf{VALUE IS} \\ \textbf{VALUES ARE} \end{array} \right\} \text{literal–1} \left[\left\{ \begin{array}{l} \textbf{THROUGH} \\ \textbf{THRU} \end{array} \right\} \text{literal–2} \right]$$

$$\left[\text{literal–3} \left[\left\{ \begin{array}{l} \textbf{THROUGH} \\ \textbf{THRU} \end{array} \right\} \text{literal–4} \right] \right] \; \ldots$$

The condition-name can only refer to an elementary item, so an 88 level entry can only follow an elementary item or another 88 entry. An 88 level entry may occur in the FILE SECTION or the WORKING-STORAGE SECTION.

The format looks very complicated but in practice the use of a condition name entry is relatively simple. Let us take as an example a data item MARITAL-STATUS which is described as a single digit numeric item. It may contain one of three values, 1 indicating that a person is single, 2 indicating that a person is married and 3 indicating that a person is divorced. We set up the data item description as follows:

```
03 MARITAL-STATUS    PIC 9.
   88 SINGLE       VALUE IS 1.
   88 MARRIED      VALUE IS 2.
   88 DIVORCED  VALUE IS 3.
```

If we wished to test the contents of MARITAL-STATUS to find if a person is single, we can write either

```
IF MARITAL-STATUS = 1 PERFORM PROCESS-SINGLE.
        or
IF SINGLE PERFORM PROCESS-SINGLE.
```

Similarly, if we wanted to determine the other conditions we can write

```
IF MARRIED PERFORM PROCESS-MARRIED.
IF DIVORCED PERFORM PROCESS-DIVORCED.
```

Condition-names simplify IF statements and can be used to make the program code easier to understand. IF MARITAL-STATUS = 1 may not mean very much to someone who does not know the marital status coding system but IF SINGLE immediately conveys the meaning of the statement.

A level 88 entry may specify a range of values using the THROUGH/THRU option.

Example: 03 ITEM-CODE   PICTURE 9.
           88 STEEL   VALUE 1 THRU 4.
           88 IRON   VALUE 5.
           88 ALUMINIUM   VALUE 6 7 9 THRU 11.

In this example IF STEEL is equivalent to writing

IF ITEM-CODE = 1 OR ITEM-CODE = 2 OR ITEM-CODE = 3 OR ITEM-CODE = 4

ALUMINIUM is indicated when ITEM-CODE contains either 6, 7, 9, 10 or 11.

10.9 COBOL 85 Additions

The COBOL 85 format of the IF statement includes scope terminators for situations where a full-stop cannot be used, but otherwise makes no changes to the operation of the statement.

It has the format:

$$\underline{IF}\ condition\text{--}1\ \textbf{THEN} \left\{ \begin{array}{l} \{\ \textbf{statement-1}\ \}\ \cdots \\ \underline{\textbf{NEXT}}\ \underline{\textbf{SENTENCE}} \end{array} \right\}$$

$$\left\{ \begin{array}{l} \underline{\textbf{ELSE}}\ \{\ \textbf{statement-2}\ \}\ \cdots\ [\ \underline{\textbf{END--IF}}\ ] \\ \underline{\textbf{ELSE}}\ \underline{\textbf{NEXT}}\ \underline{\textbf{SENTENCE}} \\ [\ \underline{\textbf{END--IF}}\ ] \end{array} \right\}$$

10.10 Case Statement

In the program PRINT-DAY in Fig 9.1, the selection of the weekday name is carried out by a series of nested IF statements.

```
IF WEEKDAY IS EQUAL TO 0
   DISPLAY "Saturday"
ELSE
     IF WEEKDAY IS EQUAL TO 1
        DISPLAY "Sunday"
     ELSE
          IF WEEKDAY IS EQUAL TO 2
             DISPLAY "Monday"
          ELSE
```

```
    IF WEEKDAY IS EQUAL TO 3
        DISPLAY "Tuesday"
    ELSE
        IF WEEKDAY IS EQUAL TO 4
            DISPLAY "Wednesday"
        ELSE
            IF WEEKDAY IS EQUAL TO 5
                DISPLAY "Thursday"
            ELSE
                DISPLAY "Friday".
```

Here we are selecting from among several cases as shown in Fig. 10.1. The selection process tests the state of WEEKDAY. The first IF determines whether WEEKDAY contains 0. If it does, we select the first case and DISPLAY "Saturday". If the first case is not TRUE, we test for the second case, that WEEKDAY is equal to 1. If it is, we DISPLAY "Sunday" and so on. After a case is successfully selected the program proceeds to the next sentence.

WEEKDAY	NAME
0	Saturday
1	Sunday
2	Monday
3	Tuesday
4	Wednesday
5	Thursday
6	Friday

Fig. 10.1

Notice that all the nesting is done in the ELSE part of statement. This is characteristic of case selection. Several programming languages provide a special case statement to handle this type of selection easily but COBOL 74 has no such special facility. However, COBOL 85 contains a case statement.

10.11 EVALUATE Statement

The EVALUATE statement provides a neat way of making multiple choices.

It has the format:

95

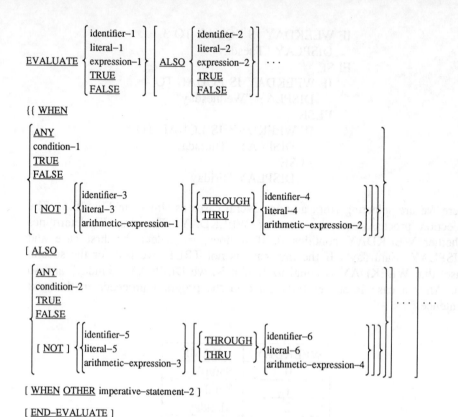

All this looks very complicated, indeed it is, but we can extract from the complete format the options which are most immediately useful to novice programmers. The set of IF statements which looked for the correct day name in the previous example can be rewritten as follows

```
EVALUATE WEEKDAY
      WHEN 0 DISPLAY "Saturday"
      WHEN 1 DISPLAY "Sunday"
      WHEN 2 DISPLAY "Monday"
      WHEN 3 DISPLAY "Tuesday"
      WHEN 4 DISPLAY "Wednesday"
      WHEN 5 DISPLAY "Thursday"
      WHEN 6 DISPLAY "Friday"
END-EVALUATE.
```

The statement tests the contents of the identifier WEEKDAY, this is called the selection subject, the elements after WHEN are the selection objects. Depending on which of the WHEN clauses are true the appropriate action is taken. The same results can be achieved in another way.

```
EVALUATE TRUE
      WHEN WEEKDAY = 0 DISPLAY "Saturday"
      WHEN WEEKDAY = 1 DISPLAY "Sunday"
      WHEN WEEKDAY = 2 DISPLAY "Monday""
      WHEN WEEKDAY = 3 DISPLAY "Tuesday""
      WHEN WEEKDAY = 4 DISPLAY "Wednesday"
      WHEN WEEKDAY = 5 DISPLAY "Thursday"
      WHEN WEEKDAY = 6 DISPLAY "Friday"
END-EVALUATE.
```

EVALUATE allows ranges of values to be tested,

```
EVALUATE MONTH
      WHEN 1 THRU 3 PERFORM FIRST-QUARTER
      WHEN 4 THRU 6 PERFORM SECOND-QUARTER
      WHEN 7 THRU 9 PERFORM THIRD-QUARTER
      WHEN OTHER PERFORM FOURTH-QUARTER.
```

In the first WHEN clause, 1,2 and 3 would cause FIRST-QUARTER to be performed, 4, 5 and 6 would cause SECOND-QUARTER and so on. Notice the catch-all condition WHEN OTHER. Any value which does not fall within the ranges specified in the previous WHEN clauses would satisfy OTHER and cause FOURTH-QUARTER to be performed. In this example, the statement is terminated by a full-stop, not by the scope terminator END-EVALUATE. Whether the scope terminator or a full-stop is used is up to the programmer, depending on personal preference or the context of the program.

CHAPTER 11

Interactive Processing

11.1 Creating Files

In the program PRINT-PRODUCTS (Fig. 7.3) we used a file of data which already existed. Now we will look at the facilities available in COBOL for interactive processing and use these to create data files. There are a variety of means of transferring data from a document to a computer. Data may be encoded using a key-to-disk data entry system, read directly from written documents or entered through a keyboard to a file creation program. Some old systems may still be using punched cards. When there is a large amount of data to be input it is usually formed into batches of records on a magnetic tape or disk file and input as a transaction file. We will use the direct interactive method of file creation by using a VDU to a mainframe. A microcomputer works in a similar way. Data items will be input, one item at a time, in response to a request displayed on the screen. The COBOL statements which will handle this are DISPLAY and ACCEPT.

11.2 DISPLAY Statement

The DISPLAY statement causes data to be written to a terminal.

It has the format:

$$\underline{\text{DISPLAY}} \left\{ \begin{array}{l} \text{identifier--1} \\ \text{literal--1} \end{array} \right\} \dots \left[\underline{\text{UPON}} \left\{ \begin{array}{l} \underline{\text{CONSOLE}} \\ \text{mnemonic--name--1} \end{array} \right\} \right]$$

[WITH $\underline{\text{NO}}$ $\underline{\text{ADVANCING}}$]

In its simplest form, DISPLAY causes the contents of an identifier or the literal character string to be output on a terminal.

Example: DISPLAY "Type your name please - ".

The same result could be achieved by placing the message "Type your name please - " in an identifier, MESSAGE, either by a MOVE statement or by using a VALUE clause in the WORKING-STORAGE SECTION and writing the statement

DISPLAY MESSAGE.

Both types of display are often combined as in

DISPLAY "Todays date is " CURRENT-DATE.

In this statement the message "Todays date is " is output followed by the contents of CURRENT-DATE. If the UPON CONSOLE option is used the data is output to the operator's console as in

DISPLAY "Please load tape MS302 " UPON CONSOLE.

The UPON mnemonic-name-1 option causes the message to be display on a device which has been named in the SPECIAL-NAMES paragraph of the ENVIRONMENT DIVISION.

SPECIAL-NAMES.
   CONSOLE IS CRT.
      .
      .
      .

PROCEDURE DIVISION.
      .
      .

DISPLAY MESSAGE UPON CRT.

The position of the cursor after the execution of a DISPLAY statement is not specified in COBOL 74. COBOL 85 specifies that the cursor must be placed on the left-most position of the next line of the display. It also has the additional WITH NO ADVANCING clause which allows the programmer to specify that the cursor remains on the same line as the displayed message.

Example: DISPLAY "Please enter your password " WITH NO ADVANCING.

11.3 ACCEPT Statement

The ACCEPT statement obtains data from the user's terminal and places it in an identifier. It has two formats.

Format 1:

$$\underline{\textbf{ACCEPT}} \text{ identifier--1} \left[\underline{\textbf{FROM}} \left\{ \begin{array}{l} \underline{\textbf{CONSOLE}} \\ \text{mnemonic--name--1} \end{array} \right\} \right]$$

When an ACCEPT statement is executed the program waits for data to be typed in from the keyboard and when the return or enter key is pressed the data is transferred into the identifier. If the FROM option is used the program looks either for data from the operator's console or from the device named in mnemonic-name. The mnemonic-name has to be specified in a SPECIAL-NAMES paragraph. No checking is done on the data so it is possible to enter letters into a numeric field. It is also possible to enter a decimal point into a numeric field which will cause a run-time error as soon as any operations are carried out on it, so a decimal number must be entered without the decimal point with the exact number of digits.

Example: ACCEPT PRODUCT-NUMBER.

When a five digit string is typed and the return key pressed, the five digits are placed in PRODUCT-NUMBER. Since numeric input is treated as if it is characters, no alignment on the decimal point takes place. Each character is placed in the next available position starting from the left. If only four digits are entered they occupy the first four places and the fifth is a space. When used as a numeric value for arithmetic purposes the space will be treated as a digit and this will not produce the same value as expected. Obviously ACCEPT, though very useful has some very unfriendly habits! The reason is that the original designers of COBOL never conceived of the interactive use of their creation. ACCEPT was used to input simple data such as date or file generation numbers at run time by the computer operator. Consequently the ACCEPT and DISPLAY statements have had considerable non-standard extensions added which we will look at later. Also a number of utility packages are available to aid the programmer in capturing data from a VDU or microcomputer. But for the present we will restrict ourselves to the standard ACCEPT and DISPLAY with their attendant limitations.

The second format of ACCEPT has three special functions, extracting two forms of date and the time from the operating system.

$$\underline{\textbf{ACCEPT}} \text{ identifier--2 } \underline{\textbf{FROM}} \left\{ \begin{array}{l} \underline{\textbf{DATE}} \\ \underline{\textbf{DAY}} \\ \underline{\textbf{DAY--OF--WEEK}} \\ \underline{\textbf{TIME}} \end{array} \right\}$$

If the FROM DATE option is used the current date in the format YYMMDD is placed in the identifier. If the date is to be printed then it will have to be reorganised into a day, month, year sequence, however it is worth remembering that if there is any possibility that the date is to be used for sorting a file into date sequence then the date should be stored on the record in the original YYMMDD format. The FROM DAY option places the current year number and the number of days in the year since the 1st January in the format YYDDD. The FROM TIME option places the time held in the operating system into the identifier in the format HHMMSSFF, where FF is hundredths of a second.

The DAY-OF-WEEK option is only available in COBOL 85. This option places a one-digit character in the identifier which stands for the day of the week, 1 for Monday, 2 for Tuesday and so on up to 7 for Sunday. This can be useful for handling data related data stored in a table. (See Chapter 15).

11.4 GO TO Statement

The GO TO statement transfers control from one part of a program to another.

It has the format:

<u>GO</u> <u>TO</u> procedure–name–1

This statement causes the program flow logic to proceed directly to the procedure specified. The procedure-name is either a paragraph name or a section name.

Example: GO TO ABANDON-INPUT.

The GO TO statement is much criticised and some writers go as far as to condemn any use of this statement, maintaining that it is unnecessary in a well designed program following modern structured programming techniques. However, it is the indiscriminate use of GO TO that has lead to the bad programming habits of the past. COBOL was designed before the modern ideas of structured programming were developed but the language allows most of these ideas to be accommodated effectively without the use of GO TO. We require a means of prematurely ending processing in a procedure when a condition arises which prevents any further processing. This situation most commonly occurs when validating input data. This happens in the program CREATE-PRODUCT. If a correct entry cannot be made of a data item, the input of data for that record is abandoned. The GO TO statement is used to jump past the coding to input other items and proceed directly to the end of the procedure where an "Entry abandoned" message is printed. The GO TO is also used to jump round the paragraph ABANDON-INPUT so that this paragraph is not entered when data is valid. The GO TO should always jump forwards, never backwards.

11.5 Program CREATE-PRODUCT

This program demonstrates the use of ACCEPT and DISPLAY and the straightforward validation of data.

11.5.1 Data Validation

There is a saying in computing, "Garbage in, garbage out", which is a blunt American way of saying that the quality of the output from a computer program can only be as good as that of the input data. If the input data is wrong to start with, no amount of processing is going to produce the right output. It is, therefore, of crucial importance that a programmer ensures that all data is thoroughly checked according to a set of rules to ensure that any incorrect or suspect data is rejected and only correct data presented for processing. This is why the program which inputs raw data into a computer processing system must contain extensive data vetting operations. In a batch system any incorrect data is rejected and an error report produced. A file containing the correct data is then entered into the processing stream. In an interactive system, data items must be checked immediately on input and any errors reported to the terminal user for correction before any further processing takes place.

11.5.2 Program Logic

This program creates a record by issuing a series of requests on a VDU and accepting data from the keyboard in response to these requests. The data items are placed in fields of the record PRODUCT-RECORD. The partial pseudocode for the program is as follows:

```
MAIN
     initialise
     while the product number is not equal to the terminator
          process data
     close-down
INITIALISE
     open output file
     initialise data fields
     input product number
```

102

PROCESS DATA
    input description
    input unit price
    input unit cost
    input quantity on hand
    input quantity on order
    if date of delivery is required
      input date
    write record
    input next product number
CLOSE-DOWN
    close file

PROCESS-DATA contains a repetition of a section ENTER-RECORD which contains a sequence of statements to input and check data. The description can contain any character and is not checked, but all numeric fields are checked to see if the data entered is numeric. The program asks for an item, checks it, and if it is correct, proceeds to the next item. If a field is not numeric the program asks for it again. This continues until either a correct item is input or the entry is aborted. Each entry, except the description, can be aborted by typing 99999. The quantity items are input to a five character alphanumeric field, INPUT-ITEM-5, then tested for numeric and if correct, moved to the numeric field in the output-record. This arrangement may seem rather complicated but some compilers allow alphabetic data to be entered into a numeric field with ACCEPT but the program crashes if a special character such as a hyphen or a question mark is entered. The coding arrangement in the program avoids this problem for integers but not for decimal data descriptions. So there is no protection in the program against a program crash if a special character is input to the UNIT-PRICE or UNIT-COST fields. The IS NUMERIC test only prevents alphabetic characters being entered into these fields. Obviously this is unsatisfactory situation but we have not yet dealt with the parts of COBOL which can be used to check decimal numbers effectively. The date is extensively checked to ensure a valid one is entered. You cannot enter the 30th February, and leap years are coped with. When the user aborts an entry, all the data which has already been entered is erased from the program which starts again at a new product number. All previous correct records are written to disk and are unaffected. The PRODUCT-CODE as the key to each record entry is handled differently. The abort has the effect of ending all processing and terminating the program.

When all the data making up the record is input, the record is written to the file UNSPROD. This file is defined as an output file held on magnetic disk. The IDENTIFICATION DIVISION, ENVIRONMENT DIVISION and DATA DIVISION of the program require no comment. The PROCEDURE DIVISION has the same general logic as previous programs. There are two sections MAIN and ENTER-RECORD. MAIN contains three paragraphs, INITIALISE, PROCESS-DATA and CLOSE-DOWN. INITIALISE contains statements to open the output file then ask for a product number. This is the priming read. In previous programs the end of processing has occurred when all the records on the input file have been read and the AT END path taken. This set a switch which stopped the processing of data and executed the closing statements. In the present program we are not reading from an existing file so we must adopt some other procedure to stop the program. This is done by entering a special value which tells the program to terminate. In this program the typing of a product number of zero causes the program to go to CLOSE-DOWN. Paragraph PROCESS-DATA contains the single statement

PERFORM ENTER-RECORD UNTIL PRODUCT-NUMBER = ZERO.

which repeats the record creation and writing cycle until a product number of zero is entered then the program procedes to the next paragraph CLOSE-DOWN. CLOSE-DOWN closes the file, prints a terminating message and stops the run. ENTER-RECORD SECTION contains one paragraph INPUT-DATA which contains a series of DISPLAYs and ACCEPTs to fill the fields of PRODUCT-RECORD. The date of delivery is an optional field so the user is given the choice of entering one or not. When all the data is entered the whole record is written to UNSPROD and the next product number is requested and input.

```
000100 IDENTIFICATION DIVISION.
000110 PROGRAM-ID. CREATE-PRODUCT.
000120 AUTHOR. D WATSON.
000130 INSTALLATION. UNIVERSITY OF ABERDEEN.
000140 DATE-WRITTEN. APRIL 1985.
000150 SECURITY. NONE.
000160*
000170 ENVIRONMENT DIVISION.
000180 CONFIGURATION SECTION.
000190 SOURCE-COMPUTER.  ABC-1.
000200 OBJECT-COMPUTER.  ABC-1.
000210 INPUT-OUTPUT SECTION.
000220 FILE-CONTROL.
000230     SELECT OUTPUT-FILE ASSIGN TO DISK.
000250*
000260 DATA DIVISION.
000270 FILE SECTION.
000280 FD    OUTPUT-FILE
000290       LABEL RECORDS ARE STANDARD
000300       VALUE OF FILE-ID IS "UNSPROD".
000310 01    OUTPUT-FILE-REC              PIC X(66).
000320*
000330 WORKING-STORAGE SECTION.
```

```
000340 01    PRODUCT-RECORD.
000350       03 PRODUCT-NUMBER         PIC 9(5).
000360       03 DESCRIPTION            PIC X(30).
000370       03 UNIT-PRICE             PIC 999V99.
000380       03 UNIT-COST              PIC 999V99.
000390       03 QUANTITY-ON-HAND       PIC 9(5).
000400       03 QUANTITY-ON-ORDER      PIC 9(5).
000410       03 DATE-OF-DELIVERY.
000420          05 DD                  PIC 99.
000430          05 MM                  PIC 99.
000440          05 YY                  PIC 99.
000450       03 QUANTITY-SOLD          PIC 9(5).
000460*
000470 01    WS-WORK-ITEMS.
000480       03 REPLY                  PIC X VALUE "N".
000490       03 ERROR-SWITCH           PIC 9.
000500          88 CORRECT   VALUE 0.
000510          88 INCORRECT VALUE 1.
000520          88 ABANDON   VALUE 2.
000530       03 ERROR-MESSAGE          PIC X(24)
000535          VALUE "This item is not numeric".
000540       03 LEAP-YEAR-FLAG         PIC X.
000550          88 LEAP-YEAR VALUE "T".
000560       03 YEAR-REM               PIC 9.
000570       03 INPUT-ITEM-5           PIC X(5).
000580 PROCEDURE DIVISION.
000590 MAIN SECTION.
000600 INITIALISE.
000610       OPEN OUTPUT OUTPUT-FILE.
000620       PERFORM CLEAR-RECORD.
000630       MOVE 1 TO ERROR-SWITCH.
000640       PERFORM INPUT-PRODUCT-NUMBER UNTIL CORRECT OR ABANDON.
000650       IF CORRECT
000660          MOVE INPUT-ITEM-5 TO PRODUCT-NUMBER
000670       ELSE
000680          MOVE ZERO TO PRODUCT-NUMBER.
000690 PROCESS-DATA.
000700       PERFORM ENTER-RECORD UNTIL PRODUCT-NUMBER = ZERO.
000710 CLOSE-DOWN.
000720       CLOSE OUTPUT-FILE.
000730       DISPLAY "End of entry program".
000740       STOP RUN.
000750 ENTER-RECORD SECTION.
000760 INPUT-DATA.
000770       DISPLAY "Description".
000780       ACCEPT DESCRIPTION.
000790       MOVE 1 TO ERROR-SWITCH.
000800       PERFORM INPUT-UNIT-PRICE UNTIL CORRECT OR ABANDON.
000810       IF ABANDON
000820          GO TO ABANDON-INPUT.
```

```
000830        MOVE 1 TO ERROR-SWITCH.
000840        PERFORM INPUT-UNIT-COST UNTIL CORRECT OR ABANDON.
000850        IF ABANDON
000860            GO TO ABANDON-INPUT.
000870        MOVE 1 TO ERROR-SWITCH.
000880        PERFORM INPUT-QUANTITY-ON-HAND UNTIL CORRECT
000885            OR ABANDON.
000890        IF CORRECT
000900            MOVE INPUT-ITEM-5 TO QUANTITY-ON-HAND
000910        ELSE
000920            GO TO ABANDON-INPUT.
000930        MOVE 1 TO ERROR-SWITCH.
000940        PERFORM INPUT-QUANTITY-ON-ORDER UNTIL CORRECT
000945            OR ABANDON.
000950        IF CORRECT
000960            MOVE INPUT-ITEM-5 TO QUANTITY-ON-ORDER
000970        ELSE
000980            GO TO ABANDON-INPUT.
000990        MOVE 1 TO ERROR-SWITCH.
001000        PERFORM INPUT-DATE UNTIL CORRECT OR ABANDON.
001010        IF ABANDON
001020            GO TO ABANDON-INPUT.
001030        MOVE 1 TO ERROR-SWITCH.
001040        PERFORM INPUT-QUANTITY-SOLD UNTIL CORRECT OR ABANDON.
001050        IF CORRECT
001060            MOVE INPUT-ITEM-5 TO QUANTITY-SOLD
001070        ELSE
001080            GO TO ABANDON-INPUT.
001090        WRITE OUTPUT-FILE-REC FROM PRODUCT-RECORD.
001100            GO TO READ-NEXT-RECORD.
001110 ABANDON-INPUT.
001120        DISPLAY "Entry abandoned".
001130 READ-NEXT-RECORD.
001140        PERFORM CLEAR-RECORD.
001150        MOVE 1 TO ERROR-SWITCH.
001160        PERFORM INPUT-PRODUCT-NUMBER UNTIL CORRECT OR ABANDON.
001170        IF CORRECT
001180            MOVE INPUT-ITEM-5 TO PRODUCT-NUMBER
001190        ELSE
001200            MOVE ZERO TO PRODUCT-NUMBER.
001210*
001220 SUPPORT SECTION.
001230 INPUT-PRODUCT-NUMBER.
001240        DISPLAY "Enter product number"
001250        PERFORM CHECK-DATA.
001260 INPUT-UNIT-PRICE.
001270        DISPLAY "Unit price - five digits - 3 before & 2 after".
001280        ACCEPT UNIT-PRICE.
001290        IF UNIT-PRICE = 999.99
001300            MOVE 2 TO ERROR-SWITCH
```

```
001310        ELSE
001320            IF UNIT-PRICE IS NUMERIC
001330                MOVE 0 TO ERROR-SWITCH
001340            ELSE
001350                DISPLAY ERROR-MESSAGE.
001360 INPUT-UNIT-COST.
001370        DISPLAY "Cost price - five digits - 3 before & 2 after".
001380        ACCEPT UNIT-COST.
001390        IF UNIT-COST = 999.99
001400            MOVE 2 TO ERROR-SWITCH
001410        ELSE
001420            IF UNIT-PRICE IS NUMERIC
001430                MOVE 0 TO ERROR-SWITCH
001440            ELSE
001450                DISPLAY ERROR-MESSAGE.
001460 INPUT-QUANTITY-ON-HAND.
001470        DISPLAY "Quantity on hand "
001480        PERFORM CHECK-DATA.
001490 INPUT-QUANTITY-ON-ORDER.
001500        DISPLAY "Quantity on order "
001510        PERFORM CHECK-DATA.
001520 INPUT-DATE.
001530        DISPLAY "Do you wish to enter the Date of Delivery? Y/N)".
001540        ACCEPT REPLY.
001550        IF REPLY = "Y" OR REPLY = "y"
001560            PERFORM INPUT-DATE-1
001570        ELSE
001580            MOVE 0 TO ERROR-SWITCH.
001590 INPUT-QUANTITY-SOLD.
001600        DISPLAY "Quantity sold".
001610        PERFORM CHECK-DATA.
001620 CLEAR-RECORD.
001630        MOVE SPACES TO DESCRIPTION.
001640        MOVE ZEROS TO PRODUCT-NUMBER UNIT-PRICE UNIT-COST
001650                QUANTITY-ON-HAND QUANTITY-ON-ORDER
001660                DATE-OF-DELIVERY.
001670 CHECK-DATA.
001680        ACCEPT INPUT-ITEM-5.
001690        IF INPUT-ITEM-5 = 99999
001700            MOVE 2 TO ERROR-SWITCH
001710        ELSE
001720            IF INPUT-ITEM-5 IS NUMERIC
001730                MOVE 0 TO ERROR-SWITCH
001740            ELSE
001750                DISPLAY ERROR-MESSAGE.
001760 INPUT-DATE-1.
001770        DISPLAY "DATE - Day 2 digits between 01 and 31"
001780        ACCEPT DD
001790        DISPLAY "      Month 2 digits between 01 and 12"
001800        ACCEPT MM
```

107

```
001810          DISPLAY "      Year 2 digits between 84 and 99"
001820          ACCEPT YY
001830          IF DATE-OF-DELIVERY = 999999
001840              MOVE 2 TO ERROR-SWITCH
001850          ELSE
001860              PERFORM CHECK-DATE.
001870 CHECK-DATE.
001880           MOVE 0 TO ERROR-SWITCH.
001890           PERFORM CHECK-IF-LEAP-YEAR.
001900           IF MM < 01 OR DD < 01
001910              MOVE 1 TO ERROR-SWITCH.
001920           IF MM > 12 OR DD > 31
001930              MOVE 1 TO ERROR-SWITCH.
001940           IF (MM = 04 OR MM = 06 OR MM = 09 OR MM = 11) AND DD > 30
001950              MOVE 1 TO ERROR-SWITCH.
001960           IF MM = 02 AND DD > 29
001970              MOVE 1 TO ERROR-SWITCH.
001980           IF NOT LEAP-YEAR AND MM = 02 AND DD = 28
001990              MOVE 1 TO ERROR-SWITCH.
002000           IF INCORRECT
002010              DISPLAY "Invalid date".
002020 CHECK-IF-LEAP-YEAR.
002030           DIVIDE 4 INTO YY GIVING YY REMAINDER YEAR-REM.
002040           IF YEAR-REM = ZERO
002050              MOVE "T" TO LEAP-YEAR-FLAG
002060           ELSE
002070              MOVE "F" TO LEAP-YEAR-FLAG.
```

Fig. 11.1

CHAPTER 12

Ordering Data

12.1 Introduction

The program in Chapter 11 created a file called UNSPROD with records stored in the order in which they were input. To use this file efficiently the records have to be in ascending sequence of the part number. The source documents containing the data input by CREATE-PRODUCT could be sorted in order but this is a waste of time and very unreliable. It is essential to sort the file we have just created by program into the correct sequence. COBOL contains its own sort instruction.

12.2 SORT Statement

The SORT statement accepts records from one or more files and sorts them according to a set of keys. There are two versions, a simple one and a more sophisticated one.

The simple version has the format:

$$\underline{SORT} \quad \text{file–name–1} \; \{ \; ON \; \left\{ \begin{array}{l} \underline{ASCENDING} \\ \underline{DESCENDING} \end{array} \right\} \; KEY \; \{ \; \text{data–name–1} \; \} \ldots \} \ldots$$

$$[\; WITH \; \underline{DUPLICATES} \; IN \; ORDER \;]$$

$$\left[\; ON \; \left\{ \begin{array}{l} \underline{ASCENDING} \\ \underline{DESCENDING} \end{array} \right\} \; KEY \; \text{data–name–3} \; [\text{data–name–4}] \ldots \right] \ldots$$

$$\underline{USING} \; \{ \; \text{filename–2} \; \} \; \ldots$$

$$\underline{GIVING} \; \{ \; \text{filename–3} \; \} \ldots$$

The SORT statement accepts records from an input file specified in the

USING clause, passes them to a sort file and sorts the records into ascending or descending order of their keys. The sorted records are passed out to the file in the GIVING clause. File-name-1 is the sort file. The sort file is selected in the INPUT-OUTPUT SECTION and has a special SD (sort-merge description) entry in the FILE SECTION. This entry also contains the description of the records to be sorted including the key fields. When ASCENDING KEY is specified the file will be sorted so that the record with the lowest value in the key field is output first and the record with the highest key value is output last. When DESCENDING KEY is specified the file will be sorted so that the record with the highest value in the key field is output first, and the record with the lowest key value is output last. If the WITH DUPLICATES IN ORDER clause is present, any records with duplicate keys will be placed in the output file in the same order as they were input. This is a COBOL 85 addition. In COBOL 74, duplicate records can be output in any order.

In COBOL 85 the sorted records can be output to more than one file and this need not be a sequential file. The other permissible file organisations are dealt with in Chapter 17.

12.3 Program SORT-PRODUCT

The SORT statement sounds rather more complicated than it is. UNSPROD contains records in no particular sequence. The program sorts the records on input file UNSPROD into ascending sequence of the contents of PRODUCT-NUMBER and outputs them on the file PRODUCT. UNSPROD and PRODUCT are declared as INPUT-FILE and OUTPUT-FILE in the INPUT-OUTPUT SECTION. The extra sort file is also declared. The FILE SECTION contains an FD for both INPUT-FILE and OUTPUT-FILE. Both files have their records specified as a single field. The sort file has an SD entry containing only the record entry. The PROCEDURE DIVISION contains the SORT statement. The SORT statement in this format does not require OPEN and CLOSE statements for any of its files. If the SORT statement is used in a program which contains file processing then you must ensure that any files used by the SORT are closed before the SORT statement is executed.

000100 IDENTIFICATION DIVISION.

000110 PROGRAM-ID. SORT-PRODUCT.

000120 AUTHOR. D WATSON.

000130 INSTALLATION. UNIVERSITY OF ABERDEEN.

000140 DATE-WRITTEN. APRIL 1985.

000150 SECURITY. NONE.

```
000160*
000170 ENVIRONMENT DIVISION.
000180 CONFIGURATION SECTION.
000190 SOURCE-COMPUTER.  ABC-1.
000200 OBJECT-COMPUTER.   ABC-1.
000210 INPUT-OUTPUT SECTION.
000220 FILE-CONTROL.
000230        SELECT INPUT-FILE ASSIGN TO DISK.
000250        SELECT OUTPUT-FILE ASSIGN TO PFILE.
000270        SELECT SORT-FILE ASSIGN TO SFILE.
000290*
000300 DATA DIVISION.
000310 FILE SECTION.
000320 FD    INPUT-FILE
000330        LABEL RECORDS ARE STANDARD
000340        VALUE OF FILE-ID IS "UNSPROD".
000350 01    INPUT-FILE-REC            PIC X(66).
000360 FD    OUTPUT-FILE
000370        LABEL RECORDS STANDARD
000380        VALUE OF FILE-ID IS "PRODUCT".
000390 01    OUTPUT-FILE-REC           PIC X(66).
000400 SD    SORT-FILE.
000410 01    PRODUCT-RECORD.
000420        03 PRODUCT-NUMBER        PIC 9(5).
000430        03 DESCRIPTION           PIC X(30).
000440        03 UNIT-PRICE            PIC 999V99.
000450        03 UNIT-COST             PIC 999V99.
000460        03 QUANTITY-ON-HAND      PIC 9(5).
000470        03 QUANTITY-ON-ORDER     PIC 9(5).
000480        03 DATE-OF-DELIVERY.
000490           05 DD                 PIC 99.
000500           05 MM                 PIC 99.
000510           05 YY                 PIC 99.
000520        03 QUANTITY-SOLD         PIC 9(5).
000530 PROCEDURE DIVISION.
000540 PARA-1.
000550        SORT SORT-FILE ON ASCENDING KEY PRODUCT-NUMBER
000560               USING INPUT-FILE
000570               GIVING OUTPUT-FILE.
000580        STOP RUN.
```

Fig. 12.1

111

12.4 More Advanced Sorting

Sometimes it is necessary to carry out some operation on the keys of a file before a record is presented for sorting or after sorting has taken place. There is a second version of SORT which allows us to do this.

It has the format:

SORT file-name-1 ON $\left\{ \begin{array}{l} \underline{ASCENDING} \\ \underline{DESCENDING} \end{array} \right\}$ KEY data-name-1 [data-name-2] ...

[WITH <u>DUPLICATES</u> IN ORDER]

$\left[ON \left\{ \begin{array}{l} \underline{ASCENDING} \\ \underline{DESCENDING} \end{array} \right\} KEY \ data-name-3 \ [data-name-4] \ ... \right] \ ...$

<u>INPUT PROCEDURE</u> IS section-name-1 $\left[\left\{ \begin{array}{l} \underline{THROUGH} \\ \underline{THRU} \end{array} \right\} section-name-2 \right]$

<u>OUTPUT PROCEDURE</u> IS section-name-3 $\left[\left\{ \begin{array}{l} \underline{THROUGH} \\ \underline{THRU} \end{array} \right\} section-name-4 \right]$

12.4.1 INPUT PROCEDURE

The INPUT PROCEDURE can contain any set of statements needed to select, create or amend records before they are presented for sorting. In the INPUT PROCEDURE the input file has to be opened and records read in the normal way but there is a special statement to pass a record to a sort file.

It has the format:

<u>RELEASE</u> record-name-1 [<u>FROM</u> identifier-1]

This statement operates in exactly the same way as a WRITE statement. A WRITE statement cannot be used to pass a record to a sort file. The input file must be closed before sorting. In COBOL 74 the input procedure must not contain any explicit transfers outside the input procedure, but in COBOL 85, procedures outwith INPUT PROCEDURE can be performed and any procedure within INPUT PROCEDURE can also be performed from anywhere else in the program.

12.4.2 OUTPUT PROCEDURE

The OUTPUT PROCEDURE contains any set of statements needed to select, amend or copy records returned, one at a time in sorted order, from the sort file. In the OUTPUT PROCEDURE, the file which is to receive the records

112

from the sort file is opened and records written to it in the normal way but a special statement is used to read a record from the sort file.

It has the format:

RETURN file–name–1 RECORD [**INTO** identifier–1]

       AT **END** imperative–statement–1

       [**NOT** AT **END** imperative–statement–2]

       [**END–RETURN**]

This acts in exactly the same way as a READ. A READ statement cannot be used on a sort file. The output file must be closed. In COBOL 74 the output procedure must not contain any explicit transfers outside that procedure, but in COBOL 85, procedures outwith OUTPUT PROCEDURE can be performed and any procedure within OUTPUT PROCEDURE can also be performed from anywhere else in the program.

12.5 Program SORT-NAMES

Program SORT-NAMES takes a file of student records and sorts them into ascending surname, first name and initial order. A problem arises in the handling of the surnames starting with Mac or Mc. If we sorted the surnames in ascending alphabetic sequence all the Macs would be grouped together and the Mcs would form a separate group later in the sequence. Therefore, Macdonald, John and Mcdonald, John would not appear together. However, common usage requires that they do. If you want proof, take a look in the telephone directory! One solution to this problem is to use the facility in SORT to convert all the Mcs to Macs before sorting, carry out the sort, then change the amended records back to their original state. The INPUT PROCEDURE transfers control to FIRST-PASS SECTION where the records are amended before being released for sorting. The first two letters of each surname are tested to see if they are Mc. If this is the case, they are converted to Mac and an indicator is set at the end of the record to show that a conversion has taken place. The statement RELEASE SORT-RECORD passes the input record to the sort file. This continues until all the records from the input file have been read and processed. The input file is closed and the program returns to carry out the sorting process. Once this is completed the OUTPUT PROCEDURE LAST-PASS is executed. LAST-PASS SECTION opens the output file to receive the sorted records. Each record from the sort file is returned and tested to see if Mac needs to be converted back to Mc. The record is then written to the output file. This continues until all the records from sort-file have been read, processed and written to the output file.

```
000100 IDENTIFICATION DIVISION.
000110 PROGRAM-ID. SORT-NAMES.
000120 AUTHOR. D WATSON.
000130 DATE-WRITTEN. APRIL 1985.
000140***********************************************
000160*    This program sorts a file into ascending
000170*    sequence of student name.
000190***********************************************
000200 ENVIRONMENT DIVISION.
000210 CONFIGURATION SECTION.
000220 SOURCE-COMPUTER. ABC-1.
000230 OBJECT-COMPUTER. ABC-1.
000240 INPUT-OUTPUT SECTION.
000250 FILE-CONTROL.
000260      SELECT MASTER-FILE ASSIGN TO MFILE.
000280      SELECT SORTED-MASTER ASSIGN TO SFILE.
000300      SELECT SORT-FILE ASSIGN TO WORK.
000310 DATA DIVISION.
000320 FILE SECTION.
000330 FD   MASTER-FILE
000340      LABEL RECORDS STANDARD
000350      VALUE OF FILE-ID "USTUDENT".
000360 01   MASTER-RECORD.
000370      03 FILLER                   PIC X(292).
000380 SD  SORT-FILE.
000390 01  SORT-RECORD.
000400      03 STUDENT-NO               PIC X(5).
000410      03 LAST-NAME.
000420         05 PREF                  PIC XX.
000430         05 REST                  PIC X(18).
000440      03 FIRST-NAME               PIC X(20).
000450      03 INIT                     PIC X.
000460      03 FILLER                   PIC X(246).
000470      03 IND                      PIC X.
000480 FD   SORTED-MASTER
000490      LABEL RECORDS STANDARD
000500      VALUE OF FILE-ID "SSTUDENT".
000510 01   SORTED-RECORD.
000520      03 FILLER                   PIC X(5).
000530      03 S-LAST-NAME  PIC X(20).
000540      03 FILLER                   PIC X(267).
000550 WORKING-STORAGE SECTION.
```

```
000560 01    MORE-DATA                        PIC X VALUE "Y".
000570       88 NO-MORE-DATA VALUE "N".
000580 01    TEMP.
000590       03 WS-NAME.
000600          05 WS-P                        PIC XXX.
000610          05 WS-R                         PIC X(17).
000620       03 WWS-NAME REDEFINES WS-NAME.
000630          05 WWS-P                        PIC XX.
000640          05 WWS-R                        PIC X(18).
000650 01  TEMP1.
000660       03 FILLER                          PIC X.
000670       03 T-NAME                          PIC X(17).
000680 PROCEDURE DIVISION.
000690 MAIN SECTION.
000700*
000710 SORT-RECORDS.
000720       SORT SORT-FILE ON ASCENDING KEY
000730           LAST-NAME FIRST-NAME INIT
000740           INPUT PROCEDURE IS FIRST-PASS
000750           OUTPUT PROCEDURE IS LAST-PASS.
000760       STOP RUN.
000770 FIRST-PASS SECTION.
000780 FIRST-PASS-SEQ.
000790       OPEN INPUT MASTER-FILE.
000800       READ MASTER-FILE INTO SORT-RECORD
000810           AT END  MOVE "N" TO MORE-DATA.
000820       PERFORM RELEASE-RECORD UNTIL NO-MORE-DATA.
000830       CLOSE MASTER-FILE.
000835       GO TO FIRST-PASS-END.
000840 RELEASE-RECORD.
000850       IF PREF = "Mc"
000860           MOVE "Mac" TO WS-P
000870           MOVE REST TO WS-R
000880           MOVE WS-NAME TO LAST-NAME
000890           MOVE "*" TO IND.
000900       RELEASE SORT-RECORD.
000910       READ MASTER-FILE INTO SORT-RECORD
000920           AT END  MOVE "N" TO MORE-DATA.
000930 FIRST-PASS-END.
000940*
000950 LAST-PASS SECTION.
000960 LAST-PASS-SEQ.
000970       OPEN OUTPUT SORTED-MASTER.
000980       MOVE "Y" TO MORE-DATA.
```

```
000990        RETURN SORT-FILE INTO SORTED-RECORD
001000             AT END  MOVE "N" TO MORE-DATA.
001010        PERFORM WRITE-RECORD UNTIL NO-MORE-DATA.
001020        CLOSE SORTED-MASTER.
001030        GO TO LAST-PASS-END.
001040 WRITE-RECORD.
001050        IF IND = "*"
001060             MOVE "Mc" TO WWS-P
001070             MOVE REST TO TEMP1
001080             MOVE T-NAME TO WWS-R
001090             MOVE WWS-NAME TO S-LAST-NAME.
001100        WRITE SORTED-RECORD.
001110        RETURN SORT-FILE INTO SORTED-RECORD
001120             AT END  MOVE "N" TO MORE-DATA.
001130 LAST-PASS-END.
```

Fig. 12.2

CHAPTER 13

Picture Editing

13.1 Inputing Numeric Data

In Chapter 5 we saw the way in which numeric data is described. Now we must look in more detail at how COBOL handles numbers in different situations.

13.1.1 Integers

Each value has to be allocated a maximum number of digit places, that is

        03 A-NUMBER   PIC 9999.

means that A-NUMBER can hold any value from 0000 to 9999. The value always occupies the number of places specified in the PICTURE clause so 5 would be stored in A-NUMBER as 0005.

13.1.2 Decimal Numbers

COBOL uses a system of implied decimal points. When a decimal number is described with a PICTURE clause the position of the decimal point is indicated by the letter V. The V does not take up any character position, rather it shows where a decimal point would be if it were present. Let us take the example of a numeric field described as

        03 D-NUMBER   PIC 999V99.

If we passed the number 35560 into this field it would be interpreted as 355.60 for all storage and arithmetical purposes in the program. Conversely, if we wish to read a numeric value directly into a program we must omit the actual decimal point. If we wished to input 355.60 then we have to input 35560. When an integer field is described, such as A-NUMBER, the decimal point implicitly follows the last 9. We do not have to write it ourselves.

13.2 Editing a Numeric Field

When we are outputting numbers we must convert the data from the format in which it is held internally to the format in which we wish it to be output. The output format is described by the report form of the PICTURE clause.

13.2.1 Integers

The description

        03 C-NUMBER   PIC 9999.

holds a four digit number. So the value 50 is held as 0050. The zeros preceding the digit 5 are eliminated in normal usage. We can do this in COBOL by editing the field using zero suppression. This allows us to replace leading zeros but retain zeros elsewhere in the number. We can describe C-NUMBER as follows:

        03 C-NUMBER   PIC ZZZZ.
            or
        03 C-NUMBER   PIC Z(4).

This means that all the zeros before the first non-zero digit are converted to spaces. If the number 0050 was placed in C-NUMBER and then printed, the number output would occupy four print positions on the line but the first two are spaces. The zero following the 5 is not suppressed even though a Z appears in its PICTURE position. All the leading zero positions of C-NUMBER are suppressed so if each digit position were occupied by zero then four spaces would appear. This is dangerous in almost every case. When we are printing out numeric data we normally wish to suppress every leading zero except the last one and show a field containing zero as at least one zero. The description

        03 C-NUMBER   PIC ZZZ9.
            or
        03 C-NUMBER   PIC Z(3)9.

is better. With this picture 0000 will be printed as   0. A character Z cannot appear to the right of a 9.

13.2.2 Inserting Decimal Points

When decimal numbers are printed, the decimal point must be present. Therefore, we must replace the implied decimal point with an actual one. This is done by using the report form of the PICTURE clause with the decimal point written in the place we wish it to appear in the number. The report form of the PICTURE clause can only be used for outputting data. It cannot be used for arithmetic purposes. The conversion from input format to output format is achieved simply by moving the data from its source field to the edited field.

MOVE SOURCE-FIELD TO RECEIVING-FIELD.

In all the following examples this statement is used to pass data from the unedited SOURCE-FIELD into the edited RECEIVING-FIELD.

SOURCE-FIELD		RECEIVING-FIELD	
PICTURE	VALUE	PICTURE	VALUE
99V99	2550	999.99	025.50
9V99	023	9.99	0.23
9V99	023	9.9999	0.2300
999V999	185378	99.999	85.378
999V999	185378	999.99	185.37

Alignment always takes place on the decimal point. If there are fewer character positions before the decimal point in the receiving field than the source field, the leading numbers for which there is no room are simply lost - a disaster in most cases. Similarly, though less disastrous, if the number of digit places following the decimal point is fewer than the sending field then the rightmost digits are lost. The last two examples illustrate this.

13.2.3 Insertion of Commas, Blanks and Zeros

A comma, blank (space) or a zero can be inserted into a numeric field. Each occurrence of any of these characters in the PICTURE clause represents one actual occurrence of the specified character in the receiving field.

SOURCE-FIELD		RECEIVING-FIELD	
PICTURE	VALUE	PICTURE	VALUE
9(7)	1234567	9,999,999	1,234,567
9(5)	35712	9,999,999	0,035,712
9(5)	35712	Z,ZZZ,ZZ9	35,712

Notice that when zero suppression is used the unnecessary commas are also omitted.

Blanks can be inserted by putting the letter B in the place where a space or blank has to be inserted. Zero can be inserted by putting 0 in the place where a zero has to be inserted.

SOURCE-FIELD		RECEIVING-FIELD	
PICTURE	VALUE	PICTURE	VALUE
9(6)	250385	99B99B99	25 03 85
9(4)	1234	990099	120034
9(4)	1234	999900	123400
9(4)	0012	ZZZZ00	1200

13.3 Inserting Signs

+ or − signs can be inserted into a picture entry of a signed numeric item, that is, one with S in front of the leftmost 9, either in a fixed position or in a floating position depending on the number of digits the value occupies. When a single + or − sign is present, the appropriate sign is inserted at the position indicated. If there is a series of signs, the actual sign is inserted immediately in front of the first non-zero digit. In fact, zero suppression takes place as well. A single sign may be inserted following the value. If a + sign is used in the picture, a positive value is preceded or followed by + and a negative number is preceded or followed by -. If - is inserted in the picture and the value is positive then a space is placed in the sign position.

SOURCE-FIELD		RECEIVING-FIELD	
PICTURE	VALUE	PICTURE	VALUE
S9(4)	-1234	+9(4)	-1234
S999	006	+ZZZ	+ 6
S999	006	+++9	+6
S99V99	4275	99.99+	42.75+
S9(4)	-1234	-9(4)	-1234
S9(4)	+1234	-9(4)	1234
S999	006	-ZZZ	6
S99V99	-1275	99.99-	12.75-

13.4 Editing Money Fields

Fields containing money values can be edited to insert credit or debit symbols, currency signs or cheque protection characters. The credit and debit

120

symbols are CR and DB. These can only appear at the end of a PICTURE clause. They occupy two character positions on the output and are only output if the value is negative. So if you are accumulating values to be credited to a customer account the sum of credits which is to be printed must be set negative in order to force the printing of CR after the amount. No minus sign is printed. A currency sign can be floated or fixed in front of a value in the same way as the + and − signs. The standard currency sign is the $ as one would expect from a language originating in the USA. When cheques are being printed it is undesirable to allow leading spaces in front of the amount for which the cheque is drawn. So leading zeros are replaced by asterisks in the same way as zeros are suppressed to spaces using Z.

SOURCE-FIELD		RECEIVING-FIELD	
PICTURE	VALUE	PICTURE	VALUE
S9(4)	-1234	9(4)CR	1234CR
S99V99	1275	99.99DB	12.75
S999	-002	ZZZCR	2CR
9(4)	1234	$9999	$1234
9(4)	0054	$$$9	$54
9(4)	0054	$ZZ9	$ 54
9(6)	000391	*****9	***391

The appearance of a floating sign string or a fixed plus or minus insertion character precludes the appearance of any other sign control character. When you are editing data items in a program remember the rules about moving numeric data from one PICTURE to another, especially if the two fields are of different sizes. If you are not careful you may lose either leading or trailing numbers.

CHAPTER 14

Writing A Report Program

14.1 Program PRINT-REPORT

One of the commonest requests a programmer receives is for a program to produce a report. This is normally printed although it may also be output on a VDU. We have already looked at a very simple report program, PRINT-PRODUCTS in Chapter 7, but now we have covered enough COBOL to write a much better report program. The program will be written in a way that will allow it to be adapted to handle a wide range of simple reports. A useful practice is to design shell programs which can be used as a framework for other programs.

Data is held on a sequential file, on disk in this case, but it could just as easily be on magnetic tape. We will write a report program which selects records from a file and prints data items from each selected record. There are a number of points which must be dealt with when planning a well written report program. First of all the organisation of the input file must be known, the format of the records and, very importantly, the sequence of the records. The format of each record is as follows;

```
01  PRODUCT-RECORD.
    03 PRODUCT-NUMBER        PIC 9(5).
    03 DESCRIPTION           PIC X(30).
    03 UNIT-PRICE            PIC 999V99.
    03 UNIT-COST             PIC 999V99.
    03 QUANTITY-ON-HAND      PIC 9(5).
    03 QUANTITY-ON-ORDER     PIC 9(5).
    03 DATE-OF-DELIVERY.
       05 DD                 PIC 99.
       05 MM                 PIC 99.
       05 YY                 PIC 99.
```

In this example the input file is sequential, that means the records are ordered in ascending sequence of PRODUCT-NUMBER. So the first record has the lowest product number and each following record has a higher value than the previous one. PRODUCT-NUMBER is a key field, that means it contains the data value which uniquely identifies each record. So each product number appears only once in the file. Duplicate keys within the file would mean that a program which had previously processed the file had an error in it. Unfortunately the appearance of duplicate keys is a recurring problem in file processing and the programmer must be particularly careful when writing programs which generate or amend records.

We want to print a report containing data from records of products where the quantity on hand i.e. the amount of the product in the warehouse, has fallen below 200 and no more products have been ordered, i.e. the QUANTITY-ON-ORDER field is zero. To do this we must read each record in turn from the file and test the QUANTITY-ON-HAND and QUANTITY-ON-ORDER fields to see if they satisfy the selection criteria. This can be done by the statement

IF QUANTITY-ON-HAND < 200 AND QUANTITY-ON-ORDER = ZERO
    PERFORM PRINT-RECORD.

14.2 Report Design

When a report is printed we must have headings at the top of each page. It is a very poorly designed report that has one heading at the beginning and the data printed on succeeding pages without a break. Apart from being awkward to use, data may be lost or made illegible when the individual sheets are torn along the perforations. We must also leave space around the borders of the document to allow it to be filed in such a way that data is not covered by the spine of the binder or lost when binding holes are punched. Output may also have to be photocopied, so margins reduce the risk of data being lost in the copying process because the original document was not placed in the copier properly. It is much better to have headings at the top of each page of the report and a fixed number of lines on the page leaving margins at each side of a page and blank lines at the top and foot of each page. In program PRINT-REPORT (Fig. 14.1) two blank lines are left at the top of the page.

In order to design a report we use a layout sheet of squared paper. Each square represents a printed character position. The commonest length of a line of print on a line printer is 132 characters. 80 is common on microcomputer printers, but the line length obviously depends on that of the available printer or display. The number of lines available for printing depends on the size of the output document. The number of lines in our program is set to 22 to allow each page to fit on a VDU display. By using a layout sheet several different layouts can be shown to future users and they can decide which one is most useful for their purposes. To indicate the position and contents of data fields the standard practice is to write the full headings and any field descriptions but indicate the position of a variable data field by writing an X in each of the print positions to be occupied by alphabetic or alphanumeric the data and 9 for each print position of a numeric field. Any suppression or insertion editing characters should also be written. The layout for the report we are to be printing is given in Fig. 14.2.

14.3 Files and Data

In Chapter 7 we saw how a record is read from a file into a record area set aside for it in WORKING-STORAGE, The data items from that record are then moved to an output record which specifies the format of the line to be output. Each line with a different format has its own record description. In this program the data from one record becomes one line of print - the detail line. After all the data has been placed in the fields of the detail line, the WRITE statement causes the record to be passed into the FD output record area and then output to the printer or other output device. In mainframe systems printed output from a program does not go directly to a printer. It will be spooled on to a print file then printed when the operating system decides a printer is available. In many installations, irrespective of the operating system, it is standard practice for all report programs to output to a print file and the actual printing be handled by another special print program.

The actual reading and processing of the data takes only a small part of the program, the rest is taken up with describing the formats of the input and output data. The INPUT-OUTPUT SECTION describes the two files. They are named INPUT-FILE and OUTPUT-FILE. INPUT-FILE is to be found on a disk and OUTPUT-FILE is assigned to the printer. In the FILE SECTION of the DATA DIVISION, INPUT-FILE is declared as having standard labels as is normal with a disk file and the name of the file is PRODUCT. The length of each record on this file is 66 characters. Since OUTPUT-FILE is going to be printed there are no labels to be processed so these are described as OMITTED and there is no file name. The record length is 80 characters. This is the line length of the printer. On a line-printer this could be 132 and the format of the report adjusted to utilise the extra space available. A point worth noting is that certain implementations of COBOL require the first character of a record which is to be sent to a printer to be reserved as a print control character. This character is described as a FILLER with PIC X.

Though it is described in the record this character is not otherwise referenced in the program. None of the computers used to produce the report programs in this book have this requirement.

The WORKING-STORAGE SECTION contains the full description of the records as well as extra data items, such as date and line count, which are needed in the program. The input record is set up in PRODUCT-RECORD. There are four different formats for the output record. PAGE-HEADING describes the first line of the page. This consists of the date in the format of day, month and year. The COBOL program can accept the current date from the operating system. In a mainframe computer this is set up as part of the operator's job and does not concern the programmer. On some microcomputers either the date must be entered when it is switched on, or, prior to running a program requiring the date, a system utility is run to input and store a date. Other microcomputers have a battery backup system which allows the date to be permanently held in memory even when the computer is switched off. COBOL supplies the date in the format of year, month and day, so our program re-orders the date and inserts a stroke (/) between day and month and month and year. The page number is also printed, so this must be accumulated in the program. The headings on the columns of data in the report are written on two lines to save space. Each line is a separate record and are described in SUB-HEADING-1 and SUB-HEADING-2. DETAIL-LINE contains the fields which receive the data from each selected record. The quantity and price fields are edited to suppress leading zeros and insert decimal points where necessary. The numeric product code is always five characters long and any leading zeros are significant so no zero suppression is specified.

TOTALS-LINE contains the format of the last line of the report. The record WS-WORK-ITEMS contains data items required for processing the pages and lines of print and for handling the end of file condition.

14.4 PROCEDURE DIVISION

The partial pseudocode for the program is as follows:

```
    MAIN
        initialise
        while the input file is not at end of file
            process records
        close-down
    INITIALISE
        open files
```

```
                set up date
                set end-of-file marker to "N"
                read a record
                if end of file reached
                    set end-of-file marker to "Y"
            PROCESS RECORDS
                if quantity-on-hand < 200 and quantity-on-order = 0
                    set up detail line
                    add 1 to item count
                    write out detail line
                read next record
                if end of file reached
                    set end-of-file marker to "Y"
            CLOSE-DOWN
                set up final totals
                write out final totals
                close files
```

The pseudocode gives the logical control sequence of operations in the program. It is not a line by line specification of the coding. This is written by the programmer according to the rules of COBOL and to achieve the most effective use of the facilities of the language.

The Procedure Division is divided into three sections, MAIN containing the high-level logic of the program, PROCESS-RECORDS processing each record and SUPPORT containing the procedures required to handle the page setup and printing.

14.4.1 MAIN SECTION

MAIN Section contains the paragraphs INITIALISE, PROCESS-DATA and CLOSE-DOWN. INITIALISE contains statements to open the input and output files, get the current date from the operating system, reorganise it and place it in PAGE-HEADING. Next, the priming read is executed so that the first record of the file is available for processing. PROCESS-DATA paragraph contains one statement, a PERFORM, which is repeated until the end of the input file is detected by a READ statement. When this happens EOF-SWITCH is set to "Y" having been pre-set to "N" in the WORKING-STORAGE SECTION. The condition name END-OF-INPUT-FILE is given to EOF-SWITCH when it is set to "Y". So PERFORM PROCESS-RECORDS is repeated until the condition name END-OF-INPUT-FILE is true.

14.4.2 PROCESS-RECORDS SECTION

This section contains one paragraph, PROCESS-A-RECORD. Remember that a section must contain at least one paragraph so in this case a paragraph name must be present even though it is never used. PROCESS-A-RECORD contains the tests on the QUANTITY-ON-HAND and QUANTITY-ON-ORDER fields to see if they satisfy the selection criteria. If the record is selected the data items which are to be printed are moved from the input record area to the output record area. In the process the data is automatically edited. The count of the items selected is increased by one. The next record from the file is now read. If there are no more records on the file the AT END path is taken and EOF-SWITCH is set to "Y" and the repetition of PROCESS-RECORDS stops. If there is another record on the file PROCESS-RECORDS is performed again.

The process of outputting a record is not a straightforward one. Before a record can be printed the program must determine whether there is enough room on the page. If there is, the record is written out. If not, a new page is thrown, the page number increased by one and the relevant page heading lines output. The line count is updated and the detain record is output. When all the records on the input file have been read the program stops performing PROCESS-RECORDS and proceeds to paragraph CLOSE-DOWN where the final totals are printed, the files closed and the run terminated.

14.4.3 SUPPORT SECTION

This section contains six paragraphs consisting of statements mainly concerned with organising the page printing. The exception is READ-A-RECORD which consists of a READ statement. OUTPUT-A-RECORD contains statements to see if a new page is required. If so, then paragraph NEW-PAGE is performed and the detail line written out. If no new heading is required the detail line is output. A count of the lines printed is increased by the number of lines used. The coding is slightly complicated by the need to deal with the first heading of the report. In this case LINE-SPACING contains 1 and LINE-COUNT is zero so OUTPUT-HEADINGS would be executed with the page number set to 1. The coding also allows the programmer the extra facility of forcing a new page should that be required in the program by separating some of the statements as paragraph NEW-PAGE. PERFORM NEW-PAGE would ensure that next time anything was printed it would appear on a new page with the correct headings.

14.5 OUTPUT-HEADINGS

This paragraph prints the three lines of headings, increments the line count by six - the number of lines taken up by the headings, and sets the line spacing to two. This causes a blank line to be output between the last heading line and the first detail line. The detail lines have single spacing. two blank lines are left at the top of the page.

14.6 FINAL-TOTALS

This paragraph moves the item count to the field on the output record. TOTALS-LINE, sets the spacing to three so that two blank lines are output before the totals line is printed.

14.7 Summing up

PRINT-REPORT is an example of a straightforward report program with no control breaks. It is easy to adapt to handle different input data and output it in different format. The changes involve putting different input and output record descriptions in the WORKING-STORAGE SECTION, writing the PROCESS-RECORDS SECTION to suit the processing requirements and adjusting OUTPUT-HEADINGS to suit the number of heading lines required.

```
000100 IDENTIFICATION DIVISION.
000110 PROGRAM-ID.   PRINT-REPORT.
000120 AUTHOR.D WATSON.
000130 INSTALLATION. UNIVERSITY OF ABERDEEN.
000140 DATE-WRITTEN. APRIL 1985.
000150 SECURITY. NONE.
000160*
000170 ENVIRONMENT DIVISION.
000180 CONFIGURATION SECTION.
000190 SOURCE-COMPUTER.  ABC-1.
000200 OBJECT-COMPUTER.  ABC-1.
000210 INPUT-OUTPUT SECTION.
000220 FILE-CONTROL.
000230      SELECT INPUT-FILE ASSIGN TO DISK.
000250      SELECT OUTPUT-FILE ASSIGN TO PRINTER.
000270*
000280 DATA DIVISION.
000290 FILE SECTION.
000300 FD    INPUT-FILE
```

```
000310        LABEL RECORDS ARE STANDARD
000320        VALUE OF FILE-ID IS "PRODUCT".
000330 01     INPUT-FILE-REC              PIC X(66).
000340 FD     OUTPUT-FILE
000350        LABEL RECORDS OMITTED.
000360 01     OUTPUT-FILE-REC             PIC X(80).
000370*
000380 WORKING-STORAGE SECTION.
000390 01     PRODUCT-RECORD.
000400        03 PRODUCT-NUMBER           PIC 9(5).
000410        03 DESCRIPTION              PIC X(30).
000420        03 UNIT-PRICE               PIC 999V99.
000430        03 UNIT-COST                PIC 999V99.
000440        03 QUANTITY-ON-HAND         PIC 9(5).
000450        03 QUANTITY-ON-ORDER        PIC 9(5).
000460        03 DATE-OF-DELIVERY.
000470           05 DD                    PIC 99.
000480           05 MM                    PIC 99.
000490           05 YY                    PIC 99.
000500        03 QUANTITY-SOLD            PIC 9(5).
000510 01     PAGE-HEADING.
000520        03 FILLER                   PIC XXX VALUE SPACES.
000530        03 PH-DATE.
000540           05 PH-DD                 PIC 99.
000550           05 FILLER                PIC X VALUE "/".
000560           05 PH-MM                 PIC 99.
000570           05 FILLER                PIC X VALUE "/".
000580           05 PH-YY                 PIC 99.
000590        03 FILLER                   PIC X(17) VALUE SPACES.
000600        03 FILLER                   PIC X(32)
000610        VALUE "PRODUCTS AT CRITICAL STOCK LEVEL".
000620        03 FILLER                   PIC X(18) VALUE SPACES.
000630        03 FILLER                   PIC X(5) VALUE "PAGE ".
000640        03 PAGE-NUMBER              PIC ZZZ9.
000650 01     SUB-HEADING-1.
000660        03 FILLER                   PIC X(6) VALUE SPACES.
000670        03 FILLER                   PIC X(19) VALUE "PRODUCT       ".
000680        03 FILLER                   PIC X(11) VALUE "DESCRIPTION".
000690        03 FILLER                   PIC X(15) VALUE SPACES.
000700        03 FILLER                   PIC X(13) VALUE "QUANTITY     ".
000710        03 FILLER                   PIC X(10) VALUE "UNIT PRICE".
000720        03 FILLER                   PIC X(11) VALUE " UNIT COST".
000730 01     SUB-HEADING-2.
000740        03 FILLER                   PIC X(12) VALUE "     NUMBER".
000750        03 FILLER                   PIC X(39) VALUE SPACES.
000760        03 FILLER                   PIC X(7) VALUE "ON HAND".
000770 01     DETAIL-LINE.
000780        03 FILLER                   PIC X(6) VALUE SPACES.
000790        03 RL-PRODUCT-NUMBER        PIC 9(5).
000800        03 FILLER                   PIC X(5) VALUE SPACES.
```

```
000810          03 RL-DESCRIPTION              PIC X(30).
000820          03 FILLER                      PIC X(6) VALUE SPACES.
000830          03 RL-QUANTITY-ON-HAND         PIC Z(4)9.
000840          03 FILLER                      PIC X(8) VALUE SPACES.
000850          03 RL-UNIT-PRICE               PIC ZZ9.99.
000860          03 FILLER                      PIC X(6) VALUE SPACES.
000870          03 RL-UNIT-COST                PIC ZZ9.99.
000880 01    TOTALS-LINE.
000890          03 FILLER                      PIC X(23) VALUE SPACES.
000900          03 FILLER                      PIC X(16)
000905                                         VALUE "NUMBER OF ITEMS ".
000910          03 TL-ITEM-COUNT               PIC Z(4)9 VALUE ZERO.
000920 01    WS-WORK-ITEMS.
000930          03 PAGE-COUNT                  PIC 9(4) VALUE 1.
000940          03 LINE-COUNT                  PIC 999 VALUE ZERO.
000950          03 PAGE-SIZE                   PIC 999 VALUE 22.
000960          03 LINE-SPACING                PIC 9 VALUE 1.
000970          03 EOF-SWITCH                  PIC XX.
000980             88 END-OF-INPUT-FILE VALUE "Y".
000990          03 DATE-1.
001000             05 DATE-YY                  PIC 99.
001010             05 DATE-MM                  PIC 99.
001020             05 DATE-DD                  PIC 99.
001030          03 ITEM-COUNT                  PIC 9(5).
001040*
001050 PROCEDURE DIVISION.
001060 MAIN SECTION.
001070 INITIALISE.
001080          OPEN INPUT INPUT-FILE
001090               OUTPUT OUTPUT-FILE.
001100          PERFORM SETUP-DATE.
001110          MOVE "N" TO EOF-SWITCH.
001120          PERFORM READ-A-RECORD.
001130 PROCESS-DATA.
001140          PERFORM PROCESS-RECORDS UNTIL END-OF-INPUT-FILE.
001150 CLOSE-DOWN.
001160          PERFORM FINAL-TOTALS.
001170          CLOSE INPUT-FILE
001180               OUTPUT-FILE.
001190          STOP RUN.
001200 PROCESS-RECORDS SECTION.
001210 PROCESS-A-RECORD.
001220*******************************************************************
001230          IF QUANTITY-ON-HAND < 200 AND QUANTITY-ON-ORDER = ZERO
001240             MOVE PRODUCT-NUMBER TO RL-PRODUCT-NUMBER
001250             MOVE DESCRIPTION TO RL-DESCRIPTION
001260             MOVE QUANTITY-ON-HAND TO RL-QUANTITY-ON-HAND
001270             MOVE UNIT-PRICE TO RL-UNIT-PRICE
001280             MOVE UNIT-COST TO RL-UNIT-COST
001290             ADD 1 TO ITEM-COUNT
```

```
001300          PERFORM OUTPUT-A-RECORD.
001310          PERFORM READ-A-RECORD.
001320*****************************************************************
001330 SUPPORT SECTION.
001340 READ-A-RECORD.
001350          READ INPUT-FILE INTO PRODUCT-RECORD
001360                  AT END MOVE "Y" TO EOF-SWITCH.
001370*
001380 NEW-PAGE.
001390          IF LINE-COUNT NOT = ZERO
001400              ADD 1 TO PAGE-COUNT
001410              MOVE ZERO TO LINE-COUNT.
001420 OUTPUT-A-RECORD.
001430          IF LINE-COUNT + LINE-SPACING > PAGE-SIZE
001440              PERFORM NEW-PAGE.
001450          IF LINE-COUNT = ZERO
001460              PERFORM OUTPUT-HEADING.
001470          WRITE OUTPUT-FILE-REC FROM DETAIL-LINE
001480                  AFTER ADVANCING LINE-SPACING.
001490          ADD LINE-SPACING TO LINE-COUNT.
001500          MOVE 1 TO LINE-SPACING.
001510 OUTPUT-HEADING.
001520          MOVE PAGE-COUNT TO PAGE-NUMBER.
001530          MOVE SPACES TO OUTPUT-FILE-REC.
001540          WRITE OUTPUT-FILE-REC AFTER ADVANCING PAGE.
001550          WRITE OUTPUT-FILE-REC FROM PAGE-HEADING
001560                  AFTER ADVANCING 3 LINES.
001570          WRITE OUTPUT-FILE-REC FROM SUB-HEADING-1
001580                  AFTER ADVANCING 2 LINES.
001590          WRITE OUTPUT-FILE-REC FROM SUB-HEADING-2
001600                  AFTER ADVANCING 1 LINE.
001610          MOVE 6 TO LINE-COUNT.
001620          MOVE 2 TO LINE-SPACING.
001630 SETUP-DATE.
001640          ACCEPT DATE-1 FROM DATE.
001650          MOVE DATE-DD TO PH-DD.
001660          MOVE DATE-MM TO PH-MM.
001670          MOVE DATE-YY TO PH-YY.
001680 FINAL-TOTALS.
001690          MOVE ITEM-COUNT TO TL-ITEM-COUNT.
001700          MOVE 3 TO LINE-SPACING.
001710          MOVE TOTALS-LINE TO DETAIL-LINE.
001720          PERFORM OUTPUT-A-RECORD.
```

Fig. 14.1

PRODUCTS AT CRITICAL STOCK LEVEL   PAGE ZZZ9

99/99/99

PRODUCT NUMBER	DESCRIPTION	QUANTITY ON HAND	UNIT PRICE	UNIT COST
99999	XXXXXXXXXXXXXXXXXXXXXXXXXXXX	ZZZZ9	ZZ9.99	ZZ9.99
99999	XXXXXXXXXXXXXXXXXXXXXXXXXXXX	ZZZZ9	ZZ9.99	ZZ9.99

NUMBER OF ITEMS ZZZZ9

Fig. 14.2

CHAPTER 15

Tables

15.1 Repeated Items

When we are processing data we often find that an item or group of items have to be repeated. For example, a student registration record may contain an entry listing the courses being attended during the current year. The maximum number of courses is three. We could code this as part of a record in the DATA DIVISION as follows:

```
03 COURSE-1.
    05 COURSE-NAME-1      PIC X(10).
    05 COURSE-MARK-1      PIC 999V99.
03 COURSE-2.
    05 COURSE-NAME-2      PIC X(10).
    05 COURSE-MARK-2      PIC 999V99.
03 COURSE-3.
    05 COURSE-NAME-3      PIC X(10).
    05 COURSE-MARK-3      PIC 999V99.
```

All this is rather tedious but there is another way.

15.1.1 The OCCURS Clause

The OCCURS clause is designed to cope with this situation.

It has the format:

OCCURS integer **TIMES**

This clause is added to the description of a data group or data item and specifies the number of times the data item is repeated. We can recode the course description as follows:

```
03 COURSE OCCURS 3 TIMES.
   05 COURSE-NAME    PIC X(10).
   05 COURSE-MARK    PIC 999V99.
```

Since COURSE is a data group all the elements within the group are repeated three times. We have constructed a single dimensional table as this type of data structure is called in COBOL. A table is a set of values stored in consecutive locations in memory and assigned one data-name.

COURSE		COURSE		COURSE	
COURSE-NAME	COURSE-MARK	COURSE-NAME	COURSE-MARK	COURSE-NAME	COURSE-MARK
(1)	(1)	(2)	(2)	(3)	(3)

Since each of the identifiers, COURSE, COURSE-NAME and COURSE-MARK occurs three times, we must have a way of uniquely identifying each one. This is done by adding a subscript. This means that every time we use an identifier which is subject to an OCCURS clause, it must be followed by a subscript. A subscript must be a positive integer, the value of which points to the element which is being referred to. The subscript may either be a literal, or, more usually, an identifier and is enclosed in parenthesis. The first occurrence of COURSE is COURSE(1), the second is COURSE(2) and so on. Also each of the data elements within each occurrence of COURSE must have a subscript. COURSE-NAME(3) is a part of COURSE(3). The subscript can also be an identifier which can be varied as required.

```
Example:      MOVE 1 TO SUBSCRIPT.
              PERFORM INITIALISE-COURSE 3 TIMES.
                    . . .
                    . . .
              INITIALISE-COURSE.
                  MOVE SPACES TO COURSE-NAME(SUBSCRIPT)
                  MOVE ZEROS TO COURSE-MARK(SUBSCRIPT)
                  ADD 1 TO SUBSCRIPT.
```

This initialises each data element to either spaces or zeros depending on its type. SUBSCRIPT contains 1 in the first repetition of INITIALISE-COURSE so the data element within COURSE(1) are initialised then SUBSCRIPT is increased by 1 so the next repetition clears COURSE(2) and so on three times. An OCCURS clause cannot be written at 01 level.

15.2 Program ADD-SALES

To demonstrate the use of a single dimensional table we will take as an example a program to print the year-to-date sales figures which a company has achieved in each of its sales areas. The company divides the country into six sales areas, each the responsibility of one salesman. All customer records are kept on a customer file held on disk. Apart from the usual name, address and credit information, there is a field which contains the value of year-to-date sales made to the customer and there is also a salesman's number in the range 01 to 06 which corresponds to the salesman's sales area. The program adds the year-to-date sales amount into one of the six area totals according to salesman number. When all the records in the file have been read the program prints out the accumulated totals.

In program ADD-SALES the customer data is described in CUSTOMER-RECORD. The field YEAR-TO-DATE-SALES contains the value we wish to use in the accumulation of the sales figures. The field SALESMAN-NO contains the salesman's number which also indicates which sales area he covers. This field is used as the subscript which selects the correct element of the table SALES-TOTALS. If SALESMAN-NO contains 01 the statement

ADD YEAR-TO-DATE-SALES TO SALES-TOTAL(SALESMAN-NO)

adds the contents of YEAR-TO-DATE-SALES to the first element of SALES-TOTAL. If SALESMAN-NO contains 05 the contents of YEAR-TO-DATE-SALES are added to the fifth element of SALES-TOTAL. In COBOL 74 the OCCURS clause cannot appear in the same data description sentence as a VALUE clause so we are unable to pre-set the contents of tables in the DATA DIVISION. In this program the contents of the table SALES-TOTALS must be set to zero before the first value is added. This is done by the statement

MOVE ZERO TO SALES-TOTALS.

In COBOL 85 a VALUE clause can be specified for items within an OCCURS clause.

Examples: 01 SALES-TOTALS.
               05 SALES-TOTAL   PIC 9(7)V99 VALUE ZERO
                             OCCURS 6 TIMES.

```
000100 IDENTIFICATION DIVISION.
000110 PROGRAM-ID.  ADD-SALES.
000120 AUTHOR.  D WATSON.
000130 INSTALLATION. UNIVERSITY OF ABERDEEN.
000140 DATE-WRITTEN. APRIL 1985.
000150 SECURITY. NONE.
000160*
000170 ENVIRONMENT DIVISION.
000180 CONFIGURATION SECTION.
000190 SOURCE-COMPUTER.  ABC-1.
000200 OBJECT-COMPUTER.  ABC-1.
000210 INPUT-OUTPUT SECTION.
000220 FILE-CONTROL.
000230      SELECT INPUT-FILE ASSIGN TO DISK.
000250      SELECT OUTPUT-FILE ASSIGN TO PRINTER.
000270*
000280 DATA DIVISION.
000290 FILE SECTION.
000300 FD    INPUT-FILE
000310      LABEL RECORDS ARE STANDARD
000320      VALUE OF FILE-ID IS "CUSTOMER".
000330 01   INPUT-FILE-REC               PIC X(335).
000340 FD  OUTPUT-FILE
000350    LABEL RECORDS OMITTED.
000360 01   OUTPUT-FILE-REC              PIC X(80).
000370*
000380 WORKING-STORAGE SECTION.
000390 01   CUSTOMER-RECORD.
000400      03 CUSTOMER-NO               PIC X(5).
000410      03 CUSTOMER-NAME             PIC X(30).
000420      03 CUST-ADDRESS.
000430         05 CUST-ADDRESS-LINE1     PIC X(30).
000440         05 CUST-ADDRESS-LINE2     PIC X(30).
000450         05 CUST-ADDRESS-LINE3     PIC X(30).
000460         05 CUST-ADDRESS-LINE4     PIC X(30).
000470      03 SHIP-TO-NAME             PIC X(30).
000480      03 SHIP-TO-ADDRESS.
000490         05 SHIP-TO-ADDRESS-LINE1  PIC X(30).
000500         05 SHIP-TO-ADDRESS-LINE2  PIC X(30).
000510         05 SHIP-TO-ADDRESS-LINE3  PIC X(30).
000520         05 SHIP-TO-ADDRESS-LINE4  PIC X(30).
000530      03 CUST-CREDIT-TERMS.
000540         05 CREDIT-LIMIT           PIC 9(5)V99.
000550         05 REVISION-DATE          PIC 9(6).
```

```
000560          03 TERMS-OF-PAYMENT.
000570             05 TERMS-PERCENT          PIC 99V99.
000580             05 TERMS-DAYS             PIC 99.
000590          03 YEAR-TO-DATE-SALES        PIC 9(5)V99.
000600          03 SALES-INFO.
000610             05 SALESMAN-NO            PIC 99.
000620             05 DISTRIBUTOR-NO         PIC 99.
000630 01    PAGE-HEADER.
000640       03 FILLER                       PIC XXX VALUE SPACES.
000650       03 PH-DATE.
000660          05 PH-DD                     PIC 99.
000670          05 FILLER                    PIC X VALUE "/".
000680          05 PH-MM                     PIC 99.
000690          05 FILLER                    PIC X VALUE "/".
000700          05 PH-YY                     PIC 99.
000710       03 FILLER                       PIC X(15) VALUE SPACES.
000720       03 FILLER                       PIC X(29) VALUE
000725          "SALES FIGURES TO DATE BY AREA".
000730 01    DETAIL-LINE.
000740       03 FILLER                       PIC XX VALUE SPACES.
000750       03 DL-AREA-TOTAL OCCURS 6 TIMES
000760                                       PIC Z(6)9.99BBB.
000770 01    SALES-TOTALS.
000780       03 SALES-TOTAL OCCURS 6 TIMES
000785                                       PIC 9(7)V99.
000790 01 DATE-1.
000800       03 DATE-YY                      PIC 99.
000810       03 DATE-MM                      PIC 99.
000820       03 DATE-DD                      PIC 99.
000830 01    WORK-ITEMS.
000840       03 SUBSCRIPT                    PIC 9.
000850       03 MORE-DATA                    PIC X VALUE "Y".
000860          88 NO-MORE-DATA VALUE "N".
000870 PROCEDURE DIVISION.
000880 MAIN SECTION.
000890 INITIALISE.
000900       OPEN INPUT INPUT-FILE
000910              OUTPUT-FILE.
000920       PERFORM SETUP-DATE.
000930       MOVE ZERO TO SALES-TOTALS.
000950       PERFORM READ-A-RECORD.
000960 PROCESS-DATA.
000970       PERFORM PROCESS-RECORDS UNTIL NO-MORE-DATA.
000980       PERFORM PRINT-RESULTS.
```

```
000990 CLOSE-DOWN.
001000        CLOSE INPUT-FILE
001010              OUTPUT-FILE.
001020        STOP RUN.
001030 PROCESS-RECORDS SECTION.
001040 ADD-UP-TOTALS.
001050        ADD YEAR-TO-DATE-SALES TO SALES-TOTAL(SALESMAN-NO).
001060        PERFORM READ-A-RECORD.
001070 SUPPORT SECTION.
001080 READ-A-RECORD.
001090        READ INPUT-FILE RECORD INTO CUSTOMER-RECORD
001100              AT END MOVE "N" TO MORE-DATA.
001110 PRINT-RESULTS.
001120        MOVE SPACES TO OUTPUT-FILE-REC.
001130        WRITE OUTPUT-FILE-REC AFTER PAGE.
001140        WRITE OUTPUT-FILE-REC FROM PAGE-HEADER AFTER 2
001150        MOVE 1 TO SUBSCRIPT.
001160        PERFORM MOVE-SALES-TOTALS 6 TIMES.
001170        WRITE OUTPUT-FILE-REC FROM DETAIL-LINE AFTER 2.
001180 SETUP-DATE.
001190        ACCEPT DATE-1 FROM DATE.
001200        MOVE DATE-DD TO PH-DD.
001210        MOVE DATE-MM TO PH-MM.
001220        MOVE DATE-YY TO PH-YY.
001260 MOVE-SALES-TOTALS.
001270        MOVE SALES-TOTAL(SUBSCRIPT) TO
001280              DL-AREA-TOTAL(SUBSCRIPT).
001280        ADD 1 TO SUBSCRIPT.
```

Fig. 15.1

15.3 Multi-dimensional Tables

A single-dimensional table can be thought of as a row of data items. If we
group two or more of these rows together we form a multi-dimensional table.
So we have a data structure which is arranged in two directions which we can
refer to as rows and columns. In order to address each of the data items or
"elements" in the table, we must specify the table name followed by a double
subscript giving the intersection of the row and the column. Fig. 15.2 shows

a table with four rows, each row containing six columns.

TABLE-1						
Column	1	2	3	4	5	6
Row 1	(1, 1)	(1, 2)	(1, 3)	(1, 4)	(1, 5)	(1, 6)
Row 2	(2, 1)	(2, 2)	(2, 3)	(2, 4)	(2, 5)	(2, 6)
Row 3	(3, 1)	(3, 2)	(3, 3)	(3, 4)	(3, 5)	(3, 6)
Row 4	(4, 1)	(4, 2)	(4, 3)	(4, 4)	(4, 5)	(4, 6)

Fig. 15.2

So the first element at the top left of the table is called TABLE-1(1, 1), The fifth element of row four is TABLE-1(4, 5) and so on. The comma is, of course, optional in COBOL but the two subscripts must be separated by a space. It is often tempting to use the identifier TABLE for a table but this is a reserved word. This table is declared in the DATA DIVISION as

```
01  TABLE-OF-ITEMS.
      03 ROW OCCURS 4 TIMES.
        05 TABLE-1 OCCURS 6 TIMES PIC 9(4).
```

Notice that it is the innermost identifier that is referenced when the table is processed. The subscripts must be integers starting at 1 and ranging up to the maximum element number. In the above example the first subscript must be between 1 and 4 and the second between 1 and 6. Zero or negative subscripts are not permitted in COBOL. Subscripted data names may be used almost anywhere that identifiers are used in a program. Subscripts may be literals or identifiers.

Example: TABLE-1(SUB, IND)
           TABLE-1(4, IND)
           TABLE-1(SUB, 2)

15.4 Program SUM-TABLE

The example program SUM-TABLE is an extension of the previous program ADD-SALES. This time the customer record contains the value of sales for each month of the year. The program has to print out the accumulated total of sales for each of the six sales areas for each month of the year. The monthly

139

sales totals for each customer are described as

03 MONTHLY-SALES OCCURS 12   PIC 9(5)V99.

The area sales table is described as

01 AREA-SALES-TABLE.
    03 MONTHS OCCURS 12 TIMES.
       05 SALES-AREA OCCURS 6 TIMES PIC 9(7)V99.

This means that the table has twelve rows called MONTHS and each of these rows has six columns called SALES-AREA. To use the table we must use the identifier SALES-AREA followed by a row and column subscript enclosed in brackets. The statement

ADD MONTHLY-SALES(MONTH) TO SALES-AREA(MONTH SALES-NO).

contains a single dimensional table MONTHLY-SALES which requires a single subscript and a multidimensional table, SALES-AREA, which requires two subscripts. If you refer to a table variable in a program without the correct subscripts the compiler will be unable to decide which element of the structure you are referring to and output an appropriate error message. COBOL 74 has the facility of handling three-dimensional tables. These require three nested OCCURS clauses and three subscripts. COBOL 85 has the facility to support seven dimensions.

```
000100 IDENTIFICATION DIVISION.
000110 PROGRAM-ID.  SUM-TABLE.
000120 AUTHOR.  D WATSON.
000130 INSTALLATION. UNIVERSITY OF ABERDEEN.
000140 DATE-WRITTEN. APRIL 1985.
000150 SECURITY. NONE.
000160*
000170 ENVIRONMENT DIVISION.
000180 CONFIGURATION SECTION.
000190 SOURCE-COMPUTER.  ABC-1.
000200 OBJECT-COMPUTER.  ABC-1.
000210 INPUT-OUTPUT SECTION.
000220 FILE-CONTROL.
000230      SELECT INPUT-FILE ASSIGN TO DISK.
000250      SELECT OUTPUT-FILE ASSIGN TO PRINTER.
000270*
000280 DATA DIVISION.
000290 FILE SECTION.
000300 FD   INPUT-FILE
000310      LABEL RECORDS ARE STANDARD
000320      VALUE OF FILE-ID IS "CUSTOMER".
```

```
000330 01    INPUT-FILE-REC                      PIC X(335).
000340 FD    OUTPUT-FILE
000350       LABEL RECORDS OMITTED.
000360 01    OUTPUT-FILE-REC                     PIC X(80).
000370*
000380 WORKING-STORAGE SECTION.
000390 01    CUSTOMER-RECORD.
000400       03 CUSTOMER-NO                      PIC X(5).
000410       03 CUSTOMER-NAME                    PIC X(30).
000420       03 CUST-ADDRESS.
000430          05 CUST-ADDRESS-LINE1            PIC X(30).
000440          05 CUST-ADDRESS-LINE2            PIC X(30).
000450          05 CUST-ADDRESS-LINE3            PIC X(30).
000460          05 CUST-ADDRESS-LINE4            PIC X(30).
000470       03 SHIP-TO-NAME                     PIC X(30).
000480       03 SHIP-TO-ADDRESS.
000490          05 SHIP-TO-ADDRESS-LINE1         PIC X(30).
000500          05 SHIP-TO-ADDRESS-LINE2         PIC X(30).
000510          05 SHIP-TO-ADDRESS-LINE3         PIC X(30).
000520          05 SHIP-TO-ADDRESS-LINE4         PIC X(30).
000530       03 CUST-CREDIT-TERMS.
000540          05 CREDIT-LIMIT                  PIC 9(5)V99.
000550          05 REVISION-DATE                 PIC 9(6).
000560       03 TERMS-OF-PAYMENT.
000570          05 TERMS-PERCENT                 PIC 99V99.
000580          05 TERMS-DAYS                    PIC 99.
000590       03 MONTHLY-SALES OCCURS 12          PIC 9(5)V99.
000600       03 SALES-INFO.
000610          05 SALESMAN-NO                   PIC 99.
000620          05 DISTRIBUTOR-NO                PIC 99.
000630 01    PAGE-HEADER.
000640       03 FILLER                           PIC XXX VALUE SPACES.
000650       03 PH-DATE.
000660          05 PH-DD                         PIC 99.
000670          05 FILLER                        PIC X VALUE "/".
000680          05 PH-MM                         PIC 99.
000690          05 FILLER                        PIC X VALUE "/".
000700          05 PH-YY                         PIC 99.
000710       03 FILLER                           PIC X(17) VALUE SPACES.
000720       03 FILLER                           PIC X(29) VALUE
000725          "SALES FIGURES TO DATE BY AREA".
000730 01    DETAIL-LINE.
000740       03 DL-MONTH                         PIC Z9.
000750       03 FILLER                           PIC XX VALUE SPACES.
```

```
000760          03 DL-AREA-TOTAL OCCURS 6 TIMES
000770                                    PIC Z(6)9.99BBB.
000780 01   AREA-SALES-TABLE.
000790          03 MONTH-AREA OCCURS 12 TIMES.
000800             05 SALES-AREA OCCURS 6 TIMES
000805                                    PIC 9(7)V99.
000810 01   WORK-ITEMS.
000820          03 S-AREA                 PIC 99.
000830          03 MONTH                  PIC 99.
000840          03 MORE-DATA              PIC X VALUE "Y".
000850             88 NO-MORE-DATA VALUE "N".
000860 01   DATE-1.
000870          03 DATE-YY                PIC 99.
000880          03 DATE-MM                PIC 99.
000890          03 DATE-DD                PIC 99.
000900 PROCEDURE DIVISION.
000910 MAIN SECTION.
000920 START-UP.
000930          OPEN INPUT INPUT-FILE
000940                  OUTPUT-FILE.
000950          MOVE 1 TO MONTH.
000960          MOVE ZERO TO SALES-AREA-TABLE.
000970          PERFORM SETUP-DATE.
000980          PERFORM READ-A-RECORD.
000990 PROCESS-DATA.
001000          PERFORM PROCESS-RECORDS UNTIL NO-MORE-DATA.
001010          PERFORM PRINT-RESULTS.
001020 CLOSE-DOWN.
001030          CLOSE INPUT-FILE
001040                  OUTPUT-FILE.
001050          STOP RUN.
001060*
001070 PROCESS-RECORDS SECTION.
001080 PROCESS-DATA.
001090          MOVE 1 TO MONTH.
001100          PERFORM ADD-UP-TOTALS UNTIL MONTH > 12.
001110          PERFORM READ-A-RECORD.
001120*
001130 SUPPORT SECTION.
001140 READ-A-RECORD.
001150          READ INPUT-FILE RECORD INTO CUSTOMER-RECORD
001160                  AT END MOVE "N" TO MORE-DATA.
001170 ADD-UP-TOTALS.
001180          ADD MONTHLY-SALES(MONTH)
```

142

```
001190              TO SALES-AREA(MONTH SALESMAN-NO).
001200        ADD 1 TO MONTH.
001210 PRINT-RESULTS.
001220        MOVE SPACES TO OUTPUT-FILE-REC.
001230        WRITE OUTPUT-FILE-REC AFTER PAGE.
001240        WRITE OUTPUT-FILE-REC FROM PAGE-HEADER AFTER 2
001250        MOVE 1 TO MONTH.
001260        PERFORM PRINT-MONTH 12 TIMES.
001270 PRINT-MONTH.
001280        MOVE 1 TO S-AREA.
001290        PERFORM MOVE-SALES-TOTALS 6 TIMES.
001300        MOVE MONTH TO DL-MONTH.
001310        WRITE OUTPUT-FILE-REC FROM DETAIL-LINE AFTER 2.
001320        ADD 1 TO MONTH.
001330 MOVE-SALES-TOTALS.
001340        MOVE SALES-AREA(MONTH S-AREA) TO DL-AREA-TOTAL(S-AREA).
001350        ADD 1 TO S-AREA.
001360 SETUP-DATE.
001370        ACCEPT DATE-1 FROM DATE.
001380        MOVE DATE-DD TO PH-DD.
001390        MOVE DATE-MM TO PH-MM.
001400        MOVE DATE-YY TO PH-YY.
```

Fig. 15.3

15.5 PERFORM . . . VARYING

In the program ADD-SALES (Fig. 15.1) we used a table called SALES-
TOTALS to accumulate sales figures for six sales areas. Suppose we are
asked to write a program to go through this table and find any sales areas
which have a sales value of less than 10,000. This can be done by the
following

```
        MOVE 1 TO SUBSCRIPT.
        PERFORM TEST-TOTALS 6 TIMES.
                . . .
                . . .
                . . .
TEST-TOTALS.
        IF SALES-TOTALS(SUBSCRIPT) < 10000
            PERFORM LOW-SALES.
```

ADD 1 TO SUBSCRIPT.

The subscript is initialised to 1 before the procedure TEST-TOTALS is performed and within the procedure the subscript is incremented to point to the next element of the table which is to be processed. There is an extended version of the PERFORM statement which does this work for us.

It has the format:

$$\underline{PERFORM} \left[procedure\text{--}name\text{--}1 \left[\left\{ \begin{array}{l} \underline{THROUGH} \\ \underline{THRU} \end{array} \right\} procedure\text{--}name\text{--}2 \right] \right]$$

$$\left[WITH \; \underline{TEST} \left\{ \begin{array}{l} \underline{BEFORE} \\ \underline{AFTER} \end{array} \right\} \right]$$

$$\underline{VARYING} \left\{ \begin{array}{l} identifier\text{--}2 \\ index\text{--}name\text{--}1 \end{array} \right\} \underline{FROM} \left\{ \begin{array}{l} identifier\text{--}3 \\ index\text{--}name\text{--}2 \\ literal\text{--}1 \end{array} \right\}$$

$$\underline{BY} \left\{ \begin{array}{l} identifier\text{--}4 \\ literal\text{--}2 \end{array} \right\} \underline{UNTIL} \; condition\text{--}1$$

$$[\; imperative\text{--}statement\text{--}1 \; \underline{END\text{--}PERFORM} \;]$$

Identifier-2 is the subscript, literal-1/identifier-3 contain the start value of the subscript, literal-2/identifier-4 contain the incremental value of the subscript and condition-1 is the terminating condition for the PERFORM repetition. The previous piece of coding can be re-written as follows

```
    PERFORM TEST-TOTALS
        VARYING SUBSCRIPT FROM 1 BY 1 UNTIL SUBSCRIPT > 6.
        . . .
        . . .
        . . .
TEST-TOTALS.
    IF SALES-TOTALS(SUBSCRIPT) < 10000 PERFORM LOW-SALES.
```

The nature and purpose of index-names will be discussed in Chapter 16. There is a more complicated version of PERFORM to deal with two

144

dimensional tables.

It has the format:

$$\text{\underline{PERFORM}} \left[\text{procedure--name--1} \left[\begin{Bmatrix} \text{\underline{THROUGH}} \\ \text{\underline{THRU}} \end{Bmatrix} \text{procedure--name--2} \right] \right]$$

$$\left[\text{WITH \underline{TEST}} \begin{Bmatrix} \text{\underline{BEFORE}} \\ \text{\underline{AFTER}} \end{Bmatrix} \right]$$

$$\text{\underline{VARYING}} \begin{Bmatrix} \text{identifier--2} \\ \text{index--name--1} \end{Bmatrix} \text{\underline{FROM}} \begin{Bmatrix} \text{identifier--3} \\ \text{index--name--2} \\ \text{literal--1} \end{Bmatrix}$$

$$\text{\underline{BY}} \begin{Bmatrix} \text{identifier--4} \\ \text{literal--2} \end{Bmatrix} \text{\underline{UNTIL}} \text{ condition--1}$$

$$\left[\text{\underline{AFTER}} \begin{Bmatrix} \text{identifier--5} \\ \text{index--name--3} \end{Bmatrix} \text{\underline{FROM}} \begin{Bmatrix} \text{identifier--6} \\ \text{index--name--4} \\ \text{literal--3} \end{Bmatrix} \right. $$

$$\left. \text{\underline{BY}} \begin{Bmatrix} \text{identifier--7} \\ \text{literal--4} \end{Bmatrix} \text{\underline{UNTIL}} \text{ condition--2} \right] \quad \dots$$

[imperative--statement--1 <u>END--PERFORM</u>]

This version of the statement in effect creates two loops, one within the other. The VARYING clause sets up the first, or outer loop and the AFTER clause sets up the second or inner loop. Initially identifier-2 and identifier-5 are set to the FROM values. Then condition-1 and condition-2 are tested. If both conditions are false the procedure is performed. Identifier-5 is then increased by its BY value and condition-2 is tested again. If the condition is false, the paragraph is performed again and the process repeated. When condition-2 eventually becomes true, identifier-5 is set to its FROM value again and identifier-2 is increased by its BY value. The conditions are tested in sequence again. The whole process stops when condition-1 becomes true.

The table searching routine in the program used to process the table in ADD-SALES (Fig. 15.1) can be adapted to identify any sales area with a value of less than 10000 in the two dimensional table used in program SUM-TABLE (Fig. 15.3) as follows

```
PERFORM TEST-TOTALS
        VARYING MONTH FROM 1 BY 1 UNTIL MONTH > 12
        AFTER S-AREA FROM 1 BY 1 UNTIL S-AREA > 6.
        . . .
        . . .
```

...

TEST-TOTALS.
    IF SALES-AREA(MONTH S-AREA) < 10000
      PERFORM LOW-SALES.

You have to take great care when using PERFORM . . . VARYING . . . AFTER with two dimensional tables to make sure that the correct sequence of incrementing the subscript values is followed. In COBOL 74 there is a version of PERFORM which has two AFTER clauses for use in processing three dimensional tables. This creates three levels of loops. The order of evaluation is the same as for two dimensional tables. The inner loop is fully executed first, then the second loop followed by the first or outer loop. COBOL 85 allows up to seven nested PERFORM loops, but this is strictly for the most experienced programmer!

Example: PERFORM INITIALISE-TABLE
                VARYING SUB-1 FROM 1 BY 1 UNTIL SUB-1 = 12
                VARYING SUB-2 FROM 1 BY 1 UNTIL SUB-2 = 12
                VARYING SUB-3 FROM 1 BY 1 UNTIL SUB-3 = 12
                VARYING SUB-4 FROM 1 BY 1 UNTIL SUB-4 = 12
                VARYING SUB-5 FROM 1 BY 1 UNTIL SUB-5 = 12
                VARYING SUB-6 FROM 1 BY 1 UNTIL SUB-6 = 12
                VARYING SUB-7 FROM 1 BY 1 UNTIL SUB-7 = 12

The full format of PERFORM is given in appendix 2.

CHAPTER 16

Redefining and Searching

16.1 Redefinition

It is often useful to be able to describe the same data storage area in two or more different ways. This is implicitly allowed at record (01) level in the FILE SECTION of the DATA DIVISION. In all the example programs there is only one record format in each FD, usually referred to as INPUT-FILE-REC or OUTPUT-FILE-REC. However, COBOL allows any number of different formats to be specified so long as they are of the same length. Only one data area is set aside in the computer's primary memory to handle records from the file but the different record formats allow the data record to be looked at in different ways. An example of this is found in the processing of orders. When a customer order is input to a computer based system, it is often divided up into a header record containing such information as customer number, order number, order date etc. and detail records, each containing a product number, quantity ordered etc. The different formats of these records can be specified in the FD but refer to the same section of primary memory. However, it is a good programming habit to leave the FILE SECTION to deal with files and carry out all the record processing from WORKING-STORAGE SECTION so the facility of implicit record definition in the FILE SECTION is not recommended.

16.1.1 REDEFINES Clause

In the WORKING-STORAGE SECTION we can redefine records or data groups or data elements by using the REDEFINES clause.

It has the format:

level–number identifier–1 <u>REDEFINES</u> identifier–2

Identifier-1 is allocated the same area of memory as identifier-2.

147

Example: 01 PERSONNEL.
              03 RECORD-TYPE   PIC 9.
              03 COMMON-INFO   PIC X(20).
              03 NAME   PIC X(20).
              03 DEPT-SECT REDEFINES NAME.
                 05 DEPT-NO   PIC 9(3).
                 05 SECT-NO   PIC 99.
                 05 DESC   PIC X(15).

This allows the use of the same area for two different record formats. In this example records with types 1 and 2 contain identical data in the first 20 character positions but thereafter the two record types can contain data in different formats. A record with type 1 contains NAME in positions 21 to 40 and a record type 2 contains DEPT-NO, SECT-NO and DESC in the same area.

Another situation is where a field can have different types

Example: 03 FIELD-1   PIC X(5).
           03 INTEGER REDEFINES FIELD-1 PIC 9(5).
           03 DECIMAL REDEFINES FIELD-1 PIC 9(3)V99.

The same field can be referred to as FIELD-1, INTEGER or DECIMAL in the PROCEDURE DIVISION depending on the requirements of the program. So it is possible to read data into FIELD-1 and treat it as an alphanumeric item or a whole number or a decimal number. This also provides the possibility of placing alphabetic characters in FIELD-1 and trying to process them as a decimal number. So take care when redefining fields! But it can be useful. Remember the problem of correctness of UNIT-PRICE and UNIT-COST in program CREATE-PRODUCT (Fig. 11.1).

16.1.2 Restrictions using REDEFINES

There are a considerable number of restrictions when using the REDEFINES clause. It must be used before any other clause in the data description as in the previous example i.e REDEFINES before PIC. Both the identifiers referred to in the clause must have the same level number. Redefinition of an item continues until a level number less than or equal to that of the redefined item is encountered. REDEFINES clauses may be nested, that is, an area within a REDEFINES may itself be redefined. Entries containing or subordinate to a REDEFINES clause must not have any VALUE clauses except for condition name (88 level) entries. There must not be any entries having a higher level number than identifier-1 and identifier-2 of the REDEFINES statement between these two items. In COBOL 74, a data item which REDEFINES another data item must be the same size as the original but COBOL 85 allows the second data item to be smaller than the original one.

16.2 REDEFINES and OCCURS

REDEFINES and OCCURS can be very useful when used together. In the program PRINT-DAY (Fig. 9.1), an algorithm worked out the number of the day of the week in which a date occurred. The day number which was produced had to be converted to a day name by using a series of IF statements. We can achieve the same result in a totally different way by using REDEFINES and OCCURS. A table of names is set up in data group DAY-1 and this group is redefined as a second data group DAY-2. DAY-2 contains DAY-3 which is a table of seven elements. So DAY-3(1) occupies the same area as the first FILLER and therefore contains "SATURDAY", DAY-3(2) contains "SUNDAY" and so on.

```
000250 01  D-O-W.
000360     03 DAY-1.
000370        05 FILLER              PIC X(9) VALUE "Saturday".
000380        05 FILLER              PIC X(9) VALUE "Sunday".
000390        05 FILLER              PIC X(9) VALUE "Monday".
000500        05 FILLER              PIC X(9) VALUE "Tuesday".
000510        05 FILLER              PIC X(9) VALUE "Wednesday".
000520        05 FILLER              PIC X(9) VALUE "Thursday".
000530        05 FILLER              PIC X(9) VALUE "Friday".
000540     03 DAY-2 REDEFINES DAY-1.
000550        05 DAY-3 OCCURS 7 PIC X(9).
```

All that is required to output the day name is to use the day number produced by the algorithm as a subscript for DAY-3.

DISPLAY DAY-3(WEEKDAY).

16.3 Processing Tables

If we are unable to identify the entry in a table directly by using a subscript, we have to adopt a processing strategy similar to searching through a file. In fact, a table can be thought of as a file small enough to be stored in memory. Each entry in the table corresponds to a record in a serial file and can be treated as a single item or as a collection of data items. One of these items is the key which uniquely identifies the entry. Passing through a table looking for a specific key is called "looking up the table". We will refer to the key in a table as the target key and the data item which contains the value we are looking up in the table as the search key. Therefore, the process of looking up the table involves looking at some or all the entries in the table to see if the search key matches the target key in an entry. Two types of tables exist, one in which the target keys are not in an ordered sequence, the second in which the target keys are in ascending or descending sequence. We have to adopt different programming strategies depending on whether we are looking up an ordered or an unordered table. Let us take as an example a group of bird-watchers carrying out a survey of predator and game birds. A code is assigned to each type of bird and observers note down the name of the bird they have spotted, the numbers observed, the site and date. These observations are recorded on a file and a program is required to convert the name of the bird to a code number. This allows the data to be stored in a compact format with only three characters being required to identify each bird as opposed to thirteen if the full name is stored. The conversion is carried out by taking the bird name from the input data and using it as the search key. A table containing the code number and name of each bird is searched to find the entry where the name matches the search key. When a match is found the code number is copied to the output record. If no match is found a message is printed. Bird-watchers may write the bird names on their returns in either capital letters, small letters or with the first letter capital and the rest small. To cope with this, the table contains entries for each of these formats. Any other format would be treated as a non-match.

16.3.1 Table Description

To set up a table there is an extented version of the OCCURS clause.

It has the format:

OCCURS integer TIMES

$$\left[\left\{ \begin{array}{l} \underline{\text{ASCENDING}} \\ \underline{\text{DESCENDING}} \end{array} \right\} \text{KEY IS data–name–1} \ldots \right]$$

$$\left[\underline{\text{INDEXED}} \text{ BY index–name–1} \ldots \right]$$

The ASCENDING/DESCENDING KEY clause is only used when referring to an ordered table. The INDEXED BY index-name-1 refers to a special index item which is used as a subscript in table handling. An index-name contains a numeric value that can only be used with SET, PERFORM or SEARCH statements. It is very unusual because its size and format are determined by the compiler and it must not be described anywhere else in the DATA DIVISION.

150

16.3.2 SET Statement

$$\text{\underline{SET}} \left\{ \begin{array}{ll} \text{index--name--1} & \text{[index--name--2]} \cdots \\ \text{identifier--1} & \text{[identifier--2] ...} \end{array} \right\} \text{\underline{TO}} \left\{ \begin{array}{l} \text{index--name--3} \\ \text{identifier--3} \\ \text{integer--1} \end{array} \right\}$$

The SET statement sets the contents of index-name-1 and any other index-name items to either an integer or to the contents of index-name-3 or identifier-3. The MOVE statement cannot be used to set the contents of an index-name to a value.

Examples: SET WHICH TO 1
            SET SUBSCRIPT TO POINTER-START.

In these examples WHICH and SUBSCRIPT must have appeared in an INDEXED BY clause.

If we wish to change the contents of an index-name another version of SET must be used.

It has the format:

$$\text{\underline{SET}} \ \text{index--name--3} \ \cdots \ \left\{ \begin{array}{l} \text{\underline{UP BY}} \\ \text{\underline{DOWN BY}} \end{array} \right\} \left\{ \begin{array}{l} \text{identifier} \\ \text{integer} \end{array} \right\}$$

This statement allows a value to be added or subtracted from an index-name.

Examples: SET WHICH UP BY 2.
            SET SUBSCRIPT DOWN BY POINTER-VALUE.

16.4 Looking up a Table

The table of bird data is held as follows:

```
000590 01    LIST-BIRD-NAMES.
000600       03 B-NAMES.
000610          05 FILLER            PIC X(16) VALUE  "082MARSH HARRIER".
000620          05 FILLER            PIC X(16) VALUE  "082marsh harrier".
000630          05 FILLER            PIC X(16) VALUE  "082Marsh harrier".
000640          05 FILLER            PIC X(16) VALUE  "083HEN HARRIER  ".
000650          05 FILLER            PIC X(16) VALUE  "083Hen harrier  ".
```

000660	05 FILLER	PIC X(16) VALUE	"083hen harrier ".
000670	05 FILLER	PIC X(16) VALUE	"084GOSHAWK ".
000680	05 FILLER	PIC X(16) VALUE	"084goshawk ".
000690	05 FILLER	PIC X(16) VALUE	"084Goshawk ".
000700	05 FILLER	PIC X(16) VALUE	"085SPARROWHAWK ".
000710	05 FILLER	PIC X(16) VALUE	"085sparrowhawk ".
000720	05 FILLER	PIC X(16) VALUE	"085Sparrowhawk ".
000730	05 FILLER	PIC X(16) VALUE	"087BUZZARD ".
000740	05 FILLER	PIC X(16) VALUE	"087buzzard ".
000750	05 FILLER	PIC X(16) VALUE	"087Buzzard ".
000760	05 FILLER	PIC X(16) VALUE	"090GOLDEN EAGLE ".
000770	05 FILLER	PIC X(16) VALUE	"090golden eagle ".
000780	05 FILLER	PIC X(16) VALUE	"090Golden eagle ".
000790	05 FILLER	PIC X(16) VALUE	"091OSPREY ".
000800	05 FILLER	PIC X(16) VALUE	"091osprey ".
000810	05 FILLER	PIC X(16) VALUE	"091Osprey ".
000820	05 FILLER	PIC X(16) VALUE	"092KESTREL ".
000830	05 FILLER	PIC X(16) VALUE	"092kestrel ".
000840	05 FILLER	PIC X(16) VALUE	"092Kestrel ".
000850	05 FILLER	PIC X(16) VALUE	"094MERLIN ".
000860	05 FILLER	PIC X(16) VALUE	"094merlin ".
000870	05 FILLER	PIC X(16) VALUE	"094Merlin ".
000880	05 FILLER	PIC X(16) VALUE	"097PEREGRINE ".
000890	05 FILLER	PIC X(16) VALUE	"097peregrine ".
000900	05 FILLER	PIC X(16) VALUE	"097Peregrine ".
000910	05 FILLER	PIC X(16) VALUE	"098RED GROUSE ".
000920	05 FILLER	PIC X(16) VALUE	"098red grouse ".
000930	05 FILLER	PIC X(16) VALUE	"098Red grouse ".
000940	05 FILLER	PIC X(16) VALUE	"099PTARMIGAN ".
000950	05 FILLER	PIC X(16) VALUE	"099ptarmigan ".
000960	05 FILLER	PIC X(16) VALUE	"099Ptarmigan ".
000970	05 FILLER	PIC X(16) VALUE	"100BLACK GROUSE ".
000980	05 FILLER	PIC X(16) VALUE	"100black grouse ".
000990	05 FILLER	PIC X(16) VALUE	"100Black grouse ".
001000	05 FILLER	PIC X(16) VALUE	"101CAPERCAILLIE ".
001010	05 FILLER	PIC X(16) VALUE	"101capercaillie ".
001020	05 FILLER	PIC X(16) VALUE	"101Capercaillie ".
001030	05 FILLER	PIC X(16) VALUE	"103PARTRIDGE ".
001040	05 FILLER	PIC X(16) VALUE	"103partridge ".
001050	05 FILLER	PIC X(16) VALUE	"103Partridge ".
001060	05 FILLER	PIC X(16) VALUE	"105PHEASANT ".
001070	05 FILLER	PIC X(16) VALUE	"105pheasant ".
001080	05 FILLER	PIC X(16) VALUE	"105Pheasant ".
001090	03 TABLE-OF-NAMES REDEFINES B-NAMES OCCURS 48		

```
001100              INDEXED BY WHICH.
001110      05 T-BIRD-NO          PIC 999.
001120      05 T-BIRD-NAME        PIC X(13).
```

There are a number of different ways of looking up a table depending on the facilities available in the implementation of COBOL being used and also the sequence of data in the table. We will start by assuming that the compiler supports compound conditions.

The table TABLE-OF-NAMES can be looked up with the following statements

```
        SET WHICH TO 1.
        PERFORM FIND-MATCH
            UNTIL T-BIRD-NAME(WHICH) = BIRD-NAME OR WHICH = 48.
        IF T-BIRD-NAME(WHICH) = BIRD-NAME
            PERFORM OUTPUT-RECORD
        ELSE
            PERFORM NOT-FOUND.
    FIND-MATCH.
        SET WHICH UP BY 1.
```

These statements look at each entry in the table in turn, starting at the first one. The UNTIL clause is used to match the search key BIRD-NAME to the target key T-BIRD-NAME(WHICH). Procedure FIND-MATCH increments the index data item. PERFORM also tests for the end of the table, that is, when the value in WHICH reaches 48. Since the PERFORM statement is stopped by either of two conditions we must immediately use the IF statement to determine which condition terminated the PERFORM. The previous piece of coding can be improved by using PERFORM . . . VARYING

```
        PERFORM FIND-MATCH VARYING WHICH FROM 1 BY 1
            UNTIL T-BIRD-NAME(WHICH) = BIRD-NAME OR WHICH = 48.
        IF T-BIRD-NAME(WHICH) = BIRD-NAME
            PERFORM OUTPUT-RECORD
        ELSE
            PERFORM NOT-FOUND.
    FIND-MATCH.
```

In this case FIND-MATCH is a dummy procedure. The subscript is incremented by the PERFORM statement.

16.5 SEARCH Statement

Fuller implementations contain a SEARCH statement for looking up tables. It has two formats, the first is used when the items in the table are not in sequence of key value and the second when it is in sequence.

Format 1:

$$\underline{\text{SEARCH}} \ \text{identifier--1} \ \left[\underline{\text{VARYING}} \ \left\{ \begin{array}{l} \text{identifier--2} \\ \text{index--name--1} \end{array} \right\} \right]$$

$$[\text{AT} \ \underline{\text{END}} \ \text{imperative--statement--1}]$$

$$\left\{ \underline{\text{WHEN}} \ \text{condition--1} \ \left\{ \begin{array}{l} \text{imperative--statement--2} \\ \underline{\text{NEXT}} \ \underline{\text{SENTENCE}} \end{array} \right\} \right\} \dots$$

$$[\ \underline{\text{END--SEARCH}} \ ]$$

Identifier-1 is the name of the table being searched. The WHEN clause functions in a similar way to an IF statement. Condition-1 is tested and if it is true imperative-statement-2 is executed. If condition-1 is not satisfied, the search continues. The index item in the OCCURS clause of the table being searched is used by SEARCH as the subscript which points to the current element of the table. The VARYING option specifies that the variable or index name after VARYING is to be incremented at the same time as the index associated with the table is incremented. This allows the referencing of a second table in the WHEN condition.

16.6 Program BIRD-COUNT

Program BIRD-COUNT uses the following statements to look up the table.

```
001280 FIND-MATCH.
001290     SET WHICH TO 1.
001300     SEARCH TABLE-OF-NAMES AT END PERFORM NOT-FOUND
001310         WHEN T-BIRD-NAME(WHICH) = BIRD-NAME
001320             PERFORM OUTPUT-RECORD.
```

The SEARCH statement automatically increments the indexed identifier WHICH by 1. Searching can start anywhere in the table. All that has to be done is set WHICH at the required starting point. In this case we are starting at the first entry and searching until either a match is found or the end of the table is found without a match. In the latter case the AT END path is taken and NOT-FOUND performed.

```
000100 IDENTIFICATION DIVISION.
000110 PROGRAM-ID.  BIRD-COUNT.
000120 AUTHOR.  D WATSON.
000130 INSTALLATION. UNIVERSITY OF ABERDEEN.
000140 DATE-WRITTEN. APRIL 1985.
000150 SECURITY. NONE.
000160*
000170 ENVIRONMENT DIVISION.
000180 CONFIGURATION SECTION.
000190 SOURCE-COMPUTER.  ABC-1.
000200 OBJECT-COMPUTER.  ABC-1.
000210 INPUT-OUTPUT SECTION.
000220 FILE-CONTROL.
000230      SELECT INPUT-FILE ASSIGN TO DISK.
000250      SELECT OUTPUT-FILE ASSIGN TO D2.
000270      SELECT PRINT-FILE ASSIGN TO PRINTER.
000290*
000300 DATA DIVISION.
000310 FILE SECTION.
000320 FD   INPUT-FILE
000330      LABEL RECORDS ARE STANDARD
000340      VALUE OF FILE-ID IS "BIRDS".
000350 01   INPUT-FILE-REC          PIC X(24).
000360 FD   OUTPUT-FILE
000370      LABEL RECORDS STANDARD
000380      VALUE OF FILE-ID "NAMED".
000390 01   OUTPUT-FILE-REC         PIC X(14).
000400 FD   PRINT-FILE
000410      LABEL RECORDS OMITTED.
000420 01   PRINT-RECORD            PIC X(48).
000430*
000440 WORKING-STORAGE SECTION.
000450 01   BIRD-RECORD.
000460      03 BIRD-NAME            PIC X(13).
000470      03 NUMBER-SEEN          PIC 9(3).
000480      03 SITE                 PIC 99.
000490      03 DATE-SEEN            PIC 9(6).
000500 01   NEW-BIRD-RECORD.
000510      03 N-BIRD-NUMBER        PIC 999.
000520      03 N-NUMBER-SEEN        PIC 9(3).
000530      03 N-SITE               PIC 99.
000540      03 N-DATE-SEEN          PIC 9(6).
000550 01 ERROR-RECORD.
000560      03 OUT-NAME             PIC X(13).
```

000570	03 FILLER	PIC XXX VALUE SPACES.
000580	03 ERROR-MESSAGE	PIC X(32).
000590 01	LIST-BIRD-NAMES.	
000600	03 B-NAMES.	
000610	05 FILLER	PIC X(16) VALUE "082MARSH HARRIER".
000620	05 FILLER	PIC X(16) VALUE "082marsh harrier".
000630	05 FILLER	PIC X(16) VALUE "082Marsh harrier".
000640	05 FILLER	PIC X(16) VALUE "083HEN HARRIER ".
000650	05 FILLER	PIC X(16) VALUE "083Hen harrier ".
000660	05 FILLER	PIC X(16) VALUE "083hen harrier ".
000670	05 FILLER	PIC X(16) VALUE "084GOSHAWK ".
000680	05 FILLER	PIC X(16) VALUE "084goshawk ".
000690	05 FILLER	PIC X(16) VALUE "084Goshawk ".
000700	05 FILLER	PIC X(16) VALUE "085SPARROWHAWK ".
000710	05 FILLER	PIC X(16) VALUE "085sparrowhawk ".
000720	05 FILLER	PIC X(16) VALUE "085Sparrowhawk ".
000730	05 FILLER	PIC X(16) VALUE "087BUZZARD ".
000740	05 FILLER	PIC X(16) VALUE "087buzzard ".
000750	05 FILLER	PIC X(16) VALUE "087Buzzard ".
000760	05 FILLER	PIC X(16) VALUE "090GOLDEN EAGLE ".
000770	05 FILLER	PIC X(16) VALUE "090golden eagle ".
000780	05 FILLER	PIC X(16) VALUE "090Golden eagle ".
000790	05 FILLER	PIC X(16) VALUE "091OSPREY ".
000800	05 FILLER	PIC X(16) VALUE "091osprey ".
000810	05 FILLER	PIC X(16) VALUE "091Osprey ".
000820	05 FILLER	PIC X(16) VALUE "092KESTREL ".
000830	05 FILLER	PIC X(16) VALUE "092kestrel ".
000840	05 FILLER	PIC X(16) VALUE "092Kestrel ".
000850	05 FILLER	PIC X(16) VALUE "094MERLIN ".
000860	05 FILLER	PIC X(16) VALUE "094merlin ".
000870	05 FILLER	PIC X(16) VALUE "094Merlin ".
000880	05 FILLER	PIC X(16) VALUE "097PEREGRINE ".
000890	05 FILLER	PIC X(16) VALUE "097peregrine ".
000900	05 FILLER	PIC X(16) VALUE "097Peregrine ".
000910	05 FILLER	PIC X(16) VALUE "098RED GROUSE ".
000920	05 FILLER	PIC X(16) VALUE "098red grouse ".
000930	05 FILLER	PIC X(16) VALUE "098Red grouse ".
000940	05 FILLER	PIC X(16) VALUE "099PTARMIGAN ".
000950	05 FILLER	PIC X(16) VALUE "099ptarmigan ".
000960	05 FILLER	PIC X(16) VALUE "099Ptarmigan ".
000970	05 FILLER	PIC X(16) VALUE "100BLACK GROUSE ".
000980	05 FILLER	PIC X(16) VALUE "100black grouse ".
000990	05 FILLER	PIC X(16) VALUE "100Black grouse ".
001000	05 FILLER	PIC X(16) VALUE "101CAPERCAILLIE ".

```
001010          05 FILLER              PIC X(16) VALUE "101capercaillie ".
001020          05 FILLER              PIC X(16) VALUE "101Capercaillie ".
001030          05 FILLER              PIC X(16) VALUE "103PARTRIDGE      ".
001040          05 FILLER              PIC X(16) VALUE "103partridge    ".
001050          05 FILLER              PIC X(16) VALUE "103Partridge    ".
001060          05 FILLER              PIC X(16) VALUE "105PHEASANT      ".
001070          05 FILLER              PIC X(16) VALUE "105pheasant      ".
001080          05 FILLER              PIC X(16) VALUE "105Pheasant      ".
001090       03 TABLE-OF-NAMES REDEFINES B-NAMES OCCURS 48
001100                 INDEXED BY WHICH.
001110          05 T-BIRD-NO           PIC 999.
001120          05 T-BIRD-NAME         PIC X(13).
001130 01    MORE-DATA                 PIC X VALUE "Y".
001140          88 NO-MORE-DATA VALUE "N".
001150 PROCEDURE DIVISION.
001160 MAIN SECTION.
001170 START-UP.
001180       OPEN INPUT INPUT-FILE
001190             OUTPUT OUTPUT-FILE
001191                   PRINT-FILE.
001200 PROCESS-DATA.
001210       PERFORM READ-A-RECORD.
001220       PERFORM PROCESS-OUTPUT-INPUT UNTIL NO-MORE-DATA.
001230 CLOSE-DOWN.
001240       CLOSE INPUT-FILE
001250             OUTPUT-FILE.
001260       STOP RUN.
001270 PROCESS-OUTPUT-INPUT SECTION.
001280 FIND-MATCH.
001290       SET WHICH TO 1.
001300       SEARCH TABLE-OF-NAMES AT END PERFORM NOT-FOUND
001310          WHEN T-BIRD-NAME(WHICH) = BIRD-NAME
001320             PERFORM OUTPUT-REC.
001330       PERFORM READ-A-RECORD.
001340 SUPPORT SECTION.
001350 OUTPUT-REC.
001360       MOVE T-BIRD-NO(WHICH) TO N-BIRD-NUMBER.
001370       MOVE NUMBER-SEEN TO N-NUMBER-SEEN.
001380       MOVE SITE TO N-SITE.
001390       MOVE DATE-SEEN TO N-DATE-SEEN.
001400       WRITE OUTPUT-FILE-REC FROM NEW-BIRD-RECORD.
001410 NOT-FOUND.
001420       MOVE BIRD-NAME TO OUT-NAME.
001430       MOVE "Bird name not found on code list" TO ERROR-MESSAGE.
```

157

001440   WRITE PRINT-RECORD FROM ERROR-RECORD AFTER 2.
001450 READ-A-RECORD.
001460   READ INPUT-FILE INTO BIRD-RECORD
001470   AT END MOVE "N" TO MORE-DATA.

Fig. 16.1

16.7 Binary Searching

The table in BIRD-COUNT (Fig. 15.1) is not in target key sequence. That is, the bird names are not in ascending alphabetical order. This means that a linear search has to be carried out. The program starts at the first entry in the table, tests it for the required condition and if the test is successful the searching stops. If the search is unsuccessful the search continues. Only a match or reaching the end of file stops the search. If the items in the table are in ascending sequence a binary search can be carried out. This works by finding the middle item in the table, looking at the value of the target key to see if it is higher or lower than the search key. If the middle target key value is higher, the upper half of the list is rejected and the search continues in the lower section. This is divided in two and the search process starts again. By repeatedly bisecting smaller sections of the table the program "homes in" on the entry with the target key. The maximum number of comparisons needed to find an item in a list of n items is $\log_2 n$ against the average of $(n+1)/2$ for a successful search in an unordered list and n for an unsuccessful one.

The second version of the SEARCH has the following format.

Format 2:

SEARCH **ALL** identifier–1 [AT **END** imperative–statement–1]

$$
\textbf{WHEN} \left\{ \begin{array}{l} \textbf{data–name–1} \left\{ \begin{array}{l} \text{IS } \underline{\textbf{EQUAL}} \text{ TO} \\ \textbf{IS} = \end{array} \right\} \\ \textbf{condition–name–1} \end{array} \right. \left\{ \begin{array}{l} \text{identifier–3} \\ \text{literal–1} \\ \text{arithmetic–expression–1} \end{array} \right\}
$$

$$
\left[\textbf{AND} \left\{ \begin{array}{l} \textbf{data–name–2} \left\{ \begin{array}{l} \text{IS } \underline{\textbf{EQUAL}} \text{ TO} \\ \textbf{IS} = \end{array} \right\} \\ \textbf{condition–name–2} \end{array} \right. \left\{ \begin{array}{l} \text{identifier–4} \\ \text{literal–2} \\ \text{arithmetic–expression–2} \end{array} \right\} \right] \ldots
$$

158

$$\begin{Bmatrix} \text{imperative–statement–2} \\ \text{NEXT \underline{SENTENCE}} \end{Bmatrix}$$

[END–SEARCH]

There is only one WHEN, but within a WHEN, a series of conditions joined by AND can be specified.

16.8 Program BIRD-COUNT-2

In the program BIRD-COUNT-2 (Fig. 16.2) the items in the table TABLE-OF-NAMES are in ascending sequence of bird names. Look carefully at the order. Lower case letters have higher code numbers in the ASCII and EBCDIC character coding systems. "A" comes before "a". So the lower case names are placed in alphabetical order after those in upper case or with the first letter in upper case. The OCCURS clause is accompanied by ASCENDING KEY identifier clause. The identifier is the name of the target key in each entry in the table.

```
001280 FIND-MATCH.
001290     SET WHICH TO 1.
001300     SEARCH ALL TABLE-OF-NAMES AT END PERFORM NOT-FOUND
001310         WHEN T-BIRD-NAME(WHICH) = BIRD-NAME
001320             PERFORM OUTPUT-REC.
```

This second format of SEARCH will look up a table considerably faster than the first version.

```
000100 IDENTIFICATION DIVISION.
000110 PROGRAM-ID.  BIRD-COUNT-2.
000120 AUTHOR.  D WATSON.
000130 INSTALLATION. UNIVERSITY OF ABERDEEN.
000140 DATE-WRITTEN. APRIL 1985.
000150 SECURITY. NONE.
000160*
000170 ENVIRONMENT DIVISION.
000180 CONFIGURATION SECTION.
000190 SOURCE-COMPUTER.  ABC-1.
000200 OBJECT-COMPUTER.  ABC-1.
000210 INPUT-OUTPUT SECTION.
000220 FILE-CONTROL.
000230     SELECT INPUT-FILE ASSIGN TO DISK.
000250     SELECT OUTPUT-FILE ASSIGN TO D2.
000270     SELECT PRINT-FILE ASSIGN TO PRINTER.
```

```
000290*
000300 DATA DIVISION.
000310 FILE SECTION.
000320 FD  INPUT-FILE
000330      LABEL RECORDS ARE STANDARD
000340      VALUE OF FILE-ID IS "BIRDS".
000350 01   INPUT-FILE-REC        PIC X(24).
000360 FD  OUTPUT-FILE
000370      LABEL RECORDS STANDARD
000380      VALUE OF FILE-ID "NAMED".
000390 01   OUTPUT-FILE-REC       PIC X(14).
000400 FD  PRINT-FILE
000410      LABEL RECORDS OMITTED.
000420 01   PRINT-RECORD          PIC X(48).
000430*
000440 WORKING-STORAGE SECTION.
000450 01   BIRD-RECORD.
000460      03 BIRD-NAME          PIC X(13).
000470      03 NUMBER-SEEN        PIC 9(3).
000480      03 SITE               PIC 99.
000490      03 DATE-SEEN          PIC 9(6).
000500 01   NEW-BIRD-RECORD.
000510      03 N-BIRD-NUMBER      PIC 999.
000520      03 N-NUMBER-SEEN      PIC 9(3).
000530      03 N-SITE             PIC 99.
000540      03 N-DATE-SEEN        PIC 9(6).
000550 01   ERROR-RECORD.
000560      03 OUT-NAME           PIC X(13).
000570      03 FILLER             PIC XXX VALUE SPACES.
000580      03 ERROR-MESSAGE      PIC X(32).
000590 01   LIST-BIRD-NAMES.
000600      03 B-NAMES.
000610         05 FILLER          PIC X(16) VALUE  "100BLACK GROUSE ".
000620         05 FILLER          PIC X(16) VALUE  "100Black grouse ".
000630         05 FILLER          PIC X(16) VALUE  "087BUZZARD ".
000640         05 FILLER          PIC X(16) VALUE  "087Buzzard ".
000650         05 FILLER          PIC X(16) VALUE  "101CAPERCAILLIE ".
000660         05 FILLER          PIC X(16) VALUE  "101Capercaillie ".
000670         05 FILLER          PIC X(16) VALUE  "090GOLDEN EAGLE ".
000680         05 FILLER          PIC X(16) VALUE  "090Golden eagle ".
000690         05 FILLER          PIC X(16) VALUE  "084GOSHAWK ".
000700         05 FILLER          PIC X(16) VALUE  "084Goshawk ".
000710         05 FILLER          PIC X(16) VALUE  "083HEN HARRIER  ".
000720         05 FILLER          PIC X(16) VALUE  "083Hen harrier  ".
```

```
000730          05 FILLER              PIC X(16) VALUE  "092KESTREL ".
000740          05 FILLER              PIC X(16) VALUE  "092Kestrel ".
000750          05 FILLER              PIC X(16) VALUE  "082MARSH HARRIER".
000760          05 FILLER              PIC X(16) VALUE  "082Marsh harrier".
000770          05 FILLER              PIC X(16) VALUE  "094MERLIN ".
000780          05 FILLER              PIC X(16) VALUE  "094Merlin ".
000790          05 FILLER              PIC X(16) VALUE  "091OSPREY ".
000800          05 FILLER              PIC X(16) VALUE  "091Osprey ".
000810          05 FILLER              PIC X(16) VALUE  "103PARTRIDGE     ".
000820          05 FILLER              PIC X(16) VALUE  "103Partridge     ".
000830          05 FILLER              PIC X(16) VALUE  "097PEREGRINE     ".
000840          05 FILLER              PIC X(16) VALUE  "097Peregrine     ".
000850          05 FILLER              PIC X(16) VALUE  "105PHEASANT".
000860          05 FILLER              PIC X(16) VALUE  "105Pheasant".
000870          05 FILLER              PIC X(16) VALUE  "099PTARMIGAN     ".
000880          05 FILLER              PIC X(16) VALUE  "099Ptarmigan     ".
000890          05 FILLER              PIC X(16) VALUE  "098RED GROUSE  ".
000900          05 FILLER              PIC X(16) VALUE  "098Red grouse  ".
000910          05 FILLER              PIC X(16) VALUE  "085SPARROWHAWK ".
000920          05 FILLER              PIC X(16) VALUE  "085Sparrowhawk ".
000930          05 FILLER              PIC X(16) VALUE  "100black grouse ".
000940          05 FILLER              PIC X(16) VALUE  "087buzzard ".
000950          05 FILLER              PIC X(16) VALUE  "101capercaillie ".
000960          05 FILLER              PIC X(16) VALUE  "090golden eagle ".
000970          05 FILLER              PIC X(16) VALUE  "084goshawk ".
000980          05 FILLER              PIC X(16) VALUE  "083hen harrier ".
000990          05 FILLER              PIC X(16) VALUE  "092kestrel ".
001000          05 FILLER              PIC X(16) VALUE  "082marsh harrier".
001010          05 FILLER              PIC X(16) VALUE  "094merlin ".
001020          05 FILLER              PIC X(16) VALUE  "091osprey ".
001030          05 FILLER              PIC X(16) VALUE  "103partridge     ".
001040          05 FILLER              PIC X(16) VALUE  "099peregrine     ".
001050          05 FILLER              PIC X(16) VALUE  "105pheasant".
001060          05 FILLER              PIC X(16) VALUE  "099ptarmigan     ".
001070          05 FILLER              PIC X(16) VALUE  "098red grouse  ".
001080          05 FILLER              PIC X(16) VALUE  "085sparrowhawk  ".
001090      03 TABLE-OF-NAMES REDEFINES B-NAMES OCCURS 48
001100          ASCENDING KEY T-BIRD-NAME INDEXED BY WHICH.
001110          05 T-BIRD-NO           PIC 999.
001120          05 T-BIRD-NAME         PIC X(13).
001130 01   MORE-DATA                  PIC X VALUE "Y".
001140          88 NO-MORE-DATA VALUE "N".
001150 PROCEDURE DIVISION.
001160 MAIN SECTION.
```

161

```
001170 START-UP.
001180       OPEN INPUT INPUT-FILE
001190             OUTPUT OUTPUT-FILE.
001200 PROCESS-DATA.
001210       PERFORM READ-A-RECORD.
001220       PERFORM PROCESS-OUTPUT-INPUT UNTIL NO-MORE-DATA.
001230 CLOSE-DOWN.
001240       CLOSE INPUT-FILE
001250             OUTPUT-FILE.
001260       STOP RUN.
001270 PROCESS-OUTPUT-INPUT SECTION.
001280 FIND-MATCH.
001290       SET WHICH TO 1.
001300       SEARCH ALL TABLE-OF-NAMES AT END PERFORM NOT-FOUND
001310             WHEN T-BIRD-NAME(WHICH) = BIRD-NAME
001320                   PERFORM OUTPUT-REC.
001330       PERFORM READ-A-RECORD.
001340 SUPPORT SECTION.
001350 OUTPUT-REC.
001360       MOVE T-BIRD-NO(WHICH) TO N-BIRD-NUMBER.
001370       MOVE NUMBER-SEEN TO N-NUMBER-SEEN.
001380       MOVE SITE TO N-SITE.
001390       MOVE DATE-SEEN TO N-DATE-SEEN.
001400       WRITE OUTPUT-FILE-REC FROM NEW-BIRD-RECORD.
001410 NOT-FOUND.
001420       MOVE BIRD-NAME TO OUT-NAME.
001430       MOVE "Bird name not found on code list" TO ERROR-MESSAGE.
001440       WRITE PRINT-RECORD FROM ERROR-RECORD AFTER 2.
001450 READ-A-RECORD.
001460       READ INPUT-FILE INTO BIRD-RECORD
001470             AT END MOVE "N" TO MORE-DATA.
```

Fig. 16.2

CHAPTER 17

Direct Access Files

17.1 Introduction

Up till now we have been processing files sequentially. When the storage medium for files is magnetic tape this is the only efficient way to handle files. However, magnetic disks offer additional facilities for storing and accessing records. Data is stored on the surface of a magnetic disk in a series of concentric tracks. A read/write head on a moving arm can pass across the surface of the disk from one track to another. The disk revolves at high speed and if the read/write head is positioned over a track, all the data on that track can be read into primary memory in the time it takes for the disk to perform a revolution. In practice, data is recorded as a series of records which are grouped into blocks or buckets. The number of records stored in a block depends on the size of the record and the block. There are normally several records to a block and several blocks to a track. Large capacity disk drives on mainframe computers use disk packs which contain a number of disks fixed on a central spindle. Read/write heads move over each surface of the disks except the topmost side and the bottom side. Since, on most of these types of drive, the heads move back and forth across the disk surfaces together, the same track from each recording surface is available for reading or writing. This vertical "slice" through the disk surfaces is called a cylinder. The disk handling software uses this arrangement to store data in such a way as to minimise the time taken to transfer data to and from the disk drives. On microcomputers, the usual type of disk storage is the floppy disk. These are single disks made of a plastic material which allow data to be recorded on one or both of the surfaces. The amount of data which can be stored on a diskette varies greatly with the different makes of disk drive but even the highest capacity disks hold far less than hard disks. For this reason, the type of hard disk known as the Winchester is common on business microcomputers. Indeed, a Winchester disk with at least 10 megabyte of storage is essential for the serious business user as it not only holds more, but data is transferred to and from it much faster than from a diskette. This speeds the compilation time of COBOL which can be very slow using diskettes as well as allowing programs to process files faster. There are three types of file organisation on disk with COBOL, sequential, relative and indexed sequential.

17.2 Sequential Processing on Disk

All the programs we have looked at which process files can use files stored either on magnetic tape or disk. In interactive processing in a time sharing system, files are normally on magnetic disk but sequential processing can take place as if the files were on magnetic tape. The only difference as far a program writing is concerned is that the device name in the SELECT . . . ASSIGN statement may be different for tape and disk, though in many systems there is not even this difference. The major difference between sequential files on magnetic tape and disk occurs when a file is updated. Because of the nature of magnetic tape, amending records in a file held on tape requires the creation of an updated file on another reel of tape. So, at the completion of an update program, two versions of a file exist, the original unamended version and the new amended version. Although this is a time consuming method of amending files it has the advantage of providing two generations of a file, the older one can be filed away, along with the amendments file, for security purposes. It can always be used again if something goes wrong with the current version. This updating system can be carried out on magnetic disk, but, unlike magnetic tape, disk allows records to be read, amended and written back to their original places on the file. There is also a facility to add records to the end of an existing sequential file.

17.2.1 OPEN Statement

The OPEN statement has a number of options available to open files on disk in different modes.

It has the format:

$$
\text{OPEN} \left\{ \begin{array}{l} \underline{\text{INPUT}} \\ \underline{\text{OUTPUT}} \\ \underline{\text{I-O}} \\ \underline{\text{EXTEND}} \end{array} \right\} \text{file-name-1} \ \cdots \ \left[\left\{ \begin{array}{l} \underline{\text{INPUT}} \\ \underline{\text{OUTPUT}} \\ \underline{\text{I-O}} \\ \underline{\text{EXTEND}} \end{array} \right\} \text{file-name-2} \ \cdots \ \right] \ \cdots
$$

We are already familiar with INPUT and OUTPUT. Opening a file in I-O mode allows a record to be read from the file and written back to the same position in the file. EXTEND mode allows a record written in the program to be placed after the last record currently on the file. If this facility is used, it is easy to write records which are out of sequence with the records already on the file, so it may have to be sorted.

17.2.2 REWRITE Statement

After issuing a READ statement on a file opened in I-O mode, a REWRITE is required to replace the old version of the record with the amended version.

It has the format:

REWRITE record–name–1 [FROM identifier–1]

The REWRITE statement otherwise works in the same way as the WRITE statement.

Example: OPEN I-O SEQUENTIAL-FILE.
             . . .
             . . .
            READ SEQUENTIAL-FILE RECORD INTO WORK-SPACE
                AT END MOVE "N" TO MORE-DATA.
            MOVE ZEROS TO QUANTITY.
            REWRITE SEQUENTIAL-REC FROM WORK-SPACE.

17.3 Direct Access Organisation

In sequential files processing starts at the beginning of the file and progresses record by record until the end of the file is reached. When a substantial number of records on the file are to be processed this is an effective and efficient way to handle the file. However, when only a small number of records on the file are to be processed or when only a small number of records are to be processed in a random order, sequential processing becomes, at best, intolerably slow and often plain impossible. So we need some other way of organising and accessing files which allows a single record to be accessed without any reference to records stored before or after it in the file. There are two methods available in COBOL to do this. One is relative organisation the other is indexed sequential organisation.

17.3.1 Relative Organisation

Relative organisation of a file determines the position of each record on the file by applying an algorithm to the key of the record we wish to store which produces the address of the record on the disk. This transformation is a complicated business and a considerable amount of research has gone into finding an effective and efficient algorithm.

This method is less frequently used than other file organisations and is beyond the scope of this book.

17.4 Indexed Sequential Organisation

This method maintains an index or series of indexes containing a list of the keys of the records in the file and the address of the block in which a record is stored. These indexes are searched to find the address of any required record. This has the great advantage to the programmer because all that the program has to do is to present the key of the required record and COBOL does the rest. An indexed sequential file may be processed sequentially or randomly. The setting up of the file and indexes is also easy, though this depends on the implementation. The usual method just requires records to be read from a sequential file which has been sorted into ascending primary key sequence and written to an indexed sequential file. Records on an indexed sequential file are always updated in place. Records which are to be added to the file are either inserted into vacant space in the file or are placed in overflow locations. When too many records are stored in the overflow locations, the file is reorganised by reading it sequentially and writing to another indexed sequential file. An indexed sequential file can be opened in INPUT, I-O or OUTPUT mode, but not in EXTEND mode.

17.4.1 Random Access

Random access on an indexed sequential file operates on the following principles. Each record on a file has a primary key which uniquely identifies it. We decide which record we wish to retrieve. The key value of this record must be known, either by being input on a transaction file in a batch processing system, or by being input from a terminal in an interactive system. The format of the record in the file is described in the FD which must contain the data-name of the key field. When we wish to read a record, the key value is moved into the key field on the record, then a READ statement is executed. The file handling software looks at the value in the record key field and searches through the file indexes to find the address of the block containing that record on the magnetic disk. The contents of this block are transferred into the central processing unit and the record placed in the record description area in the program. When a record is written to the file, the record is set up in the same way as in sequential file processing. When a WRITE statement is executed the software looks at the contents of the key field and, using the indexes, writes the record to its correct position on the magnetic disk.

17.4.2 Selecting an Indexed-Sequential File

The organisation of an indexed sequential file is described in the SELECT statement.

The format for an indexed sequential file is

SELECT file-name-1 ASSIGN TO device-name

    ORGANIZATION IS INDEXED

$$\text{ACCESS MODE IS} \left\{ \begin{array}{l} \text{RANDOM} \\ \text{SEQUENTIAL} \\ \text{DYNAMIC} \end{array} \right\}$$

    RECORD KEY IS data-name-1

    [ALTERNATE RECORD KEY IS data-name-2

    [WITH DUPLICATES]] . . .

The ACCESS MODE clause determines the way in which the file is to be accessed. SEQUENTIAL specifies that the file is only to be read and/or written sequentially. RANDOM specifies that the file is to read and/or written randomly. DYNAMIC specifies that the file is to be read and/or written both sequentially and randomly. Data-name-1 contains the primary key value which uniquely identifies the record being processed. The key field must have an alphanumeric picture. This is very important. Even though the field may actually contain a numeric item which has a numeric picture elsewhere, you must ensure that its picture is alphanumeric when using it as a key in an indexed sequential file. If the program has to treat the field as numeric, use a REDEFINES. If, at any time, the file processing software finds that an attempt is made to write a record whose key already exists in the file, an error condition is signaled. Sometimes a search is made through a file using a field which is not the primary key. In this case the ALTERNATE RECORD KEY clause is used. Unlike the primary key this field is often not unique, in which case the WITH DUPLICATES phrase is included.

An example of the use of these options is a customer file which is maintained with a customer code number as the primary key to each record. Each customer has his own unique customer code number. But we are asked to write a program to go through the file printing out every record of customers whose address is in Aberdeen. The field in the customer record containing the city or town name is data-name-2 in the ALTERNATE RECORD IS clause and the WITH DUPLICATES is required because there are likely to be more than one customer satisfying the selection criterion. Any number of fields of a record can be specified as alternate keys, so we will include in the example a second ALTERNATE KEY - the data-name MONEY-OWED. This will allow us to write coding which searches the file for the records of any customer, in a certain town or city, owing more than a certain amount.

Example: SELECT CUSTOMER-FILE ASSIGN TO DISK
         ORGANIZATION IS INDEXED
         RECORD KEY IS CUSTOMER-NUMBER
         ALTERNATE RECORD KEY CITY-NAME WITH DUPLICATES
         ALTERNATE RECORD KEY MONEY-OWED WITH DUPLICATES.

17.4.3 READ Statement

To read a record from an indexed sequential file the key of the record must be moved into the record key field. A special READ statement, which may be one of two formats, is then executed.

Format 1:

READ file–name–1 [NEXT] RECORD [INTO identifier–1]

    [AT END imperative–statement–1]

    [NOT AT END imperative–statement–2]

    [END–READ]

This format is used when either SEQUENTIAL or DYNAMIC access mode has been specified. The NEXT option is used for DYNAMIC access only. The READ . . . NEXT RECORD retrieves the record with the key immediately above that of the previous one accessed. This allows us to retrieve records randomly then proceed to retrieve records sequentially from that point in the file.

Example: READ CUSTOMER-FILE NEXT RECORD INTO WORK-SPACE
           AT END PERFORM READ-ERROR.

Format 2:

READ file–name–1 RECORD [INTO identifier–1] [KEY IS data–name–1]

168

[**INVALID** KEY imperative–statement–3]

[NOT INVALID KEY imperative–statement–4]

[END–READ]

This format is used for files in RANDOM access mode and also files in DYNAMIC access mode which are being read randomly. Because we are looking for a record with a particular key only two situations can arise when a READ statement is executed. Either the record is found or it is not. There is no AT END condition for an indexed sequential file opened in I-O mode, because this would be illogical, since it can only apply to a sequentially read file. If the record is found, it is read into the program in the normal way. If it is not found, the INVALID KEY path is taken and the imperative statement executed. The KEY IS option allows the specifying of an alternate key data-name. If it is omitted, the primary key is assumed.

Example: MOVE KEY-VALUE TO CUSTOMER-NUMBER.
          READ CUSTOMER-FILE RECORD INTO WORK-SPACE
          INVALID KEY PERFORM READ-ERROR.

17.4.4 WRITE Statement

To write a record to an indexed sequential file, a special WRITE statement is used. The file must be opened in I-O or OUTPUT mode.

It has the format:

WRITE record–name–1 [**FROM** identifier–1]

[**INVALID** KEY imperative–statement–1]

[NOT INVALID KEY imperative–statement–2]

[END–WRITE]

The record referred to in record-name must contain the data-name specified in the RECORD KEY clause of the SELECT entry. The WRITE statement writes out a record with a key value which does not already exist on the file. If the key value is found to be already present on the file the INVALID KEY path is taken.

Example: MOVE NEW-KEY-VALUE TO W-CUSTOMER-NUMBER.
          WRITE CUSTOMER-RECORD FROM WORK-SPACE
          INVALID KEY PERFORM WRITE-ERROR.

Notice that NEW-KEY-VALUE is moved to the key field in the WORKING-STORAGE SECTION version of the record. This is because

169

WRITE . . . FROM moves the record from WORK-SPACE to the record area in the FD before it looks at the key field prior to writing. If NEW-KEY-VALUE had been moved directly, it would have been overwritten by the move.

17.4.5 REWRITE Statement

If an existing record has been read and has to be written back to the file, REWRITE is used.

It has the format:

REWRITE record–name–1 [FROM identifier–1]

     [INVALID KEY imperative–statement–1]

     [NOT INVALID KEY imperative–statement–2]

     [END–REWRITE]

The file must be opened in I-O mode and access must be RANDOM or DYNAMIC. The INVALID KEY phrase is executed if an attempt is made to rewrite a record with a key which is not in the file.

Example: MOVE KEY-VALUE TO W-CUSTOMER-NUMBER.
            REWRITE CUSTOMER-RECORD FROM WORK-SPACE
                    INVALID KEY PERFORM REWRITE-ERROR.

17.4.6 DELETE Statement

The DELETE statement removes a record from an indexed sequential file.

It has the format:

DELETE file–name–1 RECORD

     [INVALID KEY imperative–statement–1]

     [NOT INVALID KEY imperative–statement–2]

     [END–DELETE]

The file must be opened in I-O mode and the record key must have been placed in the data item referenced by the RECORD KEY clause. If the access to the file is SEQUENTIAL, the INVALID KEY clause must not be present. To delete a record in this case, the record in question must have been read first so it must exist. The AT END condition of the READ statement would have taken care of the situation of the record not being on the file. If the file is opened in RANDOM or DYNAMIC mode, the INVALID KEY clause must be present and this path is taken if the value of the data item in the RECORD KEY clause is not the key value of a record on the file. Since no prior READ statement is required, it is the responsibility of the programmer to move the key value to RECORD KEY.

Example: MOVE KEY-VALUE TO CUSTOMER-NUMBER.
           DELETE CUSTOMER-FILE RECORD
                INVALID KEY PERFORM DELETE-ERROR.

17.4.7 START Statement

The START statement allows the sequential retrieval of records from a point on the file other than the beginning. So it is possible to commence sequential processing of the records at any point in the file.

It has the format:

$$
\text{START} \;\; \text{file--name--1} \; \left[\text{KEY} \; \left\{ \begin{array}{l} \text{IS } \underline{\text{EQUAL}} \text{ TO} \\ \text{IS } = \\ \text{IS } \underline{\text{GREATER}} \text{ THAN} \\ \text{IS } > \\ \text{IS } \underline{\text{NOT LESS}} \text{ THAN} \\ \text{IS } \underline{\text{NOT}} < \end{array} \right\} \; \text{data--name--1} \right]
$$

      [**INVALID KEY** imperative--statement--1]

      [NOT INVALID KEY imperative--statement--2]

      [END--START]

The file must be in SEQUENTIAL or DYNAMIC access mode and must be opened as either INPUT or I-O. If the KEY clause is omitted, the program assumes that IS EQUAL TO is meant. To illustrate the use of START we will take as an example a program which processes the records of overseas customers on a customer file. Each customer has an unique five digit customer number which is the primary key on the record. All overseas customers' code numbers start with 2. We wish to start processing records with the first record which has a customer code number beginning with 2. Our coding must use the START statement to process every record with a

171

key not less than 20000.

```
FD  CUSTOMER-FILE
    LABEL RECORD STANDARD
    VALUE OF FILE-ID "CUSTOMER".
01  INPUT-REC.
    03 CUSTOMER-NUMBER        PIC X(5).
    03 FILLER                 PIC X(330).
       . . .
       . . .

WORKING-STORAGE SECTION.
01  CUSTOMER-RECORD.
    03 W-CUSTOMER-NUMBER      PIC X(5).
       . . .
       . . .

PROCEDURE DIVISION.
MAIN SECTION.
START-UP.
    OPEN INPUT CUSTOMER-FILE.
    MOVE "20000" TO CUSTOMER-NUMBER.
    START CUSTOMER-FILE
        KEY IS NOT LESS THAN CUSTOMER-NUMBER
        INVALID KEY PERFORM OS-ERROR.
        . . .
        . . .
    READ CUSTOMER-FILE RECORD INTO CUSTOMER-RECORD
    AT END GO TO PROCESS-RECORD-END.
```

17.5 Programs Using Indexed Sequential Files

Two programs follow illustrating the use of indexed sequential files. The first program creates a new indexed sequential file and the second updates an existing indexed sequential file. It should be noted that the system of always processing records in the WORKING-STORAGE SECTION is still used. This is more important for processing sequential files than indexed ones, since the problems resulting from the closing of the input record area when the AT END condition is detected do not arise with an indexed sequential file (unless it is being read sequentially). However, in the interests of consistency, it is better to keep the FILE SECTION for files and the WORKING-STORAGE SECTION for records. The fact that the record key must be specified in the FD record description is a nuisance, but this is a requirement of COBOL and there is nothing we can do about it.

172

17.5.1 BLOCK CONTAINS Clause

There is an additional optional clause in the FD entry which is used to specify the size of the block or physical record.

It has the format:

$$\text{\underline{BLOCK} CONTAINS [integer--1 \underline{TO}] integer--2} \begin{Bmatrix} \text{CHARACTERS} \\ \underline{\text{RECORDS}} \end{Bmatrix}$$

The size may be specified as either characters or records. The default is characters. When this clause is omitted, the compiler assumes that one block contains one logical record. All previous programs have done this but this is rather wasteful of disk space and record transfer time. It is better to put several records in a block unless records are really large. The two programs have five records in a block. Remember that the number of records or characters specified in a program BLOCK CONTAINS clause must match the actual storage arrangement on the disk or tape.

17.5.2 Program CREATE-INDEXED

This program creates an indexed sequential version of the sequential file we created in Chapter 11 and sorted in Chapter 12. It follows the conventional sequential file processing logic. Each record is read, in turn, from the sorted sequential file PRODUCT and written to the indexed sequential file IPRODUCT. Counts of the number of records written to the indexed sequential file and the number of records rejected are printed when all the records have been processed.

```
000100 IDENTIFICATION DIVISION.
000110 PROGRAM-ID. CREATE-INDEXED.
000120*
000130***Demonstration Cobol program to create an indexed file.
000140*
000150 ENVIRONMENT DIVISION.
000160 CONFIGURATION SECTION.
000170 SOURCE-COMPUTER. ABC-1.
000180 OBJECT-COMPUTER. ABC-1.
000190*
000200 INPUT-OUTPUT SECTION.
000210 FILE-CONTROL.
000220      SELECT SEQUENTIAL-FILE ASSIGN DISK.
000240      SELECT INDEXED-FILE ASSIGN DISK
000250           ORGANIZATION IS INDEXED
000260           ACCESS RANDOM
```

173

```
000270           RECORD KEY MASTER-PRODUCT-NUMBER.
000280      SELECT REPORT-FILE ASSIGN PRINTER.
000300*
000310 DATA DIVISION.
000320 FILE SECTION.
000330 FD   SEQUENTIAL-FILE
000340      LABEL RECORDS STANDARD
000350      VALUE OF FILE-ID "PRODUCT".
000360 01   INPUT-RECORD                   PIC X(66).
000370*
000380 FD   INDEXED-FILE
000390      BLOCK 5 RECORDS
000400      LABEL RECORDS STANDARD
000405      VALUE OF FILE-ID "IPRODUCTS".
000410 01   MASTER-RECORD.
000420      03 MASTER-PRODUCT-NUMBER    PIC X(5).
000430      03 FILLER                   PIC X(61).
000440*
000450 FD   REPORT-FILE
000460      LABEL RECORDS OMITTED.
000470 01   OUTPUT-RECORD                  PIC X(100).
000480*
000490 WORKING-STORAGE SECTION.
000500 01   S-PRODUCT-RECORD.
000510      03 S-PRODUCT-NUMBER         PIC 9(5).
000520      03 S-REST                   PIC X(61).
000530*
000540 01   M-PRODUCT-RECORD.
000550      03 M-PRODUCT-NUMBER         PIC X(5).
000560      03 M-REST                   PIC X(61).
000570*
000580 01   REPORT-RECORD.
000590      03 R-PRODUCT-NUMBER         PIC 9(5).
000600      03 R-REST                   PIC X(61).
000610      03 REPORT-MESSAGE           PIC X(29)
000620              VALUE "Unable to write random record".
000630*
000640 01   SUMMARY-RECORD.
000650      03 COUNT-RECORDS            PIC Z(6)9B.
000660      03 SUMMARY-MESSAGE          PIC X(30).
000670*
000680 01   WORK-ITEMS.
000690      03 IFILE-EOF                   PIC X VALUE "N".
000700         88 NO-MORE-DATA VALUE "Y".
```

```
000710      03 PRODUCTS-ADDED              PIC 9(5) VALUE 0.
000720      03 PRODUCTS-REJECTED           PIC 9(4) VALUE 0.
000730*
000740 PROCEDURE DIVISION.
000750 MAIN SECTION.
000760 INITIALISE.
000770      OPEN INPUT SEQUENTIAL-FILE
000780              OUTPUT INDEXED-FILE
000790                      REPORT-FILE.
000800      PERFORM READ-A-RECORD.
000810 PROCESS-DATA.
000820      PERFORM PROCESS-RECORDS UNTIL NO-MORE-DATA.
000830 CLOSE-DOWN.
000840      PERFORM CONTROL-TOTALS.
000850      CLOSE SEQUENTIAL-FILE
000860            INDEXED-FILE
000870            REPORT-FILE.
000880      STOP RUN.
000890*
000900 PROCESS-RECORDS SECTION.
000910*
000920 PROCESS-A-RECORD.
000930      MOVE S-PRODUCT-NUMBER TO M-PRODUCT-NUMBER.
000940      MOVE S-REST TO M-REST.
000950      WRITE MASTER-RECORD FROM M-PRODUCT-RECORD
000960            INVALID KEY PERFORM WRITE-ERROR
000970            GO TO PROCESS-RECORDS-END.
000980      ADD 1 TO PRODUCTS-ADDED.
000990      PERFORM READ-A-RECORD.
001000*
001010 PROCESS-RECORDS-END.
001020*
001030 SUPPORT SECTION.
001040*
001050 READ-A-RECORD.
001060      READ SEQUENTIAL-FILE RECORD INTO S-PRODUCT-RECORD
001070            AT END MOVE "Y" TO IFILE-EOF.
001080*
001090 WRITE-ERROR.
001100      MOVE M-PRODUCT-NUMBER TO R-PRODUCT-NUMBER.
001110      MOVE M-REST TO R-REST.
001120      WRITE OUTPUT-RECORD FROM REPORT-RECORD AFTER 2.
001130      ADD 1 TO PRODUCTS-REJECTED.
001140 CONTROL-TOTALS.
```

```
001150    MOVE PRODUCTS-ADDED TO COUNT-RECORDS.
001160    MOVE "Products added to master file" TO SUMMARY-MESSAGE.
001170    WRITE OUTPUT-RECORD FROM SUMMARY-RECORD AFTER 3.
001180    MOVE SPACE TO SUMMARY-RECORD.
001190    MOVE PRODUCTS-REJECTED TO COUNT-RECORDS.
001200    MOVE "Products rejected" TO SUMMARY-MESSAGE.
001210    WRITE OUTPUT-RECORD FROM SUMMARY-RECORD AFTER 1.
```

Fig. 17.1

17.5.3 Program UPDATE-INDEXED

To update a file, a sequential transaction file SEQUENTIAL-FILE contains amendments which are to be applied to an indexed sequential master file INDEXED-FILE. The program UPDATE-INDEXED reads the sequential file of transactions which contains records to be added to the master file (ie. records with key values which do not already exist on the master file), records which are amendments to existing records on the master file, and records which contain the key value of records to be deleted from the master file. The transaction file is read using the conventional sequential file processing logic. The transaction records are in the same format as the master file records except for an additional record type field. This field contains a number which indicates the type of transaction that record is to carry out. If it contains a 1, the record is an amendment to an existing master file record, a 2, the record is an additional one to the master file, and a 3, the record is a deletion. An addition record contains all the values of the fields of the record to be created on the master file. A amendment record replaces a complete record. In updating programs, the update of individual fields is also commonly allowed. The deletion record contains only the value of the key field of the record to be deleted. When each transaction record is read, the type is tested and the appropriate procedure to carry out the processing of that record is performed. It is known that the values of the record type have been validated in a previous program so that only values 1, 2 or 3 are present. The program maintains a set of control totals of the various transactions on the master file which is printed at the end of the program. Also, the program prints the contents of any record deleted from the master file and the contents of any transaction file record which cannot be processed, either because an attempt has been made to process a non-existant record or because a record cannot be written to the master file. In this case, either an attempt has been made to add a record which already exists or the program cannot rewrite a record back to the master file.

176

```
000100 IDENTIFICATION DIVISION.
000110 PROGRAM-ID. UPDATE-INDEXED.
000120*
000130***Demonstration Cobol program to update an indexed file.
000140*
000150 ENVIRONMENT DIVISION.
000160 CONFIGURATION SECTION.
000170 SOURCE-COMPUTER. ABC-1.
000180 OBJECT-COMPUTER. ABC-1.
000190*
000200 INPUT-OUTPUT SECTION.
000210 FILE-CONTROL.
000220        SELECT SEQUENTIAL-FILE ASSIGN DISK.
000240        SELECT INDEXED-FILE ASSIGN DISK
000250               ORGANIZATION IS INDEXED
000260               ACCESS RANDOM
000270               RECORD KEY MASTER-PRODUCT-NUMBER.
000280        SELECT REPORT-FILE ASSIGN PRINTER.
000300*
000310 DATA DIVISION.
000320 FILE SECTION.
000330 FD    SEQUENTIAL-FILE
000340        LABEL RECORDS STANDARD.
000350 01    INPUT-RECORD                   PIC X(67).
000360*
000370 FD    INDEXED-FILE
000380        BLOCK 5 RECORDS
000390        LABEL RECORDS STANDARD.
000400 01    MASTER-RECORD.
000410        03 MASTER-PRODUCT-NUMBER    PIC X(5).
000420        03 FILLER                   PIC X(61).
000430*
000440 FD    REPORT-FILE
000450        LABEL RECORDS OMITTED.
000460 01    OUTPUT-RECORD                 PIC X(100).
000470*
000480 WORKING-STORAGE SECTION.
000490 01    S-PRODUCT-RECORD.
000500        03 S-PRODUCT-NUMBER         PIC 9(5).
000510        03 ALPHA-PRODUCT-NUMBER
000520           REDEFINES S-PRODUCT-NUMBER PIC X(5).
000530        03 S-REST                   PIC X(61).
000540        03 S-RECORD-TYPE            PIC 9.
000550           88 AMENDMENT  VALUE 1.
```

177

```
000560              88 INSERTION   VALUE 2.
000570              88 DELETION    VALUE 3.
000580*
000590 01   M-PRODUCT-RECORD.
000600      03 M-PRODUCT-NUMBER          PIC X(5).
000610      03 M-REST                    PIC X(61).
000620*
000630 01   REPORT-RECORD.
000640      03 R-PRODUCT-NUMBER          PIC 9(5).
000650      03 R-REST                    PIC X(61).
000660      03 FILLER                    PIC X VALUE SPACE.
000670      03 REPORT-MESSAGE            PIC X(30).
000680*
000690 01   SUMMARY-RECORD.
000700      03 COUNT-RECORDS             PIC Z(6)9B.
000710      03 SUMMARY-MESSAGE           PIC X(33).
000720*
000730 01   WORK-ITEMS.
000740      03 IFILE-EOF                 PIC X VALUE "N".
000750         88 NO-MORE-DATA VALUE "Y".
000760      03 PRODUCTS-ADDED            PIC 9(4) VALUE 0.
000770      03 PRODUCTS-DELETED          PIC 9(4) VALUE 0.
000780      03 PRODUCTS-REJECTED         PIC 9(4) VALUE 0.
000790      03 PRODUCTS-AMENDED          PIC 9(4) VALUE 0.
000800*
000810 PROCEDURE DIVISION.
000820 MAIN SECTION.
000830 INITIALISE.
000840      OPEN INPUT SEQUENTIAL-FILE
000850              I-O   INDEXED-FILE
000860                OUTPUT REPORT-FILE.
000870      PERFORM READ-A-RECORD.
000880 PROCESS-DATA.
000890      PERFORM PROCESS-RECORDS UNTIL NO-MORE-DATA.
000900 CLOSE-DOWN.
000910      PERFORM CONTROL-TOTALS.
000920      CLOSE SEQUENTIAL-FILE
000930               INDEXED-FILE
000940                REPORT-FILE.
000950      STOP RUN.
000960*
000970 PROCESS-RECORDS SECTION.
000980*
000990 CHECK-RECORD-TYPE.
```

```
001000      IF  AMENDMENT
001010          PERFORM AMEND-RECORD THRU AMEND-RECORD-END
001020      ELSE
001030          IF INSERTION
001040              PERFORM INSERT-RECORD THRU INSERT-RECORD-END
001050          ELSE
001060              PERFORM DELETE-RECORD THRU DELETE-RECORD-END.
001070      PERFORM READ-A-RECORD.
001080 PROCESS-RECORDS-END.
001090*
001100 SUPPORT SECTION.
001110 INSERT-RECORD.
001120      MOVE ALPHA-PRODUCT-NUMBER TO M-PRODUCT-NUMBER.
001130      MOVE S-REST TO M-REST.
001140      WRITE MASTER-RECORD FROM M-PRODUCT-RECORD
001150              INVALID KEY PERFORM WRITE-ERROR
001160                  GO TO INSERT-RECORD-END.
001170      ADD 1 TO PRODUCTS-ADDED.
001180 INSERT-RECORD-END.
001190 AMEND-RECORD.
001200      MOVE ALPHA-PRODUCT-NUMBER
001205          TO MASTER-PRODUCT-NUMBER.
001210      READ INDEXED-FILE RECORD INTO M-PRODUCT-RECORD
001220              INVALID KEY PERFORM INVALID-P-N
001230                  GO TO AMEND-RECORD-END.
001240      MOVE ALPHA-PRODUCT-NUMBER TO M-PRODUCT-NUMBER.
001250      MOVE S-REST TO M-REST.
001260      REWRITE MASTER-RECORD FROM M-PRODUCT-RECORD
001270              INVALID KEY PERFORM WRITE-ERROR
001280                  GO TO AMEND-RECORD-END.
001290      ADD 1 TO PRODUCTS-AMENDED.
001300 AMEND-RECORD-END.
001310 DELETE-RECORD.
001320      MOVE ALPHA-PRODUCT-NUMBER
001325          TO MASTER-PRODUCT-NUMBER.
001330      READ INDEXED-FILE INTO M-PRODUCT-RECORD
001340              INVALID KEY PERFORM INVALID-P-N
001350                  GO TO DELETE-RECORD-END.
001360      MOVE M-PRODUCT-NUMBER TO R-PRODUCT-NUMBER.
001370      MOVE M-REST TO R-REST.
001380      MOVE "Product deleted" TO REPORT-MESSAGE.
001385      WRITE OUTPUT-RECORD FROM REPORT-RECORD AFTER 2.
001390      DELETE INDEXED-FILE RECORD
001400              INVALID KEY PERFORM WRITE-ERROR
```

```
001410              GO TO DELETE-RECORD-END.
001420      ADD 1 TO PRODUCTS-DELETED.
001430 DELETE-RECORD-END.
001440*
001450 READ-A-RECORD.
001460      READ SEQUENTIAL-FILE RECORD INTO S-PRODUCT-RECORD
001470          AT END MOVE "Y" TO IFILE-EOF.
001480*
001490 CONTROL-TOTALS.
001500      MOVE PRODUCTS-ADDED TO COUNT-RECORDS.
001510      MOVE "Products added to master file" TO SUMMARY-MESSAGE.
001520      WRITE OUTPUT-RECORD FROM SUMMARY-RECORD AFTER 3.
001530      MOVE PRODUCTS-AMENDED TO COUNT-RECORDS
001540      MOVE "Products amended on master file" TO SUMMARY-MESSAGE.
001550      WRITE OUTPUT-RECORD FROM SUMMARY-RECORD
001555          AFTER 1.
001560      MOVE PRODUCTS-DELETED TO COUNT-RECORDS.
001570      MOVE "Products deleted from master file"
001575          TO SUMMARY-MESSAGE.
001580      WRITE OUTPUT-RECORD FROM SUMMARY-RECORD
001585          AFTER 1.
001590      MOVE PRODUCTS-REJECTED TO COUNT-RECORDS.
001600 ·    MOVE "Products rejected" TO SUMMARY-MESSAGE.
001610      WRITE OUTPUT-RECORD FROM SUMMARY-RECORD
001615          AFTER 1.
001620*
001630 INVALID-P-N.
001640      MOVE S-PRODUCT-RECORD TO REPORT-RECORD.
001650      MOVE "Product not on master file."
001660          TO REPORT-MESSAGE.
001670      WRITE OUTPUT-RECORD FROM REPORT-RECORD AFTER 2.
001680      ADD 1 TO PRODUCTS-REJECTED.
001690*
001700 WRITE-ERROR.
001710      MOVE M-PRODUCT-NUMBER TO R-PRODUCT-NUMBER.
001720      MOVE M-REST TO R-REST.
001730      MOVE "Unable to write random record" TO REPORT-MESSAGE.
001740      WRITE OUTPUT-RECORD FROM REPORT-RECORD AFTER 2.
001750      ADD 1 TO PRODUCTS-REJECTED.
```

180

CHAPTER 18

Extended Interactive Processing

18.1 Introduction

COBOL was designed in the late 1950s when only batch processing systems were in use. So it has no facilities specifically for interactive use. This remains true in COBOL 74 and COBOL 85. COBOL 85 was expected to contain the definition of a screen management facility, however, this has not materialised. The CODASYL Screen Management Committee released a Screen Management Facility in 1985. This includes an Independent Screen Definition Language (ISDL) and a Screen Manipulation Language (SML). ISDL is independent of COBOL and may be used with any host language. So COBOL itself remains without its own screen management facilities. We can, however, use DISPLAY and ACCEPT statements to output and input data interactively. But the DISPLAY statement was originally designed to send messages, such as "LOAD PAYSLIP STATIONARY" or "Input today's date", to the computer operator on a batch processing system, The ACCEPT statement was designed to receive short and simple messages via the operating console keyboard, such as "GO" or a date. In an interactive system, the DISPLAY and ACCEPT statements are normally redirected to process messages at the user's terminal. On a microcomputer the CRT screen and the keyboard are both operator's console and user's output and input device. The standard forms of DISPLAY and ACCEPT were described in Chapter 11. Standard DISPLAY and ACCEPT handle data on a line by line basis, messages always start at the left hand side of the display screen and are accepted or displayed on the line immediately following the last message. There is no facility for placing messages anywhere else on the screen or for clearing the screen of previous messages. An essential requirement for using a COBOL program to process data interactively is, therefore, a screen handling facility which will not only clear the screen of data but also place or receive messages on or from any position on the screen. Also there must be facilities to check the format of data being input and provide means of altering such data. Since all of these facilities are lacking in standard COBOL, they are provided either by special terminal handling packages or by making non-standard extensions to COBOL itself. The latter involves greatly increasing the facilities and options available with the DISPLAY and ACCEPT statements. As there are no internationally agreed standards, the way different compilers provide these facilities varies. We will look at the facilities available in two versions of COBOL commonly found on microcomputers, Micro Focus COBOL and IBM Personal Computer COBOL. Micro Focus COBOL has been marketed in a number of versions including, CIS COBOL, Level II COBOL, Personal COBOL and COBOL/2 but they all share the same screen management system.

18.2 Extensions in Micro Focus COBOL

Micro Focus COBOL considers the CRT screen as a pseudo-form which is divided up into areas where data can be displayed and areas where data can be accepted. Any area on the screen which is not programmed to receive any input data is protected. This means that inputting data into the computer is like filling in a form with a program guiding the user from one data field to the next. Headings and field descriptions are displayed and the user fills in the requested data at the appropriate place. Unlike paper form filling the computer is able to check the data being input and immediately report any errors.

18.2.1 Extended ENVIRONMENT DIVISION

An extended SPECIAL-NAMES entry in the ENVIRONMENT DIVISION is used to enable the program to display messages or accept data from the CRT screen.

It has the following format:

SPECIAL-NAMES.

      [CONSOLE IS CRT]

      [CURSOR IS data-name-1].

When CONSOLE IS CRT is specified, DISPLAY and ACCEPT statements in the PROCEDURE DIVISION process data from the CRT screen. If this statement is not specified then the default is FROM CONSOLE unless the DISPLAY and ACCEPT statements themselves specify otherwise. Data-name-1 in the CURSOR IS clause contains the address of the cursor. It must be specified as a four digit numeric data item. At the beginning of processing it contains the "home" position of the cursor, that is the top left corner of the screen. It enables a program to store the position of the cursor after an ACCEPT or to specify the initial position at the start of an ACCEPT.

18.2.2 DATA DIVISION Entry

Pseudo-forms are set up in the WORKING-STORAGE SECTION. They can be all or part of the CRT screen. The normal screen consists of 24 lines, each with 80 characters. This makes 1920 character positions in all. The area referenced can be treated as a single group item or one or more elementary items. Screen data is described in the same way as any other, with some exceptions. FILLER has a special meaning in a pseudo-form. Any part of the screen described as a FILLER entry is protected. That is nothing can be input from that part of the screen. Edited numeric data items are allowed, but they are treated as if they were alphanumeric, in spite of their picture clause. This is very useful for inputting number containing decimal points, which cause havoc with standard ACCEPT. Where a screen contains both printed messages and areas for accepting data items, the screen consists of two or sometimes more records, one overlaying the other. The REDEFINES statement is used so that these two records actually occupy the same area. Look at the following example of a pseudo-form which is used to enter a date at the beginning of a program.

```
WORKING-STORAGE SECTION.
01      HEAD-1.
        03 FILLER                PIC X(344).
        03 HEAD-1-1              PIC X(27)
            VALUE "CUSTOMER ORDER ENTRY SYSTEM".
        03 FILLER                PIC X(53).
        03 HEAD-1-2              PIC X(27)
            VALUE "--------------------------".
        03 FILLER                PIC X(269).
        03 HEAD-1-3              PIC X(80)
            VALUE "=============================
    "=================================================".
        03 FILLER                PIC X(264).
        03 HEAD-1-4              PIC X(14) VALUE "Enter the date".
        03 FILLER                PIC X(3).
        03 HEAD-1-5              PIC X VALUE "[".
        03 FILLER                PIC XX
        03 HEAD-1-6              PIC X VALUE "/".
        03 FILLER                PIC XX.
        03 HEAD-1-7              PIC X VALUE "/".
        03 FILLER                PIC XX.
```

183

03 HEAD-1-8		PIC X VALUE "]".
03 FILLER		PIC X(133).
03 HEAD-1-9		PIC X(27)
VALUE "e.g. 01/11/88 is 1 Nov 1988".		
03 FILLER		PIC X(269).
03 HEAD-1-10		PIC X(80)

```
           VALUE "==============================
  -     "===================================================".
```

03 FILLER		PIC X(184).
03 HEAD-1-11		PIC X(28)
VALUE "Press <RETURN> when complete".		
01 HEAD-2 REDEFINES HEAD-1.		
03 FILLER		PIC X(1082).
03 HEAD-2-1		PIC 99
03 FILLER		PIC X.
03 HEAD-2-2		PIC 99.
03 FILLER		PIC X.
03 HEAD-2-3		PIC 99.

Fig. 18.1

There is an extension which allows a hexadecimal value to be placed in an non-numeric data-name by declaring a literal in the format X"nn", where n is a hexadecimal character in the set 0-9 A-F. This allows the program to output control and escape characters which are used to switch on and off various screen handling and printer facilities. For example, if we wish to use the reverse video facility on one particular model of microcomputer, the program has to send Esc/70 to the screen to switch to reverse video and Esc/71 to switch back to normal. We can do this by incorporating hexadecimal values for Esc/70 and Esc/71 in the record containing the data that is to be output.

```
   01   PAGE-MESSAGE.
        03 REVERSE-ON      PIC XXX   VALUE X"1B70".
        03 P-M-1           PIC X(21) VALUE SPACES.
        03 P-M-2           PIC X(59) VALUE
           "Please press RETURN for next page".
        03 REVERSE-OFF     PIC XXX   VALUE X"1B71".
```

If the program displays PAGE-MESSAGE, the line will be displayed in reverse video. The reverse video will be switched off when the message has been displayed.

18.2.3 Extended DISPLAY

The first description of the screen is the record HEAD-1 in Fig. 18.1 which contains the headings and field descriptions. The complete record can be displayed on the CRT screen by

DISPLAY HEAD-1.

This statement causes all the data in the record to be displayed starting at the first character position at the top left of the screen. If we want to start at another position, we must add the line number and chararcter position of the starting point to the DISPLAY statement. The statement

DISPLAY HEAD-1 AT 0301

will display the record starting at the first character position of line 3 of the screen. The literal which follows AT must be a four digit one. The first two are the line number, the second two the character position of the line. 2432 means the thirty second character position of line 24. It is also possible to use a data-name to store this address. The data-name must be declared with a PIC 9(4). The first two digits are the line number, the second two the character position.

Example: DISPLAY SCREEN-IMAGE AT SCREEN-POSITION.

18.2.4 Extended ACCEPT

Having seen how to display a pseudo-form on the CRT, we now have to see how to input data from the screen. Record HEAD-1 is redefined as a second record format, HEAD-2. These two formats occupy the same space on the screen, one overlaying the other. The first field of HEAD-2 is a FILLER of 1082 characters. This is made up of 13 lines of 80 characters each and 42 characters of line 14. This area is protected, so no data can be input from it. The field HEAD-2-1 can, however, accept data as can HEAD-2-2 and HEAD-2-3. These three fields match up with the day, month and year spaces in the date in HEAD-1. When the statement

ACCEPT HEAD-2.

is executed, the cursor is automatically positioned at the first available non-protected field, starting from the top left of the screen. This means it goes to the position immediately following the [of the date field. When the two day numbers are typed the cursor automatically positions itself at the next available non-protected field. In this case, the space immediately following the /. When the two year digits are typed, the cursor jumps over the next / and waits for the two year numbers. Any attempt to type beyond the last available field will cause an audible error signal to be output. If the data typed does not completely fill a field, the cursor can be made to move to the next available field by using a cursor control key. If only one day number was input, the cursor can be moved to the first month number position by pressing the cursor control key with the arrow pointing right. When all the fields of the pseudo-form have been filled, the RETURN key is pressed to continue the program. The cursor control keys can be used to move the cursor about the pseudo-form at any time before the RETURN is pressed to change any of the data fields. The use of the cursor control keys to move from one field to another can cause trouble. Terminal users are so accustomed to pressing the RETURN key at the end of data items that they are prone to do this in the middle of a pseudo-form. In this case, the data which has been entered is accepted, any fields which remain are either filled with spaces, if they are alphanumberic or zeros, if they are numeric. The data checking statements in the program must look out for this problem and instruct the re-input of the data. The extended ACCEPT statement can be instructed to accept data from any position on the screen by using the AT option.

ACCEPT HEAD-2-1 AT 1245

would input the day part of the date as would

MOVE 1245 TO CURSOR-POSITION.
ACCEPT HEAD-2-1 AT CURSOR-POSITION.

The description of CURSOR-POSITION is

01   CURSOR-POSITION PIC 9(4).

Data can be input from an area on the screen that has already had data displayed in it. The date entry part of HEAD-1 can be rewritten as

03 HEAD-1-4 PIC X(27) VALUE "Enter the date   [DD/MM/YY]".

DD, MM and YY now appear in the areas where we wish to input the date. ACCEPT HEAD-2 will have exactly the same effect as before, but this time the day numbers will overtype DD, the month numbers will overtype MM and so on. This is a good way of indicating to a user what data is required. However, you have to be very careful to get the FILLERs and data fields of the two versions of the screen formats to match up or else you will be accepting data from the wrong positions on the screen, perhaps overwriting descriptive data by mistake. This has the effect of making the screen look a mess but it is impossible for displayed data to be accepted from the screen. So if, in the previous example, the month numbers were not typed in, zeros would be placed in HEAD-2-2 not MM.

186

18.2.5 FORMS2 Utility

The programming of pseudo-forms can be a long and tedious job. Micro Focus provide a utility program called FORMS2 which greatly speeds up the operation. FORMS2 is a code generator which allows a programmer to specify the format of a pseudo-form on the screen. The position of the messages and the general layout of the screen can be amended until the programmer is satisfied with the result. FORMS2 generates the WORKING-STORAGE SECTION record formats according to the information on the screen. The resulting record descriptions can be copied into a program (see Chapter 20). FORMS2 can also generate a program to test the use of the pseudo-form before it is incorporated into a program. It can also generate a simple program to create and maintain an indexed sequential file which may be of use in some circumstances. FORMS2 is a considerable help in designing and implementing pseudo-forms, but it has its drawbacks. In common with many code generators the coding produced is less compact than that of a programmer. For example, PICTURE X is generated as PICTURE X(0001). The data-names are very long and largely meaningless. A program using FORMS2 generated code will take up more space in the computer than one using programmer coded screens. This may be a major problem when using a computer with a small memory.

18.3 IBM Personal Computer COBOL

This version of COBOL by Microsoft tackles the screen handling problem in a different way. In contrast to Micro Focus COBOL which is marketed for a variety of different makes of computers, IBM PC COBOL is designed specifically for the IBM PC family of microcomputers. A difference which is immediately apparent is that Micro Focus COBOL requires the program to issue control characters to control the screen, cursor and peripherals. The functions of these control characters may vary from machine to machine so the hexadecimal picture clause is used to produce these characters which cannot be handled in standard COBOL. IBM PC COBOL has these facilities built in with extra reserved words such as REVERSE-VIDEO, UNDERLINE, BELL etc. This has the adverse effect of making the extensions to data descriptions, ACCEPT and DISPLAY appear very complicated.

18.3.1 Extended DATA DIVISION

IBM PC COBOL has a special extra section in the DATA DIVISION called the SCREEN SECTION where the data groups or items which are to appear on the screen are set up.

Each data group is described as

level–number screen–name [<u>AUTO</u>] [<u>SECURE</u>]
[<u>REQUIRED</u>] [<u>FULL</u>].

Each item is described as

level–number [screen–name]

    [<u>BLANK</u> <u>SCREEN</u>]

    [<u>LINE</u> NUMBER IS [<u>PLUS</u>] integer–1]

    [<u>COLUMN</u> NUMBER IS [<u>PLUS</u>] integer–2]

    [<u>BLANK</u> <u>LINE</u>]

    [<u>BELL</u>]

    [<u>UNDERLINE</u>]

    [<u>REVERSE–VIDEO</u>]

    [<u>HIGHLIGHT</u>]

    [<u>BLINK</u>]

    [<u>FOREGROUND–COLOR</u> integer–3]

    [<u>BACKGROUND–COLOR</u> integer–4]

    [<u>VALUE</u> IS literal–1]

$$
\left[\left\{ \begin{matrix} \underline{PICTURE} \\ \underline{PIC}\ IS \end{matrix} \right\} \text{picture–string} \left\{ \begin{matrix} \underline{FROM}\ \left\{ \begin{matrix} \text{literal–2} \\ \text{identifier–1} \end{matrix} \right\} \\ \underline{TO}\quad \text{identifier–2} \\ \underline{USING}\ \text{identifier–3} \end{matrix} \right\} \right]
$$

    [<u>BLANK</u> WHEN <u>ZERO</u>]

$$
\left[\left\{ \begin{matrix} \underline{JUSTIFIED} \\ \underline{JUST}\ RIGHT \end{matrix} \right\} \right]
$$

    [<u>AUTO</u>]

    [<u>SECURE</u>]

    [<u>REQUIRED</u>]

    [<u>FULL</u>]

Each item to be displayed or accepted from the screen has a line number which determines the line on the screen on which the item is to be printed. It also has a column number which determines the character position in the line where the first character of the item is to be placed. Items to be displayed have only their position and a VALUE clause - no PICTURE clause. Items to be accepted from the screen have their position, a PICTURE clause and a destination for the data.

We will use the same example of a date input screen as we did to demonstrate Micro Focus COBOL. Part of a program which contains the necessary coding is given in Fig. 18.2. There is no extended SPECIAL-NAMES paragraph in the ENVIRONMENT DIVISION. The WORKING-STORAGE SECTION contains the fields to receive the day, month and year from the screen. The screen itself is described in the SCREEN SECTION as a record DATE-SCREEN. The first entry in the SCREEN SECTION contains the screen name DATE-SCREEN. The second entry contains a level number and the words BLANK SCREEN. This clears the screen. The next entry puts the heading in line 5, starting from character position 25. The option UNDERLINE causes the whole heading to be underlined. The next entry fills the whole of line 10 with equals signs. The next entry outputs the date prompt message. The following three entries are used to receive the day, month and year fields. Each entry is two digits long and the AUTO option means that the cursor jumps to the next available input field after two digits have been typed. If AUTO was not specified the RETURN key would have to be pressed at the end of each individual field entry. The REQUIRED option means that an entry must be input before the cursor moves on. Notice that the input fields occupy the same position on the screen as part of the date prompt message. When the ACCEPT statement is executed the character positions set aside for receiving data are filled with full stops which are overtyped when alphanumeric data is input. If the field is numeric, the full stops are replaced by zeros when the cursor is positioned at the first character position of the field. These zeros are then overtyped from the right by the input data.

18.3.2 Extended ACCEPT

There are two extended versions of ACCEPT.

Format 1:

ACCEPT screen–name [ON **ESCAPE** imperative–statement]

This inputs data from a complete screen and sends it to the TO data items. The ON ESCAPE option allows a premature exit from the screen input by pressing the Esc key. When this is done, the program stops inputting data and executes the imperative statement. Data which has been entered prior to the

Esc key being pressed is stored in the receiving data fields and is available for processing.

Format 2:

$$
\text{\underline{ACCEPT}} \quad \text{position-spec identifier} \quad \text{\underline{WITH}} \quad
\left\{
\begin{array}{l}
\text{\underline{SPACE-FILL}} \\
\text{\underline{ZERO-FILL}} \\
\text{\underline{LEFT-JUSTIFY}} \\
\text{\underline{RIGHT-JUSTIFY}} \\
\text{\underline{TRAILING-SIGN}} \\
\text{\underline{PROMPT}} \\
\text{\underline{UPDATE}} \\
\text{\underline{LENGTH-CHECK}} \\
\text{\underline{AUTO-SKIP}} \\
\text{\underline{BEEP}} \\
\text{\underline{NO-ECHO}} \\
\text{\underline{EMPTY-CHECK}}
\end{array}
\right\} \cdots
$$

This allows the accepting of data from specific areas on the screen. The position-spec is the line number and the character position of the first character of the field.

Example: ACCEPT (3, 25) PRICE.

This statement accepts the contents of the field PRICE starting at the 25th character position of line 3. The position-spec can be varied by program. There are two special registers LIN and COL which are pre-defined by the compiler and which are used to contain the current line number and column character position. Arithmetic can be carried out on these registers to determine the exact position on the screen for input. The WITH options specify what actions the ACCEPT statement carries out on execution. When, for example, WITH BEEP is written, the speaker will sound when the program is ready to accept data. It is beyond the scope of this book to go into the details of the effects of these options. If you wish more information, consult the compiler manual.

18.3.3 Extended DISPLAY

The extended DISPLAY has the format:

$$
\text{\underline{DISPLAY}} \quad [\text{ position-spec }]
\left\{
\begin{array}{l}
\left\{
\begin{array}{l}
\text{identifier} \\
\text{literal}
\end{array}
\right\} \\
\text{\underline{ERASE}}
\end{array}
\right\} \cdots
\left\{
\begin{array}{l}
\text{\underline{UPON}} \text{ mnemonic-name} \\
\text{screen-name}
\end{array}
\right\}
$$

It causes output to be sent to the screen unless the UPON mnemonic is specified. This mnemonic-name is specified in the SPECIAL-NAMES paragraph as PRINTER IS mnemonic-name. The position-spec is the same as for ACCEPT. ERASE clears the screen from the current cursor point but leaves the cursor at that point for the next DISPLAY.

18.4 Program HEAD

This section of program shows the coding required to display a screen or data and accept a date.

```
000100 IDENTIFICATION DIVISION.
000110 PROGRAM-ID. HEAD.
000120 ENVIRONMENT DIVISION.
000130 CONFIGURATION SECTION.
000140 SOURCE-COMPUTER. IBM-PERSONAL-COMPUTER.
000150 OBJECT-COMPUTER. IBM-PERSONAL-COMPUTER.
000160 DATA DIVISION.
000170 WORKING-STORAGE SECTION.
000180 01    DATE-1.
000190       03 DAY-1                PIC 99.
000200       03 MONTH-1              PIC 99.
000210       03 YEAR-1               PIC 99.
000220          . . .
000230          . . .
000240 SCREEN SECTION.
000250 01    DATE-SCREEN.
000260       03 BLANK SCREEN.
000270       03 LINE 5 COLUMN 25
000280          VALUE "CUSTOMER ORDER ENTRY SYSTEM" UNDERLINE.
000290       03 LINE 10 COLUMN 1
000300          VALUE "======================================
000310-          "==============================".
000320       03 LINE 14 COLUMN 25 VALUE "Enter the date  [ / / ]".
000330       03 LINE 14 COLUMN 43 PIC 99 TO DAY-1 REQUIRED AUTO.
000340       03 LINE 14 COLUMN 46 PIC 99 TO MONTH-1 REQUIRED AUTO.
000350       03 LINE 14 COLUMN 49 PIC 99 TO YEAR-1 REQUIRED AUTO.
000360       03 LINE 16 COLUMN 25
000370          VALUE "e.g. 01/11/85 is 1 Nov 1985".
000380       03 LINE 20 COLUMN 1
000390          VALUE "======================================
000400-          "============================
000410       03 LINE 23 COLUMN 25 VALUE "Press <RETURN> when complete".
```

```
000420 PROCEDURE DIVISION.
000430 MAIN SECTION.
000440 ENTER-DATE.
000450     DISPLAY DATE-SCREEN.
000460     ACCEPT DATE-SCREEN.
           . . .
           . . .
```

Fig. 18.2

CHAPTER 19

Data Manipulation

19.1 Introduction

The COBOL statements which we have dealt with up to now have been concerned with processing whole data items. But often a data item is a character string and we want to access and manipulate single characters or groups of characters within the string. COBOL provides several statements containing a number of facilities to do this.

19.2 INSPECT Statement

INSPECT allows the counting of specified characters in a string and the replacing of one character by another. There are three formats, one for counting (tallying) occurrences of a character or characters, a second for replacing characters and a third for doing both. INSPECT gives the facility of accessing all the characters or only selected characters in a data item. INSPECT is a very complicated statement because of the large number of permutations of the different options. We will illustrate only the simpler uses of the statement to show what it can do.

Format 1:

<u>INSPECT</u> identifier–1 <u>TALLYING</u>

$$
\left\{ \begin{array}{l} \text{identifier–2 } \underline{\text{FOR}} \left\{ \begin{array}{l} \underline{\text{CHARACTERS}} \left[\left\{ \begin{array}{l} \underline{\text{BEFORE}} \\ \underline{\text{AFTER}} \end{array} \right\} \text{INITIAL} \left\{ \begin{array}{l} \text{identifier–4} \\ \text{literal–2} \end{array} \right\} \right] \cdots \\ \left\{ \begin{array}{l} \underline{\text{ALL}} \\ \underline{\text{LEADING}} \\ \underline{\text{FIRST}} \end{array} \right\} \left\{ \left\{ \begin{array}{l} \text{identifier–3} \\ \text{literal–1} \end{array} \right\} \right. \\ \left. \left[\left\{ \begin{array}{l} \underline{\text{BEFORE}} \\ \underline{\text{AFTER}} \end{array} \right\} \text{INITIAL} \left\{ \begin{array}{l} \text{identifier–4} \\ \text{literal–2} \end{array} \right\} \right] \cdots \right\} \cdots \end{array} \right\} \cdots \end{array} \right\} \cdots
$$

193

Counting the number of characters in a string.

INSPECT CHAR-STRING TALLYING
      COUNT-1 FOR ALL SPACES BEFORE INITIAL "."
      COUNT-2 FOR ALL SPACES AFTER ".".

Format 2:

INSPECT identifier–1 REPLACING

$$
\left\{
\begin{array}{l}
\text{CHARACTERS BY } \left\{ \begin{array}{l} \text{identifier--5} \\ \text{literal--3} \end{array} \right\} \left[\left\{ \begin{array}{l} \text{BEFORE} \\ \text{AFTER} \end{array} \right\} \text{INITIAL} \left\{ \begin{array}{l} \text{identifier--4} \\ \text{literal--2} \end{array} \right\} \right] \cdots \\[3ex]
\left\{ \begin{array}{l} \text{ALL} \\ \text{LEADING} \\ \text{FIRST} \end{array} \right\} \left\{ \left\{ \begin{array}{l} \text{identifier--3} \\ \text{literal--1} \end{array} \right\} \text{BY} \left\{ \begin{array}{l} \text{identifier--5} \\ \text{literal--3} \end{array} \right\} \right. \\[3ex]
\qquad \left. \left[\left\{ \begin{array}{l} \text{BEFORE} \\ \text{AFTER} \end{array} \right\} \text{INITIAL} \left\{ \begin{array}{l} \text{identifier--4} \\ \text{literal--2} \end{array} \right\} \right] \cdots \right\} \cdots
\end{array}
\right\}
$$

A common requirement in editing data is for leading spaces to be replaced by zeros. This can be done by

INSPECT CHAR-STRING REPLACING LEADING SPACES BY ZEROS.

Sometimes a character or series of characters has to be translated. Perhaps an alphabetic code has to be translated into a numeric one.

INSPECT CHAR-STRING REPLACING ALL "B" BY "1"
                       "C" BY "2"
                       "D" BY "3"
                       "F" BY "1"
                       "G" BY "2".

This is very useful when input data has been prepared on a machine which has a different character coding system from the computer on which you wish to process the data. An INSPECT statement can be used to convert each incorrect character to the correct one.

COBOL 85 has an additional format.

Format 3:

$$
\text{INSPECT identifier--1 CONVERTING} \left\{ \begin{array}{l} \text{identifier--6} \\ \text{literal--4} \end{array} \right\} \text{TO} \left\{ \begin{array}{l} \text{identifier--7} \\ \text{literal--5} \end{array} \right\}
$$

$$
\left[\left\{ \begin{array}{l} \text{BEFORE} \\ \text{AFTER} \end{array} \right\} \text{INITIAL} \left\{ \begin{array}{l} \text{identifier--4} \\ \text{literal--2} \end{array} \right\} \right] \cdots
$$

This format allows the previous example to be written in a simpler form.

INSPECT CHAR-STRING CONVERTING "BCDEF" TO "12312".

Once you have mastered the simple uses of INSPECT its closeness to normal English makes it easier to use than might be expected when looking at the general formats.

19.3 Variable Length Data Items

The conventional way of inputting data to a program is to treat the data as a series of fixed length data items. If the number of individual digits or characters in a data item is less than the number of character spaces allotted in the receiving field, the data item has spaces or zeros added to pad out the item to the length of the receiving field. This has the effect of increasing the amount of input beyond what is really necessary because the extra padding characters have to be included. In producing input data, it is a nuisance to have to remember to add these characters, whether the input is on batch medium such as cards, or being entered interactively. The alternative is to input data as variable length items with some means of determining when a particular data item is complete. This can be done either by counting the number of characters if the length of the data item is known, or testing for a special terminating character as each character is read in. There are two character string handling statements which are useful in these circumstances.

19.3.1 UNSTRING Statement

The UNSTRING statement allows a string of characters stored in a data item to be divided up and placed in two or more separate fields.

It has the format:

UNSTRING identifier−1

$$\left[\text{DELIMITED BY [ALL]} \begin{Bmatrix} \text{identifier−2} \\ \text{literal−1} \end{Bmatrix} \left[\text{OR [ALL]} \begin{Bmatrix} \text{identifier−3} \\ \text{literal−2} \end{Bmatrix} \right] \cdots \right]$$

INTO { identifier−4 [DELIMITER IN identifier−5] [COUNT IN identifier−6] } ...

[WITH POINTER identifier−7]

[TALLYING IN identifier−8]

[ON OVERFLOW imperative−statement−1]

[NOT ON OVERFLOW imperative−statement−2]

[END−UNSTRING]

UNSTRING is best illustrated with an example. Here is part of the

CUSTOMER-RECORD we used in the program ADD-SALES.

```
01    CUSTOMER-RECORD.
      03 CUSTOMER-NUMBER        PIC X(5).
      03 CUSTOMER-NAME          PIC X(30).
      03 CUST-ADDRESS.
         05 CUST-ADDRESS-LINE-1  PIC X(30).
         05 CUST-ADDRESS-LINE-2  PIC X(30).
         05 CUST-ADDRESS-LINE-3  PIC X(30).
         05 CUST-ADDRESS-LINE-4  PIC X(30).
```

The customer number is always 5 characters long, but the name can be anything from 1 to 30 characters. Similarly, each address line can be up to 30 characters long but in most cases it will be less. There may also be less than 4 lines in an address. Instead of inputting 5 characters then 5 blocks of 30 characters including a considerable number of spaces every time, we can end each name and each address line with a terminator. We will use an asterisk for this purpose. Here is some data as an example;

16328*J. Williamson & Co.*128 High Street,*Stonehaven,*Kincardineshire.*

We will use UNSTRING to separate these fields and place them in the record and also count up the number of fields in order to ascertain how many address lines there are.

```
MOVE ZERO TO LINE-COUNT.
UNSTRING FREE-DATA DELIMITED BY "*" INTO
         CUSTOMER-NUMBER
         CUSTOMER-NAME
         CUST-ADDRESS-LINE-1
         CUST-ADDRESS-LINE-2
         CUST-ADDRESS-LINE-3
         CUST-ADDRESS-LINE-4
         TALLYING IN LINE-COUNT
         ON OVERFLOW PERFORM LINE-NUMBER-ERROR.
```

The count of the number of lines is maintained by the TALLYING IN phrase and the data item used to contain the count must be initialised before the UNSTRING is executed. UNSTRING causes the characters up to the first * to be placed in CUSTOMER-NUMBER, the characters from the following group up to the *, "J. Williamson & Co." to be placed in CUSTOMER-NAME, the next group, "128 High Street," in CUST-ADDRESS-1 and so on. LINE-COUNT will contain 5 showing that the last line of the address CUST-ADDRESS-LINE-4 had no data placed in it. UNSTRING will fill it with spaces because it is an alphanumeric field. Had it been a numeric field it would have been filled with zeros. The ON OVERFLOW condition arises when there are still characters left in the sending field and the receiving fields have all been filled. The delimiter character is not stored in the receiving field.

UNSTRING will cope with more than one delimiter. If, in the above example, the end of the customer number was still signalled by an asterisk, but the address lines had either a comma or a full stop as their terminators we can write

UNSTRING FREE-DATA DELIMITED BY "*" OR "," OR "."
                CUSTOMER-NUMBER
                CUSTOMER-NAME
                CUST-ADDRESS-LINE-1
                CUST-ADDRESS-LINE-2
                CUST-ADDRESS-LINE-3
                CUST-ADDRESS-LINE-4
                TALLYING IN LINE-COUNT
                ON OVERFLOW PERFORM LINE-NUMBER-ERROR
                DELIMITER IN DELIMITER-CHARACTER.

The optional DELIMITER IN phrase places the last delimiter detected in a data-name, in this case DELIMITER-CHARACTER. This is sometimes useful when there are more than one delimiter character because it can indicate the point UNSTRING has reached. There is also a POINTER option which stores the character position following the last item read.

19.3.2 STRING Statement

The STRING statement carries out the opposite function to UNSTRING. It is used to link together two or more fixed format data items into a free format string.

It has the format:

$$\underline{\text{STRING}} \left\{ \begin{bmatrix} \text{identifier-1} \\ \text{literal-1} \end{bmatrix} \cdots \underline{\text{DELIMITED BY}} \begin{bmatrix} \text{identifier-2} \\ \text{literal-2} \\ \underline{\text{SIZE}} \end{bmatrix} \right\} \cdots$$

    INTO identifier-3

    [WITH POINTER identifier-4]

    [ON OVERFLOW imperative-statement-1]

    [NOT ON OVERFLOW imperative-statement-2]

    [END-STRING]

The statement is used to compress or concatenate fixed length fields, eliminating spaces. As an example, suppose we have a name and address which we want to print on one line. The data record is in CUSTOMER-RECORD. Inevitably most names and address data items do not fill all the space available which means that extra spaces fill the unused parts and would be output as well. STRING allows us to eliminate these spaces.

```
MOVE SPACES TO PRINT-LINE.
STRING "Number: "  CUSTOMER-NUMBER
                   DELIMITED BY SIZE
       " Name: "   CUSTOMER-NAME
       " Address: " CUST-ADDRESS-LINE-1
                   CUST-ADDRESS-LINE-2
                   CUST-ADDRESS-LINE-3
                   CUST-ADDRESS-LINE-4
                   DELIMITED BY "," "."
                   INTO PRINT-LINE
                   POINTER NEXT-CHARACTER.
```

STRING first of all puts the literal "Number: " into PRINT-LINE starting from the left-most character. Then the contents of CUSTOMER-NUMBER are moved to PRINT-LINE, starting at the character position immediately following the last character placed there. That is why "Number:" is followed by a space in the literal. DELIMITED BY SIZE means that the whole field is moved, so all five characters of CUSTOMER-NUMBER are placed in the left most character positions of PRINT-LINE. The literal " Name: " is then moved to PRINT-LINE. The contents of CUSTOMER-NAME are moved until a comma or a full-stop is encountered. The literal " Address: " is now placed in PRINT-LINE followed by the contents of each of the address lines. The delimiting character for each of these is also the comma or full-stop. The POINTER clause puts the next available character position in PRINT-LINE in NEXT-CHARACTER. Using the data which we originally placed in CUSTOMER-RECORD in the first example of UNSTRING, this STRING statement will output:

Number: 16328 Name: J. Williamson & Co. Address: 128 High Street,Stonehaven,Kincardineshire.

STRING does not place spaces in any unused character positions in the receiving data area. So PRINT-LINE is filled with spaces before the STRING is executed. If there is no delimiter character found in a field, the full field length is output, ie. it acts as if the delimited was SIZE.

CHAPTER 20

Interprogram Communication

20.1 Introduction

When we have been writing programs we have designed them with a MAIN SECTION, the purpose of which is to perform a series of procedures. Each of these procedures may cause others to be performed. The program is a series of procedures whose operations are initiated directly or indirectly by the MAIN SECTION and ultimately returning control to it to terminate processing. This allows the division of different operations within the program into a series of separate units even though each unit can only operate as part of the whole and not separately. A similar arrangement is allowed at program level. A main program can call a series of subprograms just as a MAIN SECTION can perform procedures. A main calling program and its attendant subprograms are called a run unit. There are several benefits arising from this system. Subprograms can be written and compiled independently of any other program but they can only be executed by being called from the main program. This facility allows large programming tasks to be divided up among several programmers, each of whom can write and debug his or her program independently. When the main program and the subprograms have been completed they can be run together. A subprogram can be written to perform a commonly used task and then stored in a program library. This subprogram can be called by any program which requires the task to be carried out. So there is no need to "re-invent the wheel" every time a commonly used task has to be carried out in a program. Yet another benefit of subprograms is to allow the running of large programming tasks on a microcomputer. Microcomputers have much smaller memories than mainframes and their operating systems have less sophisticated memory management facilities and therefore can only store and execute relatively small programs. A subprogram can be called into memory as required and, when the next subprogram is called, it can overlay the previous one occupying the same place in memory.

20.2 CALL Statement

The CALL statement causes control to be passed from one object program to another within a run unit.

It has the format:

$$
\underline{CALL} \left\{ \begin{array}{l} \text{identifier--1} \\ \text{literal--1} \end{array} \right\}
$$

$$
\left[\underline{USING} \left\{ \begin{array}{l} \text{[BY } \underline{REFERENCE} \text{] identifier--2} \cdots \\ \text{BY } \underline{CONTENT} \text{ identifier--2} \cdots \end{array} \right\} \cdots \right]
$$

[ON OVERFLOW imperative--statement--1]

[END--CALL]

Literal-1 must be the name of a subprogram and must be a non-numeric. Identifier-1 must be an alphanumeric data item containing the name of the subprogram. The optional USING clause is used to pass data items between the calling program and the called subprogram. Within a program the MAIN SECTION and all the performed procedures share the same DATA DIVISION, so any item of data described there is available to all procedures. But subprograms have no such common link with the calling program's DATA DIVISION. The DATA DIVISIONs of the calling program and the called subprograms are independent. However, there must be a way of passing data directly between the programs or we may as well write completely independent programs passing data between each other by means of files. This is achieved by using a LINKAGE SECTION and a system of parameters.

20.2.1 Parameters

Parameters are the interface between the calling program and the called subprogram. There are two different sets of parameters, one set in the calling program, the other in the called subprogram. They must match each other correctly before any data can be transferred between them. A simple analogy is the electrical plug and socket. The socket is one half of the interface. In order to draw on the electric power supply of the socket, a plug with the correct number, position and shape of pins must be inserted into it. If we try to put a continental two round pin plug into a British three square pin socket, the interfaces would not match and no electricity could be used. However, try a three square pin plug and the plug fits the socket and power is available. So, in our programs, the number, order and picture of the two sets of parameters must be compatible or else we are in trouble. COBOL 74 uses a parameter system known as "call by reference". This means that any changes to the contents of the parameter fields in the subprogram are passed back to the calling program. Let us take the following statement as an example:

CALL "SUBPROGRAM-A" USING QUANTITY.

If the identifier QUANTITY contains 100 in the main program and is used as a parameter to pass 100 into the called subprogram SUBPROGRAM-A where processing changes its contents to 80, then the value of QUANTITY in the calling program would similarly be changed to 80. A parameter of this kind is an external variable because it actually exists outside the called subprogram. It is a variable of the calling program. These external variables which are the parameters of the called subprogram are declared in the LINKAGE SECTION of the DATA DIVISION, however no actual space is allocated to them since space already exists in the calling program. In COBOL 85 an explicit BY REFERENCE phrase is introduced, so the previous example can be written:

CALL "SUBPROGRAM-A" USING BY REFERENCE QUANTITY

However, if the BY ... phrase is omitted, BY REFERENCE is assumed thus preserving compatibility between COBOL 74 and COBOL 85.

There are situations where we wish to retain the original value in a parameter variable in the calling program even though its value has been changed in the called subprogram. In COBOL 74 we would have to use MOVE statements to store the values in temporary identifiers but COBOL 85 allows us to specify CALL . . BY CONTENT. Let us take the following example:

CALL "SUBPROGRAM-A" USING BY CONTENT QUANTITY.

If QUANTITY contained the value 100 when the CALL statement was executed by SUBPROGRAM-A and statements in SUBPROGRAM-A changed the value of QUANTITY to 80, QUANTITY would be reset to 100 when control passed back to the calling program.

20.2.2 Overflow

The situation can arise that the called subprogram is larger than the amount of memory available. If this happens, the program passes control to the statement immediately following the CALL unless the ON OVERFLOW phrase has been specified when the imperative-statement is executed before the program passes to the next statement.

COBOL 85 has a second format for CALL.

It has the format:

$$\underline{\text{CALL}} \left\{ \begin{array}{l} \text{identifier--1} \\ \text{literal--1} \end{array} \right\} \left[\underline{\text{USING}} \left\{ \begin{array}{l} [\ \text{BY } \underline{\text{REFERENCE}}\ ]\ \{\ \text{identifier-2}\ \} \cdots \\ \text{BY } \underline{\text{CONTENT}}\ \{\ \text{identifier-2}\ \} \quad \cdots \end{array} \right\} \cdots \right]$$

[ON EXCEPTION imperative–statement–1]

[NOT ON EXCEPTION imperative–statement–2]

[END–CALL]

The operation of this version of CALL is almost identical to the first format. ON EXCEPTION works in the same way as ON OVERFLOW. The additional NOT ON EXCEPTION allows the programmer to carry out special processing if no exception arises.

20.3 PROCEDURE DIVISION USING

There is also a special version of the PROCEDURE DIVISION declaration.

It has the format:

PROCEDURE DIVISION USING data–name–1 [data–name–2] . . .

Data-name-1 etc. are the external variables. The parameters in the USING clause must match those of the USING clause of the CALL statement in the calling program. They must match in number, order and picture but not necessarily in name. This allows a subprogram to have its own data-names separate from the calling program and facilitates the incorporation of a subprogram into a number of systems.

20.4 LINKAGE SECTION

The LINKAGE SECTION must be the last section of the DATA DIVISION. It begins with the section header and contains the data items to be used in the called subprogram, though these items can only be used if they are referred to in the USING clause of the PROCEDURE DIVISION header.

20.5 Exiting a Subprogram

A subprogram always returns control to the calling program so the STOP RUN statement cannot be used. It is replaced by an EXIT PROGRAM statement.

EXIT PROGRAM.

The statement marks the logical end of a called subprogram. The statement is a complete sentence and, in COBOL 74, must be in a paragraph of its own but COBOL 85 allows the statement to be placed in a paragraph with other statements.

20.6 Calling a Subprogram

To illustrate the use of these various statements, we will take as an example a program which calls a subprogram to print a report. The parameters are the report date and the number of copies of the report that are to be printed. These are stored in the calling program as follows:

```
DATA DIVISION.
WORKING-STORAGE SECTION.
01    TODAY                      PIC X(6).
01    NUMBER-OF-COPIES           PIC 9(3).
```

We will assume that the same identifiers are used in the called subprogram, though they may, in practice, have different names as long as their pictures match. The calling program contains the following:

CALL "REPORT" USING TODAY NUMBER-OF-COPIES.

The called subprogram REPORT contains the following

```
DATA DIVISION.
WORKING-STORAGE SECTION.
      . . .
      . . .
LINKAGE SECTION.
01    TODAY                      PIC X(6).
01    NUMBER-OF-COPIES           PIC 9(3).
PROCEDURE DIVISION USING TODAY NUMBER-OF-COPIES.
         . . .
         . . .
         . . .
RETURN-TO-PROGRAM.
EXIT PROGRAM.
```

These statements cause the subprogram REPORT to be loaded into memory and executed. The contents of TODAY and NUMBER-OF-COPIES are passed from the calling program to REPORT via the LINKAGE SECTION and the PROCEDURE DIVISION USING statement. When the processing within REPORT is completed, the EXIT PROGRAM statement returns operational control back to the calling program where processing recommences at the statement immediately after the CALL. a separate sentence and, in COBOL 74, must be in a paragraph of its own. COBOL 85 allows the statement to be placed in a paragraph with other statements.

20.7 CANCEL Statement

The CANCEL Statement is used to release the memory area occupied by a subprogram.

It has the format:

$$\underline{\text{CANCEL}} \quad \left\{ \begin{array}{l} \text{identifier--1} \\ \text{literal--1} \end{array} \right\} \dots$$

Literal-1 is the subprogram name. Identifier-1 contains that name.

Example: CANCEL "REPORT".

This statement removes the link between the calling program and the subprogram for use by the operating system. When a subprogram is called, it is placed in the available free memory by the operating system. If no CANCEL statement is given for the subprogram, it permanently occupies space to the exclusion of other programs or subprograms. Where memory is limited, especially on a microcomputer, this can severely limit the size of programs. It makes sense to cancel a subprogram after it has called if it is not needed again immediately. A common arrangement is to have the main calling program permanently in memory but each subprogram being cancelled as soon as control has returned to the calling program. Sometimes, one or more of the subprograms within a run unit are frequently used. In this case, if memory size allows, these subprograms are kept permanently in memory but other subprograms are cancelled on completion.

Example: DISPLAY MAIN-MENU.
               ACCEPT MAIN-MENU.
               PERFORM PROCESS-MAIN UNTIL OPTION = 5.
                 . . .

                 . . .
           PROCESS-MAIN.
               IF OPTION = 1   CALL "CUPDATE"
                                CANCEL "CUPDATE"
                                CANCEL "PUPDATE"
               ELSE IF OPTION = 3 CALL "PRDESC1"
                                CANCEL "PRDESC1"
               ELSE IF OPTION = 4 CALL "PRDESC2"
                                CANCEL "PRDESC2"

ELSE PERFORM WRONG-OPTION.

In COBOL 74, the programmer has to ensure that any file opened in a subprogram is closed before the CANCEL statement is given and the standard specification does not specify what happens to files which have been left open. In COBOL 85 CANCEL automatically closes any open file.

20.8 COPY Statement

When programming we often find that pieces of coding are repeated in several programs. For example, an inventory control system will contain a number of programs which process the product master file. Each program, therefore, contains the same file and record descriptions. When these have to be written out for each program it is not only tedious and time wasting but also dangerous. The coding can easily be copied wrongly. COBOL provides a simple solution to this problem. A piece of coding can be stored in a file and copied into a program. The exact way this is done varies with the implementation of the language. Mainframe implementations of COBOL commonly expect these files to be stored in a special library which requires manufacturer supplied software to create and maintain it. Other versions of COBOL, notably on microcomputers, adopt a simpler approach. A section of code is created by an editor and stored in a file in the normal way, just like a program. Whichever approach is adopted, the COPY statement is used in the program to insert the contents of a file in place of the COPY statement itself.

It has the format:

<u>COPY</u> text–name.

Text-name is the name of the file containing the coding which we wish to incorporate in our program. As an example of the use of COPY let us take the product record on a product master file which is coded as follows

```
01     PRODUCT-RECORD.
       03 PRODUCT-NUMBER          PIC 9(5).
       03 DESCRIPTION             PIC X(20).
       03 UNIT-PRICE              PIC 999V99.
       03 UNIT-COST               PIC 999V99.
       03 QUANTITY-ON-HAND        PIC 9(5).
       03 QUANTITY-ON-ORDER       PIC 9(5).
       03 DATE-OF-DELIVERY.
          05 DD                   PIC 99.
          05 MM                   PIC 99.
          05 YY                   PIC 99.
```

```
                 03 QUANTITY-SOLD                    PIC 9(5).
```

This is saved on a file with the name PRODUCT.TXT. In our program we can write

```
        WORKING-STORAGE SECTION.
        COPY "PRODUCT.TXT".
```

This will have the effect of incorporating the contents of the file PRODUCT.TXT as follows

```
        WORKING-STORAGE SECTION.
        01    PRODUCT-RECORD.
              03 PRODUCT-NUMBER        PIC 9(5).
              03 DESCRIPTION           PIC X(20).
              03 UNIT-PRICE            PIC 999V99.
              03 UNIT-COST             PIC 999V99.
              03 QUANTITY-ON-HAND      PIC 9(5).
              03 QUANTITY-ON-ORDER     PIC 9(5).
              03 DATE-OF-DELIVERY.
                 05 DD                 PIC 99.
                 05 MM                 PIC 99.
                 05 YY                 PIC 99.
              03 QUANTITY-SOLD         PIC 9(5).
```

The COPY statement allows pieces of coding for any part of a program to be copied from a file. The programmer is allowed to specify when compiling a program whether the copied pieces of code are to be printed in full in a listing of the program or just the COPY statement itself. Because of the different way this statement is implemented you must consult the user manual for the version of COBOL you are using.

APPENDIX 1

COBOL 85 Reserved Words

ACCEPT	CLOCK-UNITS	DEBUG-SUB-3
ACCESS	CLOSE	DEBUGGING
ADD	COBOL	DECIMAL-POINT
ADVANCING	CODE	DECLARATIVES
AFTER	CODE-SET	DELETE
ALL	COLLATING	DELIMITED
ALPHABET	COLUMN	DELIMITER
ALPHABETIC	COMMA	DEPENDING
ALPHABETIC-LOWER	COMMON	DESCENDING
ALPHABETIC-UPPER	COMMUNICATION	DESTINATION
ALPHANUMERIC	COMP	DETAIL
ALPHANUMERIC- EDITED	COMPUTATIONAL	DISABLE
ALSO	COMPUTE	DISPLAY
ALTER	CONFIGURATION	DIVIDE
ALTERNATE	CONTAINS	DIVISION
AND	CONTENT	DOWN
ANY	CONTINUE	DUPLICATES
ARE	CONTROL	DYNAMIC
AREA	CONTROLS	EGI
AREAS	CONVERTING	ELSE
ASCENDING	COPY	EMI
ASSIGN	CORR	ENABLE
AT	CORRESPONDING	END
AUTHOR	COUNT	END-ADD
BEFORE	CURRENCY	END-CALL
BINARY	DATA	END-COMPUTE
BLANK	DATE	END-DELETE
BLOCK	DATE-COMPILED	END-DIVIDE
BOTTOM	DATE-WRITTEN	END-EVALUATE
BY	DAY	END-IF
CALL	DAY-OF-WEEK	END-MULTIPLY
CANCEL	DE	END-OF-PAGE
CD	DEBUG-CONTENTS	END-PERFORM
CF	DEBUG-ITEM	END-READ
CH	DEBUG-LINE	END-RECEIVE
CHARACTER	DEBUG-NAME	END-RETURN
CHARACTER	DEBUG-SUB-1	END-REWRITE
CLASS	DEBUG-SUB-2	END-SEARCH

END-START	INITIATE	OF
END-STRING	INPUT	OFF
END-SUBTRACT	INPUT-OUTPUT	OMITTED
END-UNSTRING	INSPECT	ON
END-WRITE	INSTALLATION	OPEN
ENTER	INTO	OPTIONAL
ENVIRONMENT	INVALID	OR
EOP	IS	ORDER
EQUAL	JUST	ORGANIZATION
ERROR	JUSTIFIED	OTHER
ESI	KEY	OUTPUT
EVALUATE	LABEL	OVERFLOW
EVERY	LAST	PACKED-DECIMAL
EXCEPTION	LEADING	PADDING
EXIT	LEFT	PAGE
EXTEND	LENGTH	PAGE-COUNTER
EXTERNAL	LESS	PERFORM
FALSE	LIMIT	PF
FD	LIMITS	PH
FILE	LINAGE	PIC
FILE-CONTROL	LINAGE-COUNTER	PICTURE
FILLER	LINE	PLUS
FINAL	LINE-COUNTER	POINTER
FIRST	LINES	POSITION
FOOTING	LINKAGE	POSITIVE
FOR	LOCK	PRINTING
FROM	LOW-VALUE	PROCEDURE
GENERATE	LOW-VALUES	PROCEDURES
GIVING	MEMORY	PROCEED
GLOBAL	MERGE	PROGRAM
GO	MESSAGE	PROGRAM-ID
GREATER	MODE	PURGE
GROUP	MODULES	QUEUE
HEADING	MOVE	QUOTE
HIGH-VALUE	MULTIPLE	QUOTES
HIGH-VALUES	MULTIPLY	RANDOM
I-O	NATIVE	RD
I-O-CONTROL	NEGATIVE	READ
IDENTIFICATION	NEXT	RECEIVE
IF	NO	RECORD
IN	NOT	RECORDS
INDEX	NUMBER	REDEFINES
INDEXED	NUMERIC	REEL
INDICATE	NUMERIC-EDITED	REFERENCE
INITIAL	OBJECT-COMPUTER	REFERENCES
INITIALIZE	OCCURS	RELATIVE

RELEASE	SEQUENCE	TERMINATE
REMINDER	SEQUENTIAL	TEST
REMOVAL	SET	TEXT
RENAMES	SIGN	THAN
REPLACE	SIZE	THAN TRUE
REPLACING	SORT	THROUGH
REPORT	SORT-MERGE	THRU
REPORTING	SOURCE	TIME
REPORTS	SOURCE-COMPUTER	TIMES
RERUN	SPACE	TO
RESERVE	SPACES	TOP
RESET	SPECIAL-NAMES	TRAILING
RETURN	STANDARD	TYPE
REVERSED	STANDARD-1	UNIT
REWIND	STANDARD-2	UNSTRING
REWRITE	START	UNTIL
RF	STATUS	UP
RH	STOP	UPON
RIGHT	STRING	USAGE
ROUNDED	SUB-QUEUE-1	USE
RUN	SUB-QUEUE-2	USING
SAME	SUB-QUEUE-3	VALUE
SD	SUBTRACT	VALUES
SEARCH	SUM	VARYING
SECTION	SUPPRESS	WHEN
SECURITY	SYMBOLIC	WITH
SEGMENT	SYNC	WORDS
SEGMENT-LIMIT	SYNCHRONIZED	WORKING-STORAGE
SELECT	TABLE	WRITE
SEND	TALLYING	ZERO
SENTENCE	TAPE	ZEROES
SEPARATE	TERMINAL	ZEROS

APPENDIX 2

COBOL 85 Statement Formats

IDENTIFICATION DIVISION.

[PROGRAM–ID. program–name.]

[AUTHOR. [comment–entry] · · ·]

[INSTALLATION. [comment–entry] · · ·]

[DATE–WRITTEN. [comment–entry] · · ·]

[DATE–COMPILED. [comment–entry] · · ·]

[SECURITY. [comment–entry] · · ·]

[ENVIRONMENT DIVISION.

[CONFIGURATION SECTION.

[SOURCE–COMPUTER. [computer–name [WITH DEBUGGING MODE].]]

[OBJECT–COMPUTER. [computer–name

$$\left[\text{MEMORY SIZE integer–1} \left\{ \begin{array}{l} \text{WORDS} \\ \text{CHARACTERS} \\ \text{MODULES} \end{array} \right\} \right]$$

[PROGRAM COLLATING SEQUENCE IS alphabetic–name–1]

[SEGMENT–LIMIT IS segment–number].]]

[SPECIAL–NAMES.

[implementor–name–1 IS mnemonic–name, · · ·]

[CURRENCY SIGN IS literal–6]

[DECIMAL–POINT IS COMMA] .]

[INPUT–OUTPUT SECTION.

FILE–CONTROL.

$$\text{SELECT [OPTIONAL] file–name–1 ASSIGN TO} \left\{ \begin{array}{l} \text{implementor–name–1} \\ \text{literal–1} \end{array} \right\} \cdots$$

$$\left[\text{RESERVE integer} \left[\begin{array}{l} \text{AREA} \\ \text{AREAS} \end{array} \right] \right]$$

$$\left[\text{[ORGANIZATION] IS} \left\{ \begin{array}{l} \text{SEQUENTIAL} \\ \text{RELATIVE} \\ \text{INDEXED} \end{array} \right\} \right]$$

$$\left[\text{PADDING CHARACTER IS} \left\{ \begin{array}{l} \text{data–name–1} \\ \text{literal–2} \end{array} \right\} \right]$$

$$\left[\underline{RECORD}\ \underline{DELIMITER}\ IS\ \left\{ \begin{array}{l} \underline{STANDARD-1} \\ implementor-name-2 \end{array} \right\} \right]$$

$$\left[\underline{ACCESS}\ MODE\ IS\ \left\{ \begin{array}{l} \underline{RANDOM} \\ \underline{SEQUENTIAL} \\ \underline{DYNAMIC} \end{array} \right\} \right]$$

[<u>RECORD</u> KEY IS data–name–1]

[<u>ALTERNATE</u> RECORD KEY IS data–name–2 [WITH <u>DUPLICATES</u>]] $\cdots$

[FILE <u>STATUS</u> IS data–name–3] .]

[<u>DATA</u> <u>DIVISION</u>.

[<u>FILE</u> <u>SECTION</u>.

<u>FD</u> file–name–1

    [IS <u>EXTERNAL</u>]

    [IS <u>GLOBAL</u>]

$$\left[\underline{BLOCK}\ CONTAINS\ [\ integer-1\ \underline{TO}\ ]\ integer-2 \left\{ \begin{array}{l} \underline{RECORDS} \\ CHARACTERS \end{array} \right\} \right]$$

$$\left[\underline{RECORD} \left\{ \begin{array}{l} CONTAINS\ integer-3\ CHARACTERS \\ IS\ \underline{VARYING}\ IN\ SIZE\ [[\ FROM\ integer-4\ ]\ [\ \underline{TO}\ integer-5\ ]\ CHARACTERS\ ] \\ \quad [\ \underline{DEPENDING}\ ON\ data-name-1\ ] \\ CONTAINS\ integer-6\ \underline{TO}\ integer-7\ CHARACTERS \end{array} \right\} \right] \quad i$$

$$\left[\underline{LABEL} \left\{ \begin{array}{l} \underline{RECORD}\ IS \\ \underline{RECORDS}\ ARE \end{array} \right\} \left\{ \begin{array}{l} \underline{STANDARD} \\ \underline{OMITTED} \end{array} \right\} \right]$$

$$\left[\underline{VALUE}\ \underline{OF} \left\{ implementor-name-1\ IS\ \left\{ \begin{array}{l} data-name-1 \\ literal-1 \end{array} \right\} \right\} \cdots \right]$$

$$\left[\underline{DATA} \left\{ \begin{array}{l} \underline{RECORD} \\ \underline{RECORDS}\ ARE \end{array} \right\}\ data-name-3\ \cdots \right]$$

<u>Data description entry - General format</u>

Format 1

$$level-number \left[\begin{array}{l} data-name-1 \\ FILLER \end{array} \right]$$

    [<u>REDEFINES</u> data–name–2]

    [IS <u>EXTERNAL</u>]

    [IS <u>GLOBAL</u>]

$$\left[\left\{ \begin{array}{l} \underline{PICTURE} \\ \underline{PIC} \end{array} \right\}\ IS\ character-string \right]$$

$$\left[[\ \underline{USAGE}\ IS] \left\{ \begin{array}{l} \underline{BINARY} \\ \underline{COMPUTATIONAL} \\ \underline{COMP} \\ \underline{DISPLAY} \\ \underline{INDEX} \\ \underline{PACKED-DECIMAL} \end{array} \right\} \right]$$

211

$$\left[\ [\ \underline{\text{SIGN}}\ \text{IS}\ ]\ \left\{\begin{array}{l}\underline{\text{LEADING}}\\\underline{\text{TRAILING}}\end{array}\right\}[\ \underline{\text{SEPARATE}}\ \text{CHARACTER}\ ]\ \right]$$

$$\left[\begin{array}{l}\underline{\text{OCCURS}}\ [\ \text{integer–1}\ \underline{\text{TO}}\ ]\ \text{integer–2 TIMES}\ [\ \underline{\text{DEPENDING}}\ \text{ON data–name–4}\ ]\\ \left[\left\{\begin{array}{l}\underline{\text{ASCENDING}}\\\underline{\text{DESCENDING}}\end{array}\right\}\text{KEY IS data–name–3}\ \cdots\ \right]\ \cdots\\ [\ \underline{\text{INDEXED}}\ \text{BY}\ \{\ \text{index-name-1}\}\ \dots\ ]\end{array}\right]$$

$$\left[\left[\left\{\begin{array}{l}\underline{\text{SYNCHRONIZED}}\\\underline{\text{SYNC}}\end{array}\right\}\ \left[\begin{array}{l}\underline{\text{LEFT}}\\\underline{\text{RIGHT}}\end{array}\right]\ \right]\right]$$

$$\left[\left\{\begin{array}{l}\underline{\text{JUSTIFIED}}\\\underline{\text{JUST}}\end{array}\right\}\ \text{RIGHT}\ \right]$$

[$\underline{\text{BLANK}}$ WHEN $\underline{\text{ZERO}}$]

[$\underline{\text{VALUE}}$ IS literal–1]

Format 2

$$\text{66 data–name–1}\ \underline{\text{RENAMES}}\ \text{data–name–2}\ \left[\left\{\begin{array}{l}\underline{\text{THROUGH}}\\\underline{\text{THRU}}\end{array}\right\}\text{data–name–3}\right]$$

Format 3

$$\text{88 condition–name–1}\ \left\{\begin{array}{l}\underline{\text{VALUE}}\ \text{IS}\\\underline{\text{VALUES}}\ \text{ARE}\end{array}\right\}\left\{\text{literal–1}\ \left[\left\{\begin{array}{l}\underline{\text{THROUGH}}\\\underline{\text{THRU}}\end{array}\right\}\text{literal–2]}\right]\right\}\ \cdots$$

$\underline{\text{SD}}$ sortfile–name–1.

$$\text{01 record–name}\ \left\{\begin{array}{l}\underline{\text{PIC}}\ \text{string}\\\text{data description}\end{array}\right\}\ \cdots$$

[$\underline{\text{WORKING–STORAGE}}$ $\underline{\text{SECTION}}$.

[record description entry] . . .]

[$\underline{\text{LINKAGE}}$ $\underline{\text{SECTION}}$.

[record description entry] . . .]

$\underline{\text{PROCEDURE}}$ $\underline{\text{DIVISION}}$ [$\underline{\text{USING}}$ { data-name-1 } $\cdots$].

$$\underline{\text{ACCEPT}}\ \text{identifier–1}\ \left[\ \underline{\text{FROM}}\ \left\{\begin{array}{l}\underline{\text{CONSOLE}}\\\text{mnemonic–name–1}\end{array}\right\}\right]$$

$$\underline{\text{ACCEPT}}\ \text{identifier–2}\ \underline{\text{FROM}}\ \left\{\begin{array}{l}\underline{\text{DATE}}\\\underline{\text{DAY}}\\\underline{\text{DAY–OF–WEEK}}\\\underline{\text{TIME}}\end{array}\right\}$$

$$\underline{\text{ADD}}\ \left\{\begin{array}{l}\text{identifier–1}\\\text{literal–1}\end{array}\right\}\ \cdots\ \underline{\text{TO}}\ \{\ \text{identifier–2}\ [\ \underline{\text{ROUNDED}}\ ]\ \}\ \cdots$$

[ON $\underline{\text{SIZE}}$ $\underline{\text{ERROR}}$ imperative–statement–1]

[<u>NOT</u> ON <u>SIZE</u> <u>ERROR</u> imperative–statement–1]

[<u>END–ADD</u>]

$$\underline{ADD} \left\{ \begin{array}{l} \text{identifier–1} \\ \text{literal–1} \end{array} \right\} \cdots \text{ TO } \left\{ \begin{array}{l} \text{identifier–2} \\ \text{literal–2} \end{array} \right\}$$

       <u>GIVING</u> { identifier–3 [<u>ROUNDED</u>] }

       [ON <u>SIZE</u> <u>ERROR</u> imperative–statement–1]

       [<u>NOT</u> ON <u>SIZE</u> <u>ERROR</u> imperative–statement–2]

       [<u>END–ADD</u>]

$$\underline{CALL} \left\{ \begin{array}{l} \text{identifier–1} \\ \text{literal–1} \end{array} \right\} \left[\underline{USING} \left\{ \begin{array}{l} [\text{ BY }\underline{REFERENCE}\text{] } \{ \text{identifier-2} \} \cdots \\ \text{BY }\underline{CONTENT}\text{ } \{ \text{identifier-2} \} \cdots \end{array} \right\} \cdots \right]$$

       [ON <u>EXCEPTION</u> imperative–statement–1]

       [<u>NOT</u> ON <u>EXCEPTION</u> imperative–statement–2]

       [<u>END–CALL</u>]

$$\underline{CALL} \left\{ \begin{array}{l} \text{identifier–1} \\ \text{literal–1} \end{array} \right\} \left[\underline{USING} \left\{ \begin{array}{l} [\text{ BY }\underline{REFERENCE}\text{] } \{ \text{identifier-2} \} \cdots \\ \text{BY }\underline{CONTENT}\text{ } \{ \text{identifier-2} \} \cdots \end{array} \right\} \cdots \right]$$

       [ON <u>OVERFLOW</u> imperative–statement–1]

       [<u>END–CALL</u>]

$$\underline{CANCEL} \left\{ \begin{array}{l} \text{identifier–1} \\ \text{literal–1} \end{array} \right\} \cdots$$

<u>CLOSE</u> filename–1 $\cdots$

<u>COMPUTE</u> { identifier–1 [<u>ROUNDED</u>] } $\cdots$ = arithmetic–expression–1

       [ON <u>SIZE</u> <u>ERROR</u> imperative–statement–1]

       [<u>NOT</u> ON <u>SIZE</u> <u>ERROR</u> imperative–statement–2]

       [<u>END–COMPUTE</u>]

<u>CONTINUE</u>

$$\underline{COPY} \text{ text–name–1 } \left[\left\{ \begin{array}{l} \underline{OF} \\ \underline{IN} \end{array} \right\} \text{library–name–1} \right]$$

$$\left[\underline{REPLACING} \left\{ \left\{ \begin{array}{l} = =\text{pseudo–text–1= =} \\ \text{identifier–1} \\ \text{literal–1} \\ \text{word–1} \end{array} \right\} \underline{BY} \left\{ \begin{array}{l} = =\text{pseudo–text–2= =} \\ \text{identifier–2} \\ \text{literal–2} \\ \text{word–2} \end{array} \right\} \right\} \cdots \right]$$

<u>DELETE</u> file–name–1 RECORD

       [<u>INVALID</u> KEY imperative–statement–1]

       [<u>NOT</u> <u>INVALID</u> KEY imperative–statement–2]

[END–DELETE]

$$\text{DISPLAY} \left\{ \begin{array}{l} \text{identifier--1} \\ \text{literal--1} \end{array} \right\} \cdots \left[\underline{\text{UPON}} \left\{ \begin{array}{l} \underline{\text{CONSOLE}} \\ \text{mnemomic--name--1} \end{array} \right\} \right] [\text{ WITH } \underline{\text{NO}} \underline{\text{ADVANCING}}]$$

$$\underline{\text{DIVIDE}} \left\{ \begin{array}{l} \text{identifier--1} \\ \text{literal--1} \end{array} \right\} \underline{\text{BY}} \left\{ \begin{array}{l} \text{identifier--2} \\ \text{literal--2} \end{array} \right\}$$

        $\underline{\text{GIVING}}$ { identifier–3 [$\underline{\text{ROUNDED}}$] } $\cdots$

        [$\underline{\text{REMAINDER}}$ identifier–4]

        [ON $\underline{\text{SIZE}}$ $\underline{\text{ERROR}}$ imperative-statement–1]

        [$\underline{\text{NOT}}$ ON $\underline{\text{SIZE}}$ $\underline{\text{ERROR}}$ imperative-statement–2]

        [$\underline{\text{END–DIVIDE}}$]

$$\underline{\text{DIVIDE}} \left\{ \begin{array}{l} \text{identifier--1} \\ \text{literal--1} \end{array} \right\} \underline{\text{INTO}} \left\{ \begin{array}{l} \text{identifier--2} \\ \text{literal--2} \end{array} \right\}$$

        $\underline{\text{GIVING}}$ { identifier–3 [$\underline{\text{ROUNDED}}$] } $\cdots$

        [$\underline{\text{REMAINDER}}$ identifier–4]

        [ON $\underline{\text{SIZE}}$ $\underline{\text{ERROR}}$ imperative-statement–1]

        [$\underline{\text{NOT}}$ ON $\underline{\text{SIZE}}$ $\underline{\text{ERROR}}$ imperative-statement–2]

        [$\underline{\text{END–DIVIDE}}$]

$$\text{EVALUATE} \left\{ \begin{array}{l} \text{identifier--1} \\ \text{literal--1} \\ \text{expression--1} \\ \underline{\text{TRUE}} \\ \underline{\text{FALSE}} \end{array} \right\} \left[\underline{\text{ALSO}} \left\{ \begin{array}{l} \text{identifier--2} \\ \text{literal--2} \\ \text{expression--2} \\ \underline{\text{TRUE}} \\ \underline{\text{FALSE}} \end{array} \right\} \right] \cdots$$

      {{ $\underline{\text{WHEN}}$

$$\left\{ \begin{array}{l} \underline{\text{ANY}} \\ \text{condition--1} \\ \underline{\text{TRUE}} \\ \underline{\text{FALSE}} \\ [\underline{\text{NOT}}] \left\{ \begin{array}{l} \text{identifier--3} \\ \text{literal--3} \\ \text{arithmetic--expression--1} \end{array} \right\} \left[\left\{ \begin{array}{l} \underline{\text{THROUGH}} \\ \underline{\text{THRU}} \end{array} \right\} \left\{ \begin{array}{l} \text{identifier--4} \\ \text{literal--4} \\ \text{arithmetic--expression--2} \end{array} \right\} \right] \end{array} \right\}$$

      [$\underline{\text{ALSO}}$

$$\left\{ \begin{array}{l} \underline{\text{ANY}} \\ \text{condition--2} \\ \underline{\text{TRUE}} \\ \underline{\text{FALSE}} \\ [\underline{\text{NOT}}] \left\{ \begin{array}{l} \text{identifier--5} \\ \text{literal--5} \\ \text{arithmetic--expression--3} \end{array} \right\} \left[\left\{ \begin{array}{l} \underline{\text{THROUGH}} \\ \underline{\text{THRU}} \end{array} \right\} \left\{ \begin{array}{l} \text{identifier--6} \\ \text{literal--6} \\ \text{arithmetic--expression--4} \end{array} \right\} \right] \end{array} \right\} \cdots \right] \cdots$$

      [$\underline{\text{WHEN}}$ $\underline{\text{OTHER}}$ imperative-statement–2]

214

[END–EVALUATE]

EXIT [PROGRAM].

GO TO { procedure-name-1 }

IF condition–1 THEN $\begin{Bmatrix} \{ \text{ statement-1 } \} \cdots \\ \text{NEXT SENTENCE} \end{Bmatrix}$ $\begin{Bmatrix} \text{ELSE } \{ \text{ statement-2 } \} \cdots [\text{END–IF}] \\ \text{ELSE NEXT SENTENCE} \\ [\text{END–IF}] \end{Bmatrix}$

Relation Condition

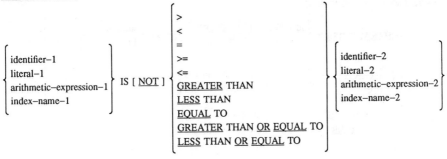

$\begin{Bmatrix} \text{identifier–1} \\ \text{literal–1} \\ \text{arithmetic–expression–1} \\ \text{index–name–1} \end{Bmatrix}$ IS [NOT] $\begin{Bmatrix} > \\ < \\ = \\ >= \\ <= \\ \text{GREATER THAN} \\ \text{LESS THAN} \\ \text{EQUAL TO} \\ \text{GREATER THAN OR EQUAL TO} \\ \text{LESS THAN OR EQUAL TO} \end{Bmatrix}$ $\begin{Bmatrix} \text{identifier–2} \\ \text{literal–2} \\ \text{arithmetic–expression–2} \\ \text{index–name–2} \end{Bmatrix}$

An expression can include OR, AND and NOT in addition to +, -, *, / and ** symbols.

Sign Condition

arithmetic–expression–1 IS [NOT] $\begin{Bmatrix} \text{POSITIVE} \\ \text{NEGATIVE} \\ \text{ZERO} \end{Bmatrix}$

Class Condition

identifier IS [NOT] $\begin{Bmatrix} \text{NUMERIC} \\ \text{ALPHABETIC} \\ \text{ALPHABETIC–LOWER} \\ \text{ALPHABETIC–UPPER} \\ \text{class–name–1} \end{Bmatrix}$

INITIALIZE { identifier-1 } $\cdots$

$\begin{bmatrix} \text{REPLACING} \begin{Bmatrix} \begin{Bmatrix} \text{ALPHABETIC} \\ \text{ALPHANUMERIC} \\ \text{NUMERIC} \\ \text{ALPHANUMERIC–EDITED} \\ \text{NUMERIC–EDITED} \end{Bmatrix} \text{DATA BY} \begin{Bmatrix} \text{identifier–2} \\ \text{literal–1} \end{Bmatrix} \cdots \end{Bmatrix} \end{bmatrix}$

INSPECT identifier–1 TALLYING

$$
\left\{ \text{identifier–2 } \underline{\text{FOR}} \left\{ \begin{array}{l} \underline{\text{CHARACTERS}} \left[\left\{ \begin{array}{l} \underline{\text{BEFORE}} \\ \underline{\text{AFTER}} \end{array} \right\} \text{INITIAL} \left\{ \begin{array}{l} \text{identifier–4} \\ \text{literal–2} \end{array} \right\} \right] \cdots \\[4mm] \left\{ \begin{array}{l} \underline{\text{ALL}} \\ \underline{\text{LEADING}} \\ \underline{\text{FIRST}} \end{array} \right\} \left\{ \begin{array}{l} \text{identifier–3} \\ \text{literal–1} \end{array} \right\} \\[4mm] \left[\left\{ \begin{array}{l} \underline{\text{BEFORE}} \\ \underline{\text{AFTER}} \end{array} \right\} \text{INITIAL} \left\{ \begin{array}{l} \text{identifier–4} \\ \text{literal–2} \end{array} \right\} \right] \cdots \end{array} \right\} \cdots \right\} \cdots
$$

INSPECT identifier–1 REPLACING

$$
\left\{ \begin{array}{l} \underline{\text{CHARACTERS}} \underline{\text{BY}} \left\{ \begin{array}{l} \text{identifier–5} \\ \text{literal–3} \end{array} \right\} \left[\left\{ \begin{array}{l} \underline{\text{BEFORE}} \\ \underline{\text{AFTER}} \end{array} \right\} \text{INITIAL} \left\{ \begin{array}{l} \text{identifier–4} \\ \text{literal–2} \end{array} \right\} \right] \cdots \\[4mm] \left\{ \begin{array}{l} \underline{\text{ALL}} \\ \underline{\text{LEADING}} \\ \underline{\text{FIRST}} \end{array} \right\} \left\{ \begin{array}{l} \text{identifier–3} \\ \text{literal–1} \end{array} \right\} \underline{\text{BY}} \left\{ \begin{array}{l} \text{identifier–5} \\ \text{literal–3} \end{array} \right\} \\[4mm] \left[\left\{ \begin{array}{l} \underline{\text{BEFORE}} \\ \underline{\text{AFTER}} \end{array} \right\} \text{INITIAL} \left\{ \begin{array}{l} \text{identifier–4} \\ \text{literal–2} \end{array} \right\} \right] \cdots \end{array} \right\} \cdots
$$

INSPECT identifier–1 TALLYING

$$
\left\{ \text{identifier–2 } \underline{\text{FOR}} \left\{ \begin{array}{l} \underline{\text{CHARACTERS}} \left[\left\{ \begin{array}{l} \underline{\text{BEFORE}} \\ \underline{\text{AFTER}} \end{array} \right\} \text{INITIAL} \left\{ \begin{array}{l} \text{identifier–4} \\ \text{literal–2} \end{array} \right\} \right] \cdots \\[4mm] \left\{ \begin{array}{l} \underline{\text{ALL}} \\ \underline{\text{LEADING}} \\ \underline{\text{FIRST}} \end{array} \right\} \left\{ \begin{array}{l} \text{identifier–3} \\ \text{literal–1} \end{array} \right\} \\[4mm] \left[\left\{ \begin{array}{l} \underline{\text{BEFORE}} \\ \underline{\text{AFTER}} \end{array} \right\} \text{INITIAL} \left\{ \begin{array}{l} \text{identifier–4} \\ \text{literal–2} \end{array} \right\} \right] \cdots \end{array} \right\} \cdots \right\} \cdots
$$

REPLACING

$$
\left\{ \begin{array}{l} \underline{\text{CHARACTERS}} \underline{\text{BY}} \left\{ \begin{array}{l} \text{identifier–5} \\ \text{literal–3} \end{array} \right\} \left[\left\{ \begin{array}{l} \underline{\text{BEFORE}} \\ \underline{\text{AFTER}} \end{array} \right\} \text{INITIAL} \left\{ \begin{array}{l} \text{identifier–4} \\ \text{literal–2} \end{array} \right\} \right] \cdots \\[4mm] \left\{ \begin{array}{l} \underline{\text{ALL}} \\ \underline{\text{LEADING}} \\ \underline{\text{FIRST}} \end{array} \right\} \left\{ \begin{array}{l} \text{identifier–3} \\ \text{literal–1} \end{array} \right\} \underline{\text{BY}} \left\{ \begin{array}{l} \text{identifier–5} \\ \text{literal–3} \end{array} \right\} \\[4mm] \left[\left\{ \begin{array}{l} \underline{\text{BEFORE}} \\ \underline{\text{AFTER}} \end{array} \right\} \text{INITIAL} \left\{ \begin{array}{l} \text{identifier–4} \\ \text{literal–2} \end{array} \right\} \right] \cdots \end{array} \right\} \cdots
$$

INSPECT identifier–1 CONVERTING $\left\{ \begin{array}{l} \text{identifier–6} \\ \text{literal–4} \end{array} \right\}$ TO $\left\{ \begin{array}{l} \text{identifier–7} \\ \text{literal–5} \end{array} \right\}$

$$
\left[\left\{ \begin{array}{l} \underline{\text{BEFORE}} \\ \underline{\text{AFTER}} \end{array} \right\} \text{INITIAL} \left\{ \begin{array}{l} \text{identifier–4} \\ \text{literal–2} \end{array} \right\} \right] \cdots
$$

216

MOVE $\left\{ \begin{array}{l} \text{identifier--1} \\ \text{literal--1} \end{array} \right\}$ <u>TO</u> { identifier-2 } $\cdots$

MULTIPLY $\left\{ \begin{array}{l} \text{identifier--1} \\ \text{literal--1} \end{array} \right\}$ <u>BY</u> { identifier-2 } [<u>ROUNDED</u>] $\cdots$

    [ON <u>SIZE</u> <u>ERROR</u> imperative--statement--1]

    [<u>NOT</u> ON <u>SIZE</u> <u>ERROR</u> imperative--statement--2]

    [<u>END--MULTIPLY</u>]

MULTIPLY $\left\{ \begin{array}{l} \text{identifier--1} \\ \text{literal--1} \end{array} \right\}$ <u>BY</u> $\left\{ \begin{array}{l} \text{identifier--2} \\ \text{literal--2} \end{array} \right\}$

    <u>GIVING</u> { identifier--3 [<u>ROUNDED</u>] } $\cdots$

    [ON <u>SIZE</u> <u>ERROR</u> imperative--statement--1]

    [<u>NOT</u> ON <u>SIZE</u> <u>ERROR</u> imperative--statement--2]

    [<u>END--MULTIPLY</u>]

<u>OPEN</u> $\left\{ \begin{array}{l} \underline{\text{INPUT}} \\ \underline{\text{OUTPUT}} \\ \underline{\text{I--O}} \\ \underline{\text{EXTEND}} \end{array} \right\}$ file--name--1 $\cdots$ $\left[\left\{ \begin{array}{l} \underline{\text{INPUT}} \\ \underline{\text{OUTPUT}} \\ \underline{\text{I--O}} \\ \underline{\text{EXTEND}} \end{array} \right\} \text{file--name--2} \cdots \right]$ $\cdots$

<u>PERFORM</u> $\left[\text{procedure--name--1} \left[\left\{ \begin{array}{l} \underline{\text{THROUGH}} \\ \underline{\text{THRU}} \end{array} \right\} \text{procedure--2} \right] \right]$

    [imperative--statement--1 <u>END--PERFORM</u>]

<u>PERFORM</u> $\left[\text{procedure--name--1} \left[\left\{ \begin{array}{l} \underline{\text{THROUGH}} \\ \underline{\text{THRU}} \end{array} \right\} \text{procedure--name--2} \right] \right]$

    $\left\{ \begin{array}{l} \text{identifier--1} \\ \text{integer--1} \end{array} \right\}$ <u>TIMES</u> [imperative--statement--1 <u>END--PERFORM</u>]

<u>PERFORM</u> $\left[\text{procedure--name--1} \left[\left\{ \begin{array}{l} \underline{\text{THROUGH}} \\ \underline{\text{THRU}} \end{array} \right\} \text{procedure--name--2} \right] \right]$

    $\left[\text{WITH } \underline{\text{TEST}} \left\{ \begin{array}{l} \underline{\text{BEFORE}} \\ \underline{\text{AFTER}} \end{array} \right\} \right]$ <u>UNTIL</u> condition--1

    [imperative--statement--1 <u>END--PERFORM</u>]

<u>PERFORM</u> $\left[\text{procedure--name--1} \left[\left\{ \begin{array}{l} \underline{\text{THROUGH}} \\ \underline{\text{THRU}} \end{array} \right\} \text{procedure--name--2} \right] \right]$

    $\left[\text{WITH } \underline{\text{TEST}} \left\{ \begin{array}{l} \underline{\text{BEFORE}} \\ \underline{\text{AFTER}} \end{array} \right\} \right]$

    <u>VARYING</u> $\left\{ \begin{array}{l} \text{identifier--2} \\ \text{index--name--1} \end{array} \right\}$ <u>FROM</u> $\left\{ \begin{array}{l} \text{identifier--3} \\ \text{index--name--2} \\ \text{literal--1} \end{array} \right\}$

$$\underline{BY} \left\{ \begin{array}{l} \text{identifier–4} \\ \text{literal–1} \end{array} \right\} \underline{UNTIL} \text{ condition–1}$$

$$\left[\begin{array}{l} \underline{AFTER} \left\{ \begin{array}{l} \text{identifier–5} \\ \text{index–name–3} \end{array} \right\} \underline{FROM} \left\{ \begin{array}{l} \text{identifier–6} \\ \text{index–name–4} \\ \text{literal–3} \end{array} \right\} \\ \qquad \underline{BY} \left\{ \begin{array}{l} \text{identifier–7} \\ \text{literal–4} \end{array} \right\} \underline{UNTIL} \text{ condition–2} \end{array} \right] \ \ldots$$

[imperative–statement–1 <u>END–PERFORM</u>]

<u>READ</u> file–name–1 [<u>NEXT</u>] RECORD [<u>INTO</u> identifier–1]

       [<u>KEY</u> IS data–name–1]

$$\left[\left\{ \begin{array}{l} \text{AT } \underline{END} \\ \underline{INVALID} \text{ KEY} \end{array} \right\} \text{ imperative–statement–1} \right]$$

       [<u>NOT</u> <u>INVALID</u> KEY imperative–statement–2]

       [<u>END–READ</u>]

<u>RELEASE</u> record–name–1 [<u>FROM</u> identifier–1]

<u>RETURN</u> file–name–1 RECORD [<u>INTO</u> identifier–1]

       AT <u>END</u> imperative–statement–1

       [<u>NOT</u> AT <u>END</u> imperative–statement–2]

       [<u>END–RETURN</u>]

<u>REWRITE</u> record–name–1 [<u>FROM</u> identifier–1]

       [<u>INVALID</u> KEY imperative–statement–1]

       [<u>NOT</u> <u>INVALID</u> KEY imperative–statement–2]

       [<u>END–REWRITE</u>]

$$\underline{SEARCH} \text{ identifier–1} \left[\underline{VARYING} \left\{ \begin{array}{l} \text{identifier–2} \\ \text{index–name–1} \end{array} \right\} \right]$$

       [AT <u>END</u> imperative–statement–1]

$$\left\{ \underline{WHEN} \text{ condition–1} \left\{ \begin{array}{l} \text{imperative–statement–2} \\ \underline{NEXT} \ \underline{SENTENCE} \end{array} \right\} \right\} \ \ldots$$

       [<u>END–SEARCH</u>]

<u>SEARCH</u> <u>ALL</u> identifier–1 [AT <u>END</u> imperative–statement–1]

$$\underline{WHEN} \left\{ \begin{array}{l} \text{data–name–1} \left\{ \begin{array}{l} \text{IS } \underline{EQUAL} \text{ TO} \\ \text{IS } = \end{array} \right\} \\ \text{condition–name–1} \end{array} \left\{ \begin{array}{l} \text{identifier–3} \\ \text{literal–1} \\ \text{arithmetic–expression–1} \end{array} \right\} \right\}$$

$$
\left[\underline{\text{AND}} \begin{Bmatrix} \text{data-name-2} \begin{Bmatrix} \text{IS } \underline{\text{EQUAL}} \text{ TO} \\ \text{IS} = \end{Bmatrix} \begin{bmatrix} \text{identifier-4} \\ \text{literal-2} \\ \text{arithmetic-expression-2} \end{bmatrix} \\ \text{condition-name-2} \end{Bmatrix} \right]
$$

$$
\begin{Bmatrix} \text{imperative-statement-2} \\ \underline{\text{NEXT}} \ \underline{\text{SENTENCE}} \end{Bmatrix}
$$

[<u>END-SEARCH</u>]

$$
\underline{\text{SET}} \begin{Bmatrix} \text{index-name-1} \\ \text{identifier-1} \end{Bmatrix} \cdots \underline{\text{TO}} \begin{Bmatrix} \text{index-name-2} \\ \text{identifier-2} \\ \text{integer-1} \end{Bmatrix}
$$

$$
\underline{\text{SET}} \text{ index-name-3} \cdots \begin{Bmatrix} \underline{\text{UP}} \ \underline{\text{BY}} \\ \underline{\text{DOWN}} \ \underline{\text{BY}} \end{Bmatrix} \begin{Bmatrix} \text{identifier-3} \\ \text{integer-2} \end{Bmatrix}
$$

$$
\underline{\text{SORT}} \text{ file-name-1} \begin{Bmatrix} \text{ON} \begin{Bmatrix} \underline{\text{ASCENDING}} \\ \underline{\text{DESCENDING}} \end{Bmatrix} \text{KEY data-name-1} \cdots \end{Bmatrix} \cdots
$$

[WITH <u>DUPLICATES</u> IN ORDER]

$$
\begin{Bmatrix} \underline{\text{INPUT}} \ \underline{\text{PROCEDURE}} \text{ IS procedure-name-1} \left[\begin{Bmatrix} \underline{\text{THROUGH}} \\ \underline{\text{THRU}} \end{Bmatrix} \text{procedure-name-2} \right] \\ \underline{\text{USING}} \ \{ \text{file-name-2} \} \ldots \end{Bmatrix}
$$

$$
\begin{Bmatrix} \underline{\text{OUTPUT}} \ \underline{\text{PROCEDURE}} \text{ IS procedure-name-3} \left[\begin{Bmatrix} \underline{\text{THROUGH}} \\ \underline{\text{THRU}} \end{Bmatrix} \text{procedure-name-4} \right] \\ \underline{\text{GIVING}} \ \{ \text{file-name-3} \} \cdots \end{Bmatrix}
$$

$$
\underline{\text{START}} \text{ file-name-1} \left[\underline{\text{KEY}} \begin{bmatrix} \text{IS } \underline{\text{EQUAL}} \text{ TO} \\ \text{IS } = \\ \text{IS } \underline{\text{GREATER}} \text{ THAN} \\ \text{IS } > \\ \text{IS } \underline{\text{NOT}} \ \underline{\text{LESS}} \text{ THAN} \\ \text{IS } \underline{\text{NOT}} < \\ \text{IS } \underline{\text{GREATER}} \text{ THAN OR } \underline{\text{EQUAL}} \text{ TO} \\ \text{IS } >= \end{bmatrix} \text{data-name-1} \right]
$$

[<u>INVALID</u> KEY imperative-statement-1]

[<u>NOT</u> <u>INVALID</u> KEY imperative-statement-1]

[<u>END-START</u>]

$$
\underline{\text{STOP}} \begin{Bmatrix} \underline{\text{RUN}} \\ \text{literal-1} \end{Bmatrix}
$$

$$
\underline{\text{STRING}} \begin{Bmatrix} \begin{Bmatrix} \text{identifier-1} \\ \text{literal-1} \end{Bmatrix} \cdots \underline{\text{DELIMITED}} \text{ BY} \begin{Bmatrix} \text{identifier-2} \\ \text{literal-2} \\ \underline{\text{SIZE}} \end{Bmatrix} \end{Bmatrix} \cdots
$$

219

INTO identifier–3

[WITH POINTER identifier–4]

[ON OVERFLOW imperative–statement–1]

[NOT ON OVERFLOW imperative-statement–2]

[END–STRING]

SUBTRACT $\left\{ \begin{array}{l} \text{identifier–1} \\ \text{literal–1} \end{array} \right\}$ $\cdots$ FROM identifier–2 [ROUNDED] $\cdots$

[ON SIZE ERROR imperative–statement–1]

[NOT ON SIZE ERROR imperative–statement–2]

[END–SUBTRACT]

SUBTRACT $\left\{ \begin{array}{l} \text{identifier–1} \\ \text{literal–1} \end{array} \right\}$ $\cdots$ FROM $\left\{ \begin{array}{l} \text{identifier–2} \\ \text{literal–2} \end{array} \right\}$

GIVING { identifier–3 [ROUNDED] } $\cdots$

[ON SIZE ERROR imperative–statement–1]

[NOT ON SIZE ERROR imperative–statement–2]

[END–SUBTRACT]

UNSTRING identifier–1

$$\left[\text{DELIMITED BY [ALL]} \left\{ \begin{array}{l} \text{identifier–2} \\ \text{literal–1} \end{array} \right\} \left[\text{OR [ALL]} \left\{ \begin{array}{l} \text{identifier–3} \\ \text{literal–2} \end{array} \right\} \right] \cdots \right]$$

INTO { identifier–4 [DELIMITER IN identifier–5] [COUNT IN identifier–6]} $\cdots$

[WITH POINTER identifier–7]

[TALLYING IN identifier–8]

[ON OVERFLOW imperative–statement–1]

[NOT ON OVERFLOW imperative–statement–2]

[END–UNSTRING]

WRITE record–name–1 [FROM identifier–1]

[INVALID KEY imperative–statement–1]

[NOT INVALID KEY imperative–statement–2]

[END–WRITE]

WRITE record–name–1 [FROM identifier–1]

$$\left[\left\{ \begin{array}{l} \text{BEFORE} \\ \text{AFTER} \end{array} \right\} \text{ADVANCING} \left\{ \begin{array}{l} \left\{ \begin{array}{l} \text{identifier–2} \\ \text{integer–1} \end{array} \right\} \left[\begin{array}{l} \text{LINE} \\ \text{LINES} \end{array} \right] \\ \left\{ \begin{array}{l} \text{mnemonic–name–1} \\ \text{PAGE} \end{array} \right\} \end{array} \right\} \right]$$

$$\left[\text{AT} \left\{ \begin{array}{l} \text{END–OF–PAGE} \\ \text{EOP} \end{array} \right\} \text{imperative-statement–1} \right]$$

$$\left[\underline{NOT} \ AT \ \left\{ \begin{array}{l} \underline{END-OF-PAGE} \\ \underline{EOP} \end{array} \right\} imperative\text{-}statement\text{-}2 \right]$$

[<u>END-WRITE</u>]

INDEX

222

Computing Books from Chartwell-Bratt

GENERAL COMPUTING BOOKS

Compiler Physiology for Beginners, M Farmer, 279pp, ISBN 0-86238-064-2
Dictionary of Computer and Information Technology, D Lynch, 225 pages, ISBN 0-86238-128-2
File Structure and Design, M Cunningham, 211pp, ISBN 0-86238-065-0
Information Technology Dictionary of Acronyms and Abbreviations, D Lynch, 270pp, ISBN 0-86238-153-3
The IBM Personal Computer with BASIC and PC-DOS, B Kynning, 320pp, ISBN 0-86238-080-4

PROGRAMMING LANGUAGES

An Intro to LISP, P Smith, 130pp, ISBN 0-86238-187-8
An Intro to OCCAM 2 Programming, Bowler, *et al,* 109pp, ISBN 0-86238-137-1
Cobol for Mainframe and Micro: 2nd Ed, D Watson, 177pp, ISBN 0-86238-211-4
Comparative Languages: 2nd Ed, J R Malone, 125pp, ISBN 0-86238-123-1
Fortran 77 for Non-Scientists, P Adman, 109pp, ISBN 0-86238-074-X
Fortran 77 Solutions to Non-Scientific Problems, P Adman, 150pp, ISBN 0-86238-087-1
Fortran Lectures at Oxford, F Pettit, 135pp, ISBN 0-86238-122-3
LISP: From Foundations to Applications, G Doukidis *et al,* 228pp, ISBN 0-86238-191-6
Programming Language Semantics, C Rattray, 135pp, ISBN 0-86238-066-9
Prolog versus You, A Johansson, *et al,* 308pp, ISBN 0-86238-174-6
Simula Begin, G M Birtwistle, *et al,* 391pp, ISBN 0-86238-009-X
The Intensive C Course, M Farmer, 167pp, ISBN 0-86238-114-2
The Intensive Pascal Course, M Farmer, 111pp, ISBN 0-86238-063-4

ASSEMBLY LANGUAGE PROGRAMMING

Coding the 68000, N Hellawell, 214pp, ISBN 0-86238-180-0
Computer Organisation and Assembly Language Programming, L Ohlsson & P Stenstrom, 128pp, ISBN 0-86238-129-0
What is machine code and what can you do with it? N Hellawell, 104pp, ISBN 0-86238-132-0

PROGRAMMING TECHNIQUES

Discrete-events simulations models in PASCAL/MT+ on a microcomputer, L P Jennergren, 135pp, ISBN 0-86238-053-7
Information and Coding, J A Llewellyn, 152pp, ISBN 0-86238-099-5
JSP - A Practical Method of Program Design, L Ingevaldsson, 204pp, ISBN 0-86238-107-X
JSD - Method for System Development, L Ingevaldsson, 248pp, ISBN 0-86238-103-7

Linear Programming: A Computational Approach: 2nd Ed, K K Lau, 150pp,
ISBN 0-86238-182-7
Programming for Beginners: the structured way, D Bell & P Scott, 178pp,
ISBN 0-86238-130-4
Software Engineering for Students, M Coleman & S Pratt, 195pp,
ISBN 0-86238-115-0
Software Taming with Dimensional Design, M Coleman & S Pratt, 164pp,
ISBN 0-86238-142-8
Systems Programming with JSP, B Sanden, 186pp, ISBN 0-86238-054-5

MATHEMATICS AND COMPUTING

Fourier Transforms in Action, F Pettit, 133pp, ISBN 0-86238-088-X
Generalised Coordinates, L G Chambers, 90pp, ISBN 0-86238-079-0
Statistics and Operations Research, I P Schagen, 300pp, ISBN 0-86238-077-4
Teaching of Modern Engineering Mathematics, L Rade (ed), 225pp,
ISBN 0-86238-173-8
Teaching of Statistics in the Computer Age, L Rade (ed), 248pp, ISBN 0-86238-090-1
The Essentials of Numerical Computation, M Bartholomew-Biggs, 241pp,
ISBN 0-86238-029-4

DATABASES AND MODELLING

Database Analysis and Design, H Robinson, 378pp, ISBN 0-86238-018-9
Databases and Database Systems, E Oxborrow, 256pp, ISBN 0-86238-091-X
Data Bases and Data Models, B Sundgren, 134pp, ISBN 0-86238-031-6
Text Retrieval and Document Databases, J Ashford & P Willett, 125pp,
ISBN 0-86238-204-1
Towards Transparent Databases, G Sandstrom, 192pp, ISBN 0-86238-095-2
Information Modelling, J Bubenko (ed), 687pp, ISBN 0-86238-006-5

UNIX

An Intro to the Unix Operating System, C Duffy, 152pp, ISBN 0-86238-143-6
Operating Systems through Unix, G Emery, 96pp, ISBN 0-86238-086-3

SYSTEMS ANALYSIS AND DEVELOPMENT

Systems Analysis and Development: 3rd Ed, P Layzell & P Loucopoulos, 284pp,
ISBN 0-86238-215-7

SYSTEMS DESIGN

Computer Systems: Where Hardware meets Software, C Machin, 200pp,
ISBN 0-86238-075-8
**Distributed Applications and Online Dialogues: a design method for application
systems,** A Rasmussen, 271pp, ISBN 0-86238-105-3

HARDWARE

Computers from First Principles, M Brown, 128pp, ISBN 0-86238-027-8
Fundamentals of Microprocessor Systems, P Witting, 525pp, ISBN 0-86238-030-8

NETWORKS

Communication Network Protocols: 2nd Ed, B Marsden, 345pp, ISBN
0-86238-106-1
Computer Networks: Fundamentals and Practice, M D Bacon *et al,* 109pp, ISBN
0-86238-028-6
Datacommunication: Data Networks, Protocols and Design, L Ewald & E
Westman, 350pp, ISBN 0-86238-092-8
Telecommunications: Telephone Networks 1, Ericsson & Televerket, 147pp, ISBN
0-86238-093-6
Telecommunications: Telephone Networks 2, Ericsson & Televerket, 176pp, ISBN
0-86238-113-4

GRAPHICS

An Introductory Course in Computer Graphics, R Kingslake, 146pp, ISBN
0-86238-073-1
Techniques of Interactive Computer Graphics, A Boyd, 242pp, ISBN 0-86238-024-3
Two-dimensional Computer Graphics, S Laflin, 85pp, ISBN 0-86238-127-4

APPLICATIONS

Computers in Health and Fitness, J Abas, 106pp, ISBN 0-86238-155-X
Developing Expert Systems, G Doukidis, E Whitley, ISBN 0-86238-196-7
Expert Systems Introduced, D Daly, 180pp, ISBN 0-86238-185-1
Handbook of Finite Element Software, J Mackerle & B Fredriksson, approx
1000pp, ISBN 0-86238-135-5
Inside **Data Processing: computers and their effective use in business,** A
deWatteville, 150pp, ISBN 0-86238-181-9
Proceedings of the Third Scandinavian Conference on Image Analysis, P
Johansen & P Becker (eds) 426pp, ISBN 0-86238-039-1
Programmable Control Systems, G Johannesson, 136pp, ISBN 0-86238-046-4
Risk and Reliability Appraisal on Microcomputers, G Singh, with G Kiangi,
142pp, ISBN 0-86238-159-2
Statistics with Lotus 1-2-3, M Lee & J Soper, 207pp, ISBN 0-86238-131-2

HCI

Human/Computer Interaction: from voltage to knowledge, J Kirakowski, 250pp,
ISBN 0-86238-179-7
Information Ergonomics, T Ivegard, 228pp, ISBN 0-86238-032-4
Computer Display Designer's Handbook, E Wagner, approx 300pp,
ISBN 0-86238-171-1

INFORMATION AND SOCIETY

Access to Government Records: International Perspectives and Trends, T Riley, 112pp, ISBN 0-86238-119-3
CAL/CBT - the great debate, D Marshall, 300pp, ISBN 0-86238-144-4
Economic and Trade-Related Aspects of Transborder Dataflow,
R Wellington-Brown, 93pp, ISBN 0-86238-110-X
Information Technology and a New International Order, J Becker, 141pp,
ISBN 0-86238-043-X
People or Computers: Three Ways of Looking at Information Systems,
M Nurminen, 1218pp, ISBN 0-86238-184-3
Transnational Data Flows in the Information Age, C Hamelink, 115pp,
ISBN 0-86238-042-1

SCIENCE HANDBOOKS

Alpha Maths Handbook, L Rade, 199pp, ISBN 0-86238-036-7
Beta Maths Handbook, L Rade, 425pp, ISBN 0-86238-140-1
Handbook of Electronics, J de Sousa Pires, approx 750pp, ISBN 0-86238-061-8
Nuclear Analytical Chemistry, D Brune *et al,* 557pp, ISBN 0-86238-047-2
Physics Handbook, C Nordling & J Osterman, 430pp, ISBN 0-86238-037-5
The V-Belt Handbook, H Palmgren, 287pp, ISBN 0-86238-111-8

Chartwell-Bratt specialise in excellent books at affordable prices.

For further details contact your local bookshop, or ring Chartwell-Bratt direct on
01-467 1956 (Access/Visa welcome.)

Ring or write for our *free* catalogue.

Chartwell-Bratt (Publishing & Training) Ltd, Old Orchard, Bickley Road,
Bromley, Kent, BR1 2NE, United Kingdom.
Tel 01-467 1956, Fax 01-467 1754, Telecom Gold 84:KJM001,
Telex 9312100451(CB)

Dictionary of Computer and Information Technology Terms

BY DON LYNCH

Sets out in a concise and easily understood manner brief explanations of over 2500 of the most common words, terms, jargon, acronyms, abbreviations and codes associated with information technology. The text provides a comprehensive and non-technical reference source and guide for users of computer and information technology in education and business. It makes the terminology and jargon of computer and information science readily understandable and available to the non-expert - at a very affordable price.

225 pages, ISBN 0-86238-128-2

CURRENT PRICE £5.95 (confirm details before ordering)

Available from your local bookshop, or direct from
Chartwell-Bratt, Old Orchard, Bickley Road, Bromley, Kent, BR1 2NE, UK. Tel 01-467 1956, Fax 01-467 1754

Information Technology Dictionary of Abbreviations and Acronyms

BY DON LYNCH

The emergence of Information Technology has produced a proliferation of jargon, much of which is expressed in the form of *abbreviations* and *acronyms,* that is confusing to all but the specialist. With the spread of this technology into seemingly every arena of life, many people are increasingly confronted by these new terms - and such is their growth that even the specialist is often left in the dark. Indeed, each specialist is also a novice in other areas.

This dictionary provides a single comprehensive, low-cost, source of reference for meanings of **over 6000** common abbreviations and acronyms associated with Information Technology. Each term is concisely defined, listed together in alphabetical order to cover an extremely wide and relevant collection - from A to ZRM.

349 pages, ISBN 0-86238-153-3

CURRENT PRICE £6.95 (confirm details before ordering)

Available from your local bookshop, or direct from Chartwell-Bratt, Old Orchard, Bickley Road, Bromley, Kent, BR1 2NE, UK. Tel 01-467 1956, Fax 01-467 1754